Lloyd George's
Secretariat

T0371478

Cambridge Studies in the History and Theory of Politics

Lloyd George's Secretariat

JOHN TURNER

Lecturer in History, Bedford College, London

CAMBRIDGE UNIVERSITY PRESS

CAMBRIDGE

LONDON NEW YORK NEW ROCHELLE
MELBOURNE SYDNEY

CAMBRIDGE UNIVERSITY PRESS
Cambridge, New York, Melbourne, Madrid, Cape Town, Singapore, São Paulo, Delhi

Cambridge University Press
The Edinburgh Building, Cambridge CB2 8RU, UK

Published in the United States of America by Cambridge University Press, New York

www.cambridge.org
Information on this title: www.cambridge.org/9780521223706

© Cambridge University Press 1980

First published 1980
This digitally printed version 2008

A catalogue record for this publication is available from the British Library

Library of Congress Cataloguing in Publication data
Turner, John, 1949–
Lloyd George's secretariat.
(Cambridge studies in the history and theory of
politics)
Bibliography: p.
Includes index.
1. Great Britain – Politics and government – 1910–1936.
2. Cabinet officers – Great Britain. 3. European War,
1914–1918 – Great Britain. 4. Lloyd George, David
Lloyd George, 1st Earl, 1863–1945. I. Title.
DA577.T87   354′.41′05   79–50510

ISBN 978-0-521-22370-6 hardback
ISBN 978-0-521-09316-3 paperback

Contents

Acknowledgements

I wish to thank the owners and trustees of copyright material for access to the private papers on which this study is based, in particular Mr A. J. P. Taylor and the First Beaverbrook Foundation, the Marquess of Lothian, the Trustees of the Second Viscount Astor, Mr Henry Borden and Professor H. C. Brown, Miss Ursula Slaghek, Lord Hankey, Captain S. W. Roskill, the Baroness White and Mr Tristan Jones, the Warden and Fellows of New College, Oxford, the Plunkett Foundation, and the Military Archives Centre, King's College, London. The staffs of many libraries – notably the Beaverbrook Library, Birmingham University Library, the Bodleian Library, the British Library, the House of Lords Record Office, the Hoover Library, the Humanities Research Center of the University of Texas at Austin, the Military Archives Centre at King's College, London, the National Library of Wales, Newcastle University Library, Plunkett House, the Public Record Office, the Public Archives of Canada, Reading University Library, the Scottish Record Office, and the Sterling Library at Yale University – gave help and advice for which I am most grateful.

Much of the work was carried out during the tenure first of a Harkness Fellowship and then of a research fellowship at Peterhouse, Cambridge, and I am obliged to the Commonwealth Fund of New York and to the Master and Fellows of Peterhouse both for financial support and for the opportunities which their generosity afforded me for travel and intellectual contacts. The last phase of writing was eased by the tolerance and kindness extended by members of the Department of History at Bedford College towards a new colleague.

The book has passed through a number of larval stages, with invaluable supervision from Dr Cameron Hazlehurst as it became a fellowship dissertation and Mr Martin Gilbert as it became a doctoral thesis. Dr K. O. Morgan and Mr A. J. Barnes as examiners of the thesis helped to determine the form in which it is now published. Mr Harry Pitt commented on an early draft of the manuscript.

Mr Maurice Cowling has generously encouraged its development from the fellowship dissertation stage. In the preparation of the manuscript I have been greatly helped by Mrs Hazel Dunn and Miss Sheelagh Taylor; and I have been guided through the process of publication, with great forbearance, by the staff of the Cambridge University Press.

My last-mentioned but greatest debt is to my wife who, despite the demands of her own profession, has throughout this work acted as researcher, critic and friend. To her this book is dedicated.

London, November 1978   J.A.T.

The Balkan Peninsula 1917

I

All in a garden fair

...a little body of *illuminati*, whose residence is in the Prime
Minister's garden, and their business to cultivate the Prime Minister's
mind. These gentlemen stand in no sense for a Civil Service cabinet.
They are rather of the class of travelling empirics in Empire, who
came in with Lord Milner, and whose spiritual home is fixed
somewhere between Balliol and Heidelberg. Their function is to
emerge from their huts in Downing Street, like the competitors in a
Chinese examination, with answers to our thousand questions of the
Sphinx.

H. W. Massingham in *The Nation*, 24 February 1917.

I

This book explores part of the curious and rather neglected world
where politics and administration intersect. Its subject is the personal
Secretariat set up by Lloyd George when he succeeded Asquith as
Prime Minister at the end of 1916. The new body, soon known as the
'Garden Suburb' from its location in temporary offices in the
Downing Street garden, was to be responsible for maintaining contact between the Prime Minister and the departments of government
and for writing reports on matters of special concern: in short, it was
to be an administrative intelligence department for Lloyd George.
It was disbanded at the end of the war. There are four reasons for
writing the history of this short-lived and irregular body of public
servants. First, the Garden Suburb was the earliest of a number of
attempts to strengthen the Prime Minister's hold over central government: its reputation, mistakes and limitations have conditioned later
efforts. Second, a study of its work illustrates the administrative
behaviour of wartime government after 1916, of which a critical
examination is long overdue. Third, the Secretariat helped to make
policy on a number of subjects, notably the Irish question, which are
of interest in themselves. Fourth, the Garden Suburb has acquired the
reputation of a kitchen cabinet of young imperialists, and this has

helped to strengthen a pervasive interpretation of Lloyd George's wartime government as the triumphant expression of a 'social-imperialist' coalition movement. The received account of the Secretariat contains fertile errors which call forth interesting refutations: but the principal task of this book is not to correct error. The aim is rather to describe an administrative institution at work and to comment on the significance of that work for the history of British politics and government in the latter years of the Great War.

The head of the Secretariat throughout its existence was Professor W. G. S. Adams, an Oxford don with administrative experience in the Irish Department of Agriculture and Technical Instruction and more recently in the Ministry of Munitions. The other founder members were Philip Kerr, editor of *The Round Table*, a quarterly devoted to the cause of imperial unity, David Davies, a Welsh coal-owner and philanthropist and a Liberal M.P., Waldorf Astor, proprietor of *The Observer* and a Conservative M.P., and Joseph Davies, a commercial statistician from South Wales. In May 1917 they were joined by Cecil Harmsworth, a Liberal M.P. and younger brother of Lord Northcliffe, the proprietor of the Harmsworth newspapers. In June 1917 David Davies left the Secretariat; in July 1918 Astor left to become Parliamentary Secretary at the Ministry of Food. Each secretary was given responsibility for keeping Lloyd George in touch with a number of departments. In the original scheme devised for Lloyd George by Kerr and Adams, Adams was to cover the Treasury, the Home Office, the Local Government Board, the Board of Education, the Reconstruction Committee, the Ministry of Food, the Board of Agriculture and the Ministry of Labour, and also labour matters at the Ministry of Munitions and the National Service Department. David Davies was to deal with the Board of Trade and the Shipping Controller, with supply questions at the Ministry of Munitions, the War Office, and the Admiralty, and with railways, mines, and drink control. Kerr was to watch over political and strategic questions at the Admiralty and the War Office, and cover the Foreign, Colonial, and India Offices, the Ministry of Blockade, and exchange problems at the Treasury.[1] Soon after the scheme was approved Astor was grafted on to it to take charge of drink control and act as Parliamentary Private Secretary; Joseph Davies suggested himself as an expert on commodity statistics.[2]

In the event only part of the scheme was put into practice. The collection of routine information was soon entrusted to the War Cabinet Secretariat.[3] Adams concentrated on food and labour until

March 1917, after which his time was taken up more and more by
the Irish question. After May 1917 Harmsworth took over most
labour questions from Adams, and assisted Joseph Davies with
food and shipping. David Davies worked at political and strategic
questions at the Admiralty and the War Office: of his assigned
subjects, railways, mines and shipping were covered by Adams,
Harmsworth and Joseph Davies, and the rest largely ignored. The
full distribution of military and diplomatic information in the War
Cabinet system allowed Kerr to be a commentator rather than a
collector of information. The Prime Minister's needs were served, not
by a comprehensive and regular gathering of intelligence as at first
envisaged, but by concentration on problems as they appeared. Only
a few topics, of which Ireland and the food supply were the most
important, engaged the Secretariat's attention continuously for more
than a few weeks: many questions which fell within its terms of
reference were apparently never noticed. This selection of subject
matter reflects the tension between administrative and political logic
in the Garden Suburb's work.

The Secretariat's work was also influenced by the interests and
previous experience of its members. Adams, for example, had known
Ireland since 1904. He was a moderate Home Ruler. In May 1917 he
helped to set up the Irish Convention, an heroic attempt to settle the
Irish question by consensus. He then used his position as intermediary
between Lloyd George and the chairman of the Convention to shape
the government's policy towards Ireland. His influence was sharply
reduced by the collapse of the Convention in the spring of 1918 and
the adoption of coercive policies; his attention was then turned to the
Cabinet committee which was drafting a new Home Rule Bill.
Though much of his other work was taken over by Harmsworth and
Joseph Davies, he maintained an interest in food supply and labour
questions for which his previous administrative experience had prepared him. Kerr, who had spent eight years in highbrow journalism
since his last administrative experience as secretary to the South
African commission on indigency in the Transvaal, hardly concerned
himself with specific foreign or imperial policies. He dealt instead in
grand designs, and most of his effort was devoted to an elaborate
ideological analysis of the progress of the war for Lloyd George to use
in public speeches. David Davies, without special interests, imagined
himself the scourge of Sloth and left the Secretariat when his efforts
were spurned. Astor's main responsibility in the Garden Suburb was
drink control, one of his established interests; he was unable to use

his position to promote the establishment of a Ministry of Health, which interested him even more, and he was discontented with his work. Harmsworth and Joseph Davies were both, for different reasons, satisfied to contribute what they could to efficient administration, and neither exerted himself to alter the course of government policy.

II

This apparently haphazard assumption of responsibilities and roles does not detract from the importance of the Garden Suburb as an administrative innovation. In the nineteenth century each Prime Minister had a number of private secretaries paid out of public funds. In the 1970s four distinct groups can be recognised in the Prime Minister's entourage: a private office of civil servants, a political office to deal with party and constituency matters, a press office, and an additional body of personal advisers drawn from outside the civil service and known (in 1978) as the Prime Minister's Policy Unit.[4] The process of differentiation has been neither swift nor smooth, but since Lloyd George established his Secretariat the experiment of appointing a body of independent policy advisers has been made on a number of occasions. In 1940 Churchill brought with him to Downing Street the Statistical Section under Lord Cherwell which had assisted him at the Admiralty;[5] a group of economists under Lord Balogh advised Wilson between 1964 and 1967;[6] and a Policy Unit under Dr Bernard Donoughue advised Wilson and Callaghan from 1974 to May 1979.[7] The functions of such a body have varied with the problems facing the government. Successive advisory bodies have all tried to inform the Prime Minister of what was happening in government, synthesising information from different sources and monitoring problems which have presented particular difficulties to the government. In the First World War these included problems of supply, Irish affairs, and the cultivation of public morale; in the Second the need was for usable digests of munitions, manpower and shipping statistics; more recently the emphasis appears to have been on short-term economic policy.

The growing complexity of government makes demands on its head which can only be met by optimising the quantity of information available to him. As government intervention in economy and society has increased, the policies of different departments have become more interdependent and the execution of policy has correspondingly required more careful co-ordination. War in the twentieth century has raised the problem of co-ordination in an acute form by bringing about sudden increases in the scope of government action. At the highest level, the need to impose coherent policy without undue recourse to the interdepartmental bargaining typical of peacetime Cabinets has led in both wars to the creation of small bodies with supreme authority to direct the war.[8] Lloyd George's most fundamental administrative innovation in December 1916 was the appointment of the War Cabinet, consisting of himself, Andrew Bonar Law, the Conservative leader, Arthur Henderson, leader of the Labour party, Lord Milner, and Lord Curzon.[9] This institution, which promised to impart energy to the higher direction of the war and to act as a swift and absolute arbiter in departmental disputes, followed naturally from Lloyd George's criticisms of the Asquith administration; it did not solve all the problems of information and understanding which had embarrassed the old régime. The concentration of business in the War Cabinet put an enormous and unforeseen strain on its members, who had to master the outlines of every subject referred to them, while meeting almost daily. On the other hand, the decisions made, which often involved more than one department, had to be followed up, for in the press of work War Cabinet members could not themselves be sure that their decisions would, or could, be put into effect successfully. The War Cabinet Secretariat, another new creation which worked under Lt. Col. Sir Maurice Hankey,[10] kept and circulated minutes of meetings, which had the force of instructions when they recorded a decision for departmental action; but Hankey's Secretariat confined itself to the mechanical work of distributing minutes, memoranda, and agendas. The Garden Suburb undertook the work of actively seeking information, before and after the War Cabinet made a decision, and presenting it in a useful form to the Prime Minister. The secretaries could use their access to departmental papers and permanent officials to digest essential information and comment critically on arguments put forward by the departments. Specialised knowledge and personal acquaintance with officials were particularly valuable. Some difficulties could even be resolved by the Secretariat on its own, leaving only a formal decision to be taken by the War Cabinet. After a decision, the Garden Suburb could find out whether instructions were being carried out and whether departmental action was having the desired effect. Five men could not monitor every decision, nor evaluate every area of policy; but they could at least identify some possible failures in time for preventive action.

Although such bodies of advisers, responsible to the Prime Minister and standing apart from administrative hierarchies, have been found useful also in peacetime and later in the century, there is no doubt that the condition of British government in 1916 offered particular scope to the Garden Suburb. Government departments traditionally did most of their business in isolation from one another. So long as no conflict arose over spheres of interest, no co-ordination was attempted except through Treasury control of finance and, remarkably late, through the Committee of Imperial Defence in matters of grand strategy.[11] Since the Great War various mechanisms have been devised to resolve or minimise interdepartmental conflict: functions have been shuffled from department to department, departments have been combined in 'super-ministries', the co-operative spirit has been encouraged by rotating 'high-flying' civil servants through the departments, and innumerable interdepartmental committees have enabled departments to work together without recourse to the Cabinet.[12] These expedients were not generally available in 1916 and the tradition of co-operation, which even now is established only insecurely, had not even taken root. The service departments in particular were pathologically suspicious of change and of one another, and formal interdepartmental committees were regarded with suspicion. The establishment in 1915 of the Ministry of Munitions, whose sole purpose was to perform a function for another department, had created precedents for continuous liaison, which were followed by the ministries of Shipping and, with less obvious success, Labour when they were established in December 1916. Other departments were less successful at adjusting their differences: the War Office and the Board of Agriculture had to be instructed by the War Cabinet to reach an agreement about the distribution of seed potatoes in March 1917, and a conference was held which both sides treated as a tournament.[13] The Garden Suburb frequently helped to sponsor interdepartmental committees of officials, either to settle short-term problems or to meet permanent needs. On many such occasions only the Secretariat's intervention saved the situation. Another stimulant to the development of the Secretariat's functions was the sheer novelty of the problems facing government. Lloyd George had to take ultimate political responsibility for many things which neither he nor anyone else had even attempted to control before the war or even in its first years, such as the allocation of cargoes to merchant ships, the rationing of food, and the direction of industrial labour. Day-to-day executive responsibility was delegated to a gallimaufry of controllers, directors and ministers. This motley crew could only be managed, if it could be managed at all, with the help of personal advisers who had the skill and information to brief the Prime Minister at critical moments and thus relieve him of some of the burdens of a state of constant and universal emergency.

The decision to achieve this supervision by attaching a group of additional secretaries to the Prime Minister's entourage marks a departure in the development of the Prime Minister's private staff. The private secretaries of nineteenth-century Prime Ministers served their masters' varied needs with little specialisation of function. By 1916 it had become conventional for the Prime Minister to have three private secretaries, one of them a personal appointment and at least one of the others a permanent civil servant. Vaughan Nash, who served both Campbell-Bannerman and Asquith, specified that between them these three 'must keep in close touch with the whips, must attend punctiliously to the demands of the court, to Patronage, to letters from every maniac in the country, to Memos. from Heads of Departments, to interviews'.[14] When Lloyd George came to 10 Downing Street he brought with him as secretaries J. T. Davies, Frances Stevenson, and William Sutherland, who carried on this routine work while the Garden Suburb attended to its own more specialised functions.[15] Sutherland added the systematic cultivation of the press to his other duties. After Lloyd George left Downing Street in 1922 the Prime Minister's entourage began to blossom, albeit fitfully, as an administrative institution. Since 1928 the 'private office' has been staffed exclusively by civil servants, who remain in post through changes of government; other functions have been carried out by a variety of confidential assistants and advisers. All Prime Ministers since Attlee have had press officers, and it would appear from Callaghan's decision in 1976 to retain the Donoughue Unit that groups of policy advisers have a future as well as a past. Lloyd George's expedient of adding to the number and function of his private secretaries broke an established pattern of private secretaryship and won a place in institutional history for his Garden Suburb.

III

The Garden Suburb's work also throws an unforgiving light on the quality of wartime administration. The reputation of Lloyd George's government as a supreme war-winning machine relies heavily on the fact that it was in office for the final years of the war. To improve on this opportunity, a strenuous self-congratulation began almost before Lloyd George was installed at 10 Downing Street and continued throughout the war. A predictable crescendo occupied the interval between the armistice and the general election of December 1918, and in later years it was mentioned often enough that the war had been won by vigorous government and a total commitment of the national resources to victory, organised by the Lloyd George coalition. Victory itself made this story very difficult to check, for success is the most convenient yardstick of a government's performance. Since the 1916 coalition presided over victory it was easily assumed that everything it did contributed to that victory, just as the preparatory work of Asquith's Cabinets was easily deprecated. The early historiography of war administration was largely the work of participants, and while many authors could recognise their colleagues' mistakes, and some could even admit their own, very few could resist depicting the extension of government activity as purposeful and benign.[16] Two questions are begged by this assumption. First, how far were the policies introduced effective in promoting victory? Although a mass of recent historical work has testified to the great changes wrought in British society by the war and government policy,[17] rather less attention has been paid to whether those changes were relevant to the maximisation of military and economic effort which was their justification. Second, was the central administration which supervised the transformation of Britain in fact well organised? These are deceptively short questions which can only be answered by lengthy accumulations of evidence from many quarters, but the viewpoint of the Garden Suburb has certain advantages for a preliminary reconnaissance. One of its tasks was to warn Lloyd George when the machine was about to break down, and it therefore paid special attention to weak points. Its central position also enabled it to take a larger view than that of the departments, yet unlike the War Cabinet it was not burdened by executive responsibility for every act of government. The problems of food supply, shipping and labour relations with which it grappled illustrate, in their progress through the War Cabinet and the departments, many of the weaknesses and some of the strengths of the machinery of British government; and drink control, though Astor seemed unaware of it, brought issues unconnected with the war into a policy decision represented then and later as yet another step on the road to victory. By looking at the

Garden Suburb's work the historian can take an informative, if not wholly representative, sample of governmental activity in the latter years of the war.

Some of the Secretariat's time was spent on subjects which have been studied already by historians without a full assessment of the secretaries' contribution. Their work on Ireland stands out among these questions because of the coherent advice given by Adams and the demonstrable effect it had on policy; but other areas where the advice was less definite or the influence more oblique are of similar interest. Kerr's work on war aims is of particular importance. The evolution of British war aims during the Great War is a subject of inexhaustible complexity.[18] A proper war aim could rally one's own people, demoralise the enemy, hearten allies, and attract the support of neutral countries; a bad war aim could be worse than a military defeat. As a public statement of a set of objectives whose purpose was not so much to define those objectives as to assist in their achievement, it was the joint apotheosis of all objectives and all propaganda statements. It was therefore not to be treated lightly, and British governments were reluctant to commit themselves to war aims except under extreme pressure: but when President Wilson of the United States invited all belligerents, in December 1916, to define the ends for which they were fighting, Britain and her allies, who all depended heavily on the United States for material support to continue fighting, could not afford to refuse. The joint declaration which resulted, setting out desiderata for territorial adjustments and a new political and economic order after the war, committed the British government to war aims which were good enough at the time but which were soon overtaken by events. The next year saw a constant effort of redefinition in which Lloyd George took the lead, and one of Kerr's functions was to supply the raw material for commentary on the changing international situation.

This was more than a digest of war news, and Kerr built up an interpretation of the conflict in which British self-interest, international morality, an historical account of the origins of the war, and a running commentary on the domestic politics of the belligerents, including Britain, were subtly interwoven to create a prescription for British war aims. His final contribution was one of a small number which influenced Lloyd George's carefully considered war-aims speech in January 1918 at the Caxton Hall; thereafter the accelerating pace of battle in France made war-aims speeches irrelevant. Kerr manifestly believed his own propaganda. His interpretation of the war encompassed the currents of party politics in Britain, and during the election campaign in 1918 his denunciations of the Labour party reflect clearly the powerful effect of wartime experience on the ideas about peacetime politics cherished in Lloyd George's immediate circle. During the war other members of the Secretariat joined him in interpreting the outside world to Lloyd George and Lloyd George to the outside world. The War Cabinet Report for 1917, an apologia for the first year of the coalition, was edited in the Garden Suburb by Adams, Kerr and Harmsworth. Most of the secretaries kept in touch with press acquaintances, thereby supplementing Sutherland's vigorous manipulation of the newspapers in the interest of Lloyd George's prestige. In all these activities the Secretariat had a considerable effect on contemporary notions of why the war had to be won and who was winning it.

Examples of a more direct intervention in policy may be mentioned. Kerr and David Davies made serious attempts to reverse the trend of British policy towards Greece and Serbia, which they believed was tending to ignore Serbian interests and to permit undue French influence in the Balkans. Kerr also attempted to influence policy towards the future government of India, and to foster imperial relations on the lines favoured in *The Round Table*. Neither endeavour was very successful. More success attended the Garden Suburb's efforts to modify the terms of the Corn Production Act which, when passed, was intended to herald the regeneration of British agriculture. For the most part long-term domestic policy lay outside the scope of the Secretariat's work: only those measures which promised to affect the war as well as the peace, such as drink control or the Corn Production Act, attracted Lloyd George's interest and the official attention of his secretaries.

IV

Since the Garden Suburb expired in 1918 two schools of interpretation have competed to display the relics. The first, in time and logic, sprang directly from the politics of 1914 to 1922. Its essential premise was that Lloyd George was a politician of protean force, without attachment to party or principle and indifferent to moral or constitutional conventions in his pursuit of political success: a major corollary was that he was readily influenced by those around him if their advice served to advance his own interests. This school has included the three Liberal journalists, Massingham, J. A. Spender,

and A. G. Gardiner, the early Keynes, and latterly Dr Wilson and
Mr Rowland.[19] The other school, which concentrates on the period
1900 to 1918, is exclusively the work of academics. Professor Semmel
has borrowed the concept of 'social-imperialism' from Schumpeter
to denote the anti-socialist ideologies of the pre-war years which
linked a desire for imperial greatness with domestic social reconstruction.[20] In an attempt to reify the concept Professor Scally has
proposed that the 1916 Lloyd George coalition was the political
culmination of social-imperialism, in which the diverse threads of
the 'movement' – Tariff Reform, Liberal Imperialism, 'Milnerism'
and Fabianism – were finally woven together.[21] Others, without
adopting the same grand design, have remarked on the entry into
government of confirmed believers in imperial expansion.[22] For both
schools the existence of the Garden Suburb as a source of advice for
Lloyd George is significant: the first school emphasises its irregularity
and the presence in it of politicians like David Davies who could
otherwise expect no influence on the course of events, while the
second school emphasises the presence of Kerr and Astor and the
'social-imperial' advice they are supposed to have given.

While using the Garden Suburb to confirm ready-made interpretations of the Lloyd George coalition, both schools have casually
misunderstood its real work and repeated simple factual errors. The
first school merely devalues it by treating it as an excrescence on the
body politic, staffed by hangers-on. The Secretariat's administrative
functions are ignored and the low quality of its membership established by conflating it with the rest of the Prime Minister's entourage
of secretaries and political camp-followers. The devotees of social-
imperialism present a more interesting and important thesis, but one
which in its most recent form is flawed by errors of proportion.
To assess its relevance to the Garden Suburb it is necessary to digress
into a compressed version of the social-imperialist account of British
politics from 1900 to 1916. The fullest work on the subject is by
Scally, and since it relies explicitly on other authors in the same
tradition it may be taken as an example. In a chronological treatment
of the period Scally seeks to show that social-imperialists in both
political parties converged in sentiment before the war and that the
political crisis of December 1916 produced a coalition which deliberately accommodated the common aims of social-imperialism in a
single movement. His list of social-imperialist groups is largely that
made familiar by Semmel and by Dr Searle's work on National
Efficiency: the Liberal League, Liberal Imperialism, Fabianism

under the Webbs, 'Milnerism', Tariff Reform, the Coefficients Club
and the Compatriots Club.[23] Scally adds the 'Lloyd George Radicals'.
He suggests that Rosebery and the Webbs made the first moves
towards a social-imperialist programme before 1903, only to be
upstaged by Chamberlain's creation of the Tariff Reform movement,
which sought to transform the Conservative party into a 'dynamic
anti-socialist instrument with a mass base among those segments of
the working and lower middle classes which they perceived to be
more receptive to appeals to social order and imperial security than
to militant labour unions or class conflict.'[24] Scally believes that
effective leadership of the Tariff Reform movement, which was the
apotheosis of social-imperialism, fell after Chamberlain's illness to
Milner, who had recently returned from his service as High Commissioner in South Africa: Milner's power to command loyalty
among the young men who later founded the Round Table movement added another dimension to the movement. Scally then brings
in Lloyd George, who entered the competition for the central anti-
socialist constituency first as President of the Board of Trade, then at
the Treasury, where he combined schemes for non-socialist reform
with a firm stance against German naval and commercial competition. At this period, he says, Lloyd George was Tariff Reform's most
dangerous opponent, but Tariff Reformers came to admire him for
his readiness to abandon Liberal idols, to eschew Little Englandism,
and to seek national regeneration wherever it could be found. The
constitutional crisis of 1909–10 is seen as an opportunity for Lloyd
George to suggest a coalition to settle outstanding problems with a
programme of military preparation and social reconstruction through
state intervention: but this was skilfully evaded by the old guard in
both parties. The election of December 1910, and the crises over the
Parliament Bill, the National Insurance Bill, and the Home Rule
Bill then intervened, it is argued, to freeze the development of the
social-imperialist alliance. The war, by isolating Lloyd George in the
Liberal Cabinet and demanding the organisation and effort for
which the social-imperialists had been pleading in quieter times,
increased the pressure on the old party system. The 1915 coalition
relieved the pressure without making any fundamental changes: the
crisis of December 1916, engineered by the followers of Milner and
Sir Edward Carson[25] with the deliberate intention of enthroning
social-imperialism, created the new politics which had been foreshadowed since 1900.

At this point historians writing in the social-imperialist school have

run into difficulties while trying to present the Lloyd George coalition
as a full-fledged social-imperialist government. The strongest evidence they put forward is the presence of Milner, whose influence
through highly placed associates they believe to have been very great.
Dr Lockwood has written at length on Milner's entry into the War
Cabinet[26] and Professor Naylor, discussing the establishment of the
War Cabinet Secretariat, has remarked in passing on the importance
of Milnerites in the 'organised administration'.[27] Both mention the
Garden Suburb incidentally, as does Professor Gollin in his biography of Milner.[28] Scally takes up the same theme, though even
more than Lockwood, and on a larger canvas, he is mistaken in
many of the critical details on which he rests his argument about
social-imperialists in the new government.[29] The authors all agree
that Milner's close associates were given positions in the new government, some in direct contact with the Prime Minister. They go on to
suggest, with differing degrees of reservation, that with Milner in the
War Cabinet, Carson at the Admiralty, and Milnerite disciples in key
positions the ideas espoused by Milner – which Lockwood calls
'Milnerism' and Scally 'social-imperialism' – exerted a strong influence on the coalition.

The history of the Garden Suburb speaks directly to this question.
Milner's significance for the historians of social-imperialism rests
largely on two groups, which looked to him for leadership and
inspiration, in which future members of the Garden Suburb were
involved. In South Africa he gathered about him a body of young
men, disrespectfully called the 'Kindergarten', who imbibed his
views on the importance of imperial unity while working in various
capacities on reconstruction after the Boer War. Returning severally
from South Africa the young men came together in 1910 to form the
Round Table, a 'study group' on imperial affairs, which recruited
a few other sympathisers and began to publish a quarterly of the
same name. Under the editorship of Philip Kerr, who had served in
South Africa and then edited a journal, *The State*, at Cape
Town, *The Round Table* was devoted to imperial and international
questions, with occasional forays into domestic politics. A massive
study of the institutions necessary for closer imperial unity was put
in hand under Lionel Curtis.[30] Meanwhile Milner, who had returned
to England in 1905, took up Tariff Reform and made a point of
linking it to social reform and extending it beyond simple protection-
ism to a genuine effort to promote imperial unity. These concerns
brought him close to J. L. Garvin,[31] a journalist who became a

leading propagandist for Tariff Reform Conservatism as editor of
Outlook and *The Observer*, and also to a number of Conservative
M.P.s who wanted to strengthen their party's following among the
working classes. His explicit distaste for the Liberal government, in
particular its Home Rule and Parliament Bills, won him a reputation
as a prominent and extreme reactionary. During the war, with
Garvin and other political associates, he helped to float the British
Workers' National League, which set out to oppose the Independent
Labour party in working-class constituencies by an appeal to imperial
patriotism coupled with a programme of social reform.[32] Waldorf
Astor, whose father had bought *The Observer* from Northcliffe to
allow Garvin to continue his support for Tariff Reform, took over the
newspaper and also financed the B.W.N.L. From early 1916 he also
offered regular hospitality to a 'ginger group' of M.P.s and others,
including Milner and Carson, which met regularly to plot the downfall of the Asquith government.

Lockwood and Scally make much of these old associations of Kerr
and Astor, but in doing so they do not give a full account of the
personnel of the Garden Suburb, about which both have misinformed
themselves, nor do they examine its work. They raise the important
point that in 1916 new jobs were created and given to new men.
They ask about the derivation of the new policies of the 1916
coalition, about how far the new men influenced policy and how far
they co-operated with one another to impose particular views on the
rump of an 'old guard'. All these are questions of the highest
importance, and it is unfortunate that the 'social-imperialist' answers
they give should exaggerate the significance of the network of
acquaintances of one man, Milner, while trying to demonstrate the
important point that December 1916 was more than just a recom-
bination of politicians. Because of its central position in the administrative structure, its proximity to Lloyd George, and its place in the
demonology of Liberal criticism of Lloyd George as well as in the
pantheon of social-imperialism, the Garden Suburb is an obvious
place to look for better answers. Its personnel was varied enough: two
Welsh Liberals, another Liberal, Harmsworth, with Liberal Imperialist antecedents and strong links with the Asquith camp, a professor
whose party politics hovered between Liberal and Labour, a Conservative who followed Milner's domestic lead, and a Milnerite
journalist with no clear views on domestic politics. The group had no
collective mind, though the interests of its individual members and
their advice on policy combine, under examination, to give it an

intellectual centre of gravity which was liberal in philosophy despite the presence of two alleged social-imperialists in Kerr and Astor. Those who had given any indication of their views before 1916 had a pronounced preference for state intervention, but that was the highest common factor. Other interests set certain pairs of secretaries off from the rest: Adams and Kerr both supported, to some degree, a supranational organisation for the resolution of international conflict, while Astor and Davies shared a concern for public health. When the time came to influence the policy of the government, membership of the Secretariat conferred less direct influence than many, including some of the secretaries, expected. The Secretariat was markedly unsuccessful at insinuating 'social-imperialist' ideas into government action: Kerr, with Amery and Milner, laboured without success to make the 1917 Imperial War Conference the foundation of imperial unity, and Astor found no outlet in the Garden Suburb for preventive social reform. Where the Secretariat did exert a notable influence was in the more conventionally Liberal direction of conciliating Ireland. There were examples of secretaries working with other leading members of the government, in particular Milner: but the subjects – agriculture and state purchase of the liquor trade – were peripheral to social-imperialism. In every respect the Garden Suburb presents a more complex picture than the social-imperialist interpretation would suggest: it is but a short step to infer that under a sufficiently close inspection the coalition government would do the same.

V

Even the establishment of the Garden Suburb took place in an atmosphere which combined administrative improvisation and personal political ambition with awareness, in a small degree, of the opportunities for long-term social and political change. It was set up in January 1917 on the initiative of a small group of Lloyd George's supporters who found themselves in the weeks after the change of government without patriotic employment. The central figures were David Davies and Thomas Jones, the secretary of the Welsh National Insurance Commission, who found among their acquaintances in London in December 1916 the ideas and personnel which formed the basis of the Secretariat. Although all the secretaries except Kerr and Adams had had some sort of contact with Lloyd George before the war, the first sign of their convergence in his entourage was seen in

May 1916, when Davies and Astor approached him separately to urge him to resign and force Asquith to reorganise the government. They had both been inspired by his well-publicised success in forcing a reluctant Cabinet to extend the principle of compulsory military service, and through the mediation of Christopher Addison, one of Lloyd George's most ardent supporters and then his Parliamentary Secretary at the Ministry of Munitions, they met together on 2 May. They discussed the 'Efficiency Programme' which Lloyd George was due to announce in a speech at Conway, and both the young M.P.s agreed that resignation would be premature.[33] At the last minute the Conway speech had to be used to refute a damaging accusation by A. G. Gardiner in the *Daily News* that Lloyd George was seeking the Liberal leadership at the expense of Liberal principles,[34] and the Efficiency Programme with its network of 'Win the War Committees' came to nothing. Davies returned to his regiment in France, hoping that another political crisis would come which would overturn Asquith.[35] He returned to England in June, when Lloyd George's succcession to the War Office was first mentioned. While Lloyd George negotiated with Sir William Robertson about the powers of the C.I.G.S. and with Irish politicians about Home Rule, Davies did odd jobs for the Ministry of Munitions.[36] When Lloyd George was finally installed at the War Office in July, Davies became his Parliamentary Private Secretary.

In this new appointment Davies offended a number of civil servants and senior military officers, and kept up some political work for his master.[37] He was still anxious for a change of government, and in November confided to Lord Riddell his alarm lest Lloyd George should resign prematurely and ruin his chance to be Prime Minister.[38] When, in late November, Lloyd George invited a group of civil servants, businessmen and academics to compose a memorandum on the future conduct of the war, Davies renewed his connection with Thomas Jones.[39] Jones, formerly professor of economics at Queen's College, Belfast, had undertaken the organisation of the Welsh National Memorial to Edward VII, a campaign against tuberculosis, at Davies's request, before moving to the Insurance Commission in 1912. In the critical days of early December, while Lloyd George, Asquith, and the various elements of the Unionist party negotiated and renegotiated the terms for reorganising the government, Jones and Davies watched, waited and advised from Davies's flat in Buckingham Gate, next door to Lloyd George. Their early contribution was mostly talk, but they were able to recruit Joseph Davies, who knew Jones and had long-standing business connections with David Davies, to help put Lloyd George in touch with J. H. Thomas M.P.[40] Late in the evening of 6 December, when it became known that Lloyd George had been invited to form a government, Joseph Davies was with Thomas trying to persuade him to join a Lloyd George Cabinet, and David Davies and Jones were discussing other appointments with Addison.[41] Their preferences were for socially reforming Liberals, and their influence was consequently small in the formation of a government which had to pay special attention to Unionists and the Labour party. With the tantalising scent of power in their nostrils, they turned to a consideration of their own employment.

On 9 December Jones breakfasted with Lloyd George and arranged to be seconded from the Insurance Commission to spend a few months in some capacity in Whitehall. At the same time he discussed the future of David Davies, who had just been removed from the fray by influenza. Jones's report to his wife is particularly revealing:

DD's ambitions as you know are very pure and unselfish. He always imagines himself as filling a job where some hustling of laggards is required and no doubt he'd be good at that. Unfortunately he also fancies himself as something of a strategist. He may be – I can't judge. He has a bold mind with a great directness of vision and honesty of purpose. He would like to be secretary to the new War Council, but there is already. . .Hankey who has had long experience of such work. . .Anyhow I can't see DD as an ideal *secretary* of anything. Other jobs suggested are Junior Whip or to remain as the Parliamentary Secretary of the P.M. I think L.G. is of that opinion too, for as he said yesterday 'close and consistent access to two or three of the Chief Ministers gives a man far more power than much more conspicuous posts'. Of course the trouble of these inconspicuous intangible posts to a concrete mind like DD's is that one does not see visible results happen at once – but the 'influence' is at work all the time.[42]

Leaving aside his 'concrete mind', Davies was not at that moment in any mood to accept an inconspicuous, intangible post which would bring him into contact with the Chief Ministers. On the one hand he had a very low opinion of Lloyd George's new colleagues: in a critique of the new administration launched from his sick-bed he complained that J. H. Thomas should not have been left out, F. E. Smith should not have been put in, Wedgwood Benn should not have been offered the Chief Whip's post, and Rhondda should have been shunned as 'the negation of the moral sense'[43] which was the principal asset of the new government. On the other hand Jones suspected that Mrs Davies was pressing him to get a proper government post.[44] His disappointment with the political millennium which he had tried to bring about did not dispose him to remain in Lloyd George's service with liaison duties which were only vaguely defined.

Within a few days, though, the task envisaged for the Prime Minister's private secretary began to expand. After it had been suggested to Jones that he might himself become Lloyd George's secretary 'to keep charlatans away', he began to investigate the responsibilities of the office in discussion first with Hankey and then with Vaughan Nash, who had served both Campbell-Bannerman and Asquith. Nash alerted Jones to the manifold duties of the position and suggested that only a small organised Secretariat, led by a competent civil servant who knew Whitehall, would allow Lloyd George to establish constructive relations with the departments.[45] This was the germ of the Garden Suburb. Although the record is obscure, it is evident that the idea reached Lloyd George, probably through Hankey: the final form of the Secretariat was so close to Nash's prescription that it seems reasonable to give him the credit rather than Leopold Amery, who would later claim that he had suggested the idea through Milner.[46] Lloyd George began to look for likely candidates.

Among the first names suggested was Philip Kerr, who was nominated by Milner and given a lukewarm testimonial by Robertson, the C.I.G.S., on 15 December.[47] Soon afterwards Astor's name was brought to Lloyd George's attention by Garvin. Astor had been suggested as Parliamentary Secretary to the Local Government Board, with a concurrent appointment as chairman of the National Insurance Commission. When this was vetoed by senior Unionist politicians, Astor was left without prospects. He wrote to Garvin:

This personal matter has honestly not affected me much as I have much useful work and I was not personally pushing claims or wire-pulling. I can't help being sorry on other grounds. The job which L.G. wanted for me and which was being considered was practically the creation of a Health Department. One has only to realise that a healthy people is a contented people...to see what a genuine chance for constructive and valuable work [it] would have been for me.[48]

Garvin, who combined a sympathy for Astor's ideals with a strong preference for being left alone to run his newspaper, smoothed over a personal antagonism between Astor and Sir Max Aitken,[49] which might have interfered with Astor's advancement, then approached Lloyd George directly:

...poor Waldorf is sore and discouraged even more than I expected.

I beg you to put him on your new Secretariat. He is worth it – he wins people and is not only hard-working but absolutely thorough about detail in his gradual and persistent way. In personal loyalty he is no end of a sticker.[50]

Plans for a Secretariat remained in abeyance until 28 December, when David Davies approached the Prime Minister again. A scheme to expand Lloyd George's private office by adding Kerr and C. H. Montgomery, a Foreign Office official who had served in Asquith's private office, to Sutherland and J. T. Davies was discussed. David Davies, pardonably excited, enlisted the support of Thomas Jones, who was himself safely ensconced as assistant secretary to the War Cabinet. Jones suggested that Professor W. G. S. Adams, with whom he had been discussing the organisation of a Ministry of Labour, should transfer his allegiance from the Ministry of Munitions to the Prime Minister's Secretariat, and that Kerr should deal with foreign affairs. In this form the plan was presented to Lloyd George, and Kerr and Adams were summoned to Downing Street on 1 January.[51]

At Lloyd George's instruction and in co-operation with Hankey, Kerr and Adams drew up the memorandum on the organisation of the new Secretariat which has already been mentioned. They gave themselves wide responsibilities, which included interviewing people who wanted to see the Prime Minister, preparing special memoranda for Lloyd George or the War Cabinet, and communicating with the departments 'with a view to discovering and reporting how far the decisions of the War Cabinet have been carried out'.[52] They took up thereby a burden deliberately laid down by Hankey, who had instructed his assistants in the War Cabinet Secretariat that his office was 'neither an Intelligence Department nor a General Staff'.[53] In these early stages the emphasis was upon liaison with the departments, and the work was all to be done by Kerr, Adams, and David Davies. During the next fortnight Astor was added to the Secretariat, a statistical sub-department was created for Joseph Davies, who was almost immediately absorbed into the body of the Garden Suburb, and the position of the Secretariat was consolidated against the opposition of Whitehall. Adams's appointment came under attack from the Ministry of Munitions, where it was rumoured that he was inadequate as an administrator: Jones drummed up testimonials and intervened personally with Lloyd George.[54] Civil service suspicions were dealt with by a blatant leak to *The Times* to the effect that 'It is not of course intended that [the new secretaries] should have executive power or that their appointment should affect in any way the regular Civil Service.'[55] The Secretariat was finally launched after a brief discussion at Lloyd George's birthday dinner, celebrated one day late at the Astors' on 18 January.[56] There Lloyd George met all his new secretaries and assigned their duties according to plans laid before him by Kerr and Adams. The next day Adams took his place for the first time as an observer at the War Cabinet.[57]

The two resignations from the Garden Suburb must be reserved for a later chapter, where their context can be explained. The only addition, of Cecil Harmsworth in May 1917, deserves consideration here because it emphasises the personal and accidental way in which the Secretariat was recruited. In April 1917 Lloyd George was look-ing for a Liberal M.P. to act as a Coalition Liberal Chief Whip in succession to Neil Primrose, who had accepted the job reluctantly in December and wished to return to his regiment.[58] In making his choice Lloyd George was influenced by the importance of limiting the damage caused by the developing split in the Liberal party. Asquith's supporters had already carried off the official Liberal party organisation, which had incidentally enabled them to prevent the selection of Joseph Davies as Liberal candidate for Derby in Decem-ber 1916,[59] and were beginning to offer overt resistance to the govern-ment in the house of commons.[60] Only back-bench opposition had been obvious to the Indian Cotton Duties in March, but in April two of Asquith's closest associates, Walter Runciman and Reginald McKenna, were threatening independent action, and Runciman made a swingeing speech against the Corn Production Bill.[61] Rather than take aggressive counter-measures, Lloyd George made approaches to the Asquithians. On 1 May Addison arrived at 10 Downing Street to find that Lloyd George had invited Harmsworth to be Chief Whip.[62] To Addison's relief Harmsworth turned the offer down by letter that afternoon.

I could not at your luncheon table open out fully to you my difficulties about the office of Chief Whip. I find them insurmountable. My misgivings in regard to the financial duties are such that I should not be able to render you good and efficient service if I held it.[63]

To his friend Runciman he explained that

I thought that in that capacity I might be of some service – having regard to the warm personal friendship existing between you and Reggie McKenna and myself – in bringing about a reconciliation. However my objection to the office proved insuperable.[64]

The job was soon filled by Frederick Guest, a more robust politician who set in hand a committee of Lloyd George's supporters to discusss counter-measures against Asquithian hostility.[65] Meanwhile Harmsworth, who never quite believed that the split was permanent, was offered and accepted a post in the Garden Suburb. David Davies's resignation in June left large areas of work without a secretary to cover them: at first Harmsworth acted as a substitute for Joseph Davies, who was in the United States investigating American shipbuilding.

VI

The *illuminati* who found their way by these varied paths to Lloyd George's garden differed widely in background, education and interests. Adams was in 1916 a respected and influential member of the Oxford community. He was born in 1874, the son of the headmaster of St John's Grammar School, Hamilton, Lanark, and he had an intellectual and somewhat evangelistic upbringing. In 1893 he went up to Glasgow University and from there took a Snell Exhibition to Balliol. He took Firsts in *Literae Humaniores* in 1899 and Modern History in 1900. After going down he lectured on social questions at Manchester and Chicago, and somewhere acquired a mastery of social statistics. In 1904 Sir Horace Plunkett invited him to become Chief Statistician at the Department of Agriculture and Technical Instruction in Ireland. He was at first reluctant, but would later speak of Plunkett as the greatest influence on his life. After six years in Ireland he was lured back to Oxford by A. L. Smith, then Master of Balliol, who wanted him to set up a School of Politics in the University: in effect to create the P.P.E. course. He took up the Gladstone Professorship in 1912 and in 1914 launched the *Political Quarterly*, a publication which was intended to bring academic study into contact with real politics. In the editorial section Adams expounded, within proper scholarly limits, a progressive view of contemporary politics which was sympathetic both to Labour and to Home Rule. During the war he served the Ministry of Munitions both as a labour adviser and as chairman of the committee which laid the foundation for the *History of the Ministry of Munitions*; he also took the chair of a committee of academics in Oxford which studied labour relations on behalf of a number of ministries.[66]

Philip Kerr took his First in the History Schools only two years after Adams, but had little else in common. A Catholic Scottish aristocrat of relatively ancient lineage, he was born in London, whither his father had retired after commanding his regiment in India, and was educated at the Oratory School. He went up to New College in 1898 and read History under the guidance of H. A. L. Fisher. After failing to be elected to All Souls he went out to Africa to assist in reconstruction, eventually becoming a member of the Milner Kindergarten. He remained in South Africa when Milner was succeeded by Selborne, and took part in the discussions which led to the promulgation of the 'Federal Egg' which played a large part in the movement to secure the union of the South African colonies. In 1909 he returned to England and soon became involved in the Round Table movement with Lionel Curtis and other former associates from South Africa. When the quarterly of the same name was launched he became the first editor and regularly contributed articles on imperial questions and on Ireland. He was involved, though not deeply, in the scheme for federal devolution which won some support in Unionist circles in 1914 as a substitute for Home Rule.[67] On the question of imperial federation he came to stand in the centre of the Round Table group, resisting the powerful and rather literal enthusiasm of Curtis. He never enjoyed robust health, and overwork so weakened his constitution that he was unable to join the army; he spent the first twenty-eight months of the war in the active but unsuccessful pursuit of patriotic employment. In 1915 Lord Selborne recommended him in vain to Hankey as 'one of the most brilliant civilians living'.[68] The two most important influences in Kerr's life were Milner, for whom he had an admiration as extreme as Adams's for Horace Plunkett, and Mrs Mary Baker Eddy, for whose creed of Christian Science he had left the Catholic Church at the risk of estrangement from his family and from many of his friends.[69]

Waldorf Astor, who shared Kerr's devotion for Milner and Mrs Eddy, was the son of an eccentric scion of the New York Astors, who had fled the United States and brought up his son as an English gentleman. Waldorf went to Eton and New College, where he studied, with little distinction, under Fisher and devoted himself to sport and society. He went down in 1902 to take up the calling of a rich young man. His marriage to Nancy Langhorne, a Virginian divorcee, under whose influence he turned to Christian Science and social reform, led him into politics and he stood in 1910 as Unionist candidate for Plymouth. In 1911 he crossed the floor to vote for Lloyd George's National Insurance Bill, a gesture which earned him the suspicion of senior members of his party, including F. E. Smith and Walter Long. He owned *The Observer*, which he had bought from his father, but scarcely controlled it. He entertained on a large scale at Cliveden and was on close social terms with Curzon, Balfour and Milner, as well as with the more socially active Liberals such as Churchill and Asquith; but he did not aspire to influence the Unionist party, preferring to work on the rather suspect Unionist Social Reform Committee and the Departmental Committee on Tuberculosis, to the chair of which he was appointed by Lloyd George. Astor had come into contact with the Round Table group in 1914, and Thomas Jones believed that he helped to finance the quarterly. Meetings of the Milner–Carson 'ginger group' frequently took place at his house in St James's Square. He was not, by all accounts, a very forceful personality (though he may have suffered unfairly from the comparison with his exceptionally forceful wife) nor excessively gifted intellectually; he was distinguished rather by honesty, loyalty and, for a Unionist, extremely progressive views including a wholehearted commitment to temperance reform.[70]

David Davies, like Astor, was both rich and good. His grandfather had been a pioneer in the development of the coal and iron resources of Wales and had built an industrial empire around the Ocean Coal Company, which was consolidated by Davies's father. The young Davies went to school in Scotland and to King's College, Cambridge. He entered parliament for Montgomeryshire in 1906 in the first general election for which he was qualified by age. On that occasion Herbert Gladstone described him as a Whig, partly on the grounds that he had been nominated both by the Liberal and the Unionist Associations,[71] but his subsequent commitment to social reform belies that description. In January 1910 he comfortably defeated a Unionist and was once more returned unopposed in December. As an M.P. he divided his time between the House, his business interests, and philanthropic activity in Wales. He was particularly interested in a sanatorium which he set up at his own expense in Montgomeryshire. He was responsible for suggesting to Lloyd George that 'sanatorium benefit' should be included in the National Insurance Bill, and he continued to work closely with the National Insurance Commission when it was set up. It was thus that he met Thomas Jones and Waldorf Astor.[72]

Any Welsh Liberal was bound to have some sort of relationship, whether love or hate, with Lloyd George. Davies was wholeheartedly Lloyd George's man. A community of interest over public welfare before the war was inevitably reinforced when Davies went to France with his regiment. It was entirely to be expected that a man of his temperament and political connections should attribute the blame for the problems of a fighting army to the inefficiency of Asquith's style of government. He took this view to unusual lengths, and it sometimes seems from his letters that he saw the solution to all wartime problems in the 'hustling' of the apathetic and incompetent men whom he assumed to hold the high positions in the state. There were some who found this attitude highly suspect, and assumed in their turn that Davies was constantly intriguing. It is certainly true that few among Lloyd George's collaborators would have been so outspoken at such an early stage as was Davies in his view that Asquith must actually be replaced by Lloyd George.

The life story of Joseph Davies, as told by himself, would have edified Samuel Smiles. He left Bristol Grammar School in 1882 at the age of fifteen to become an office boy in the Cardiff Docks office of the Glamorgan Coal Company. Ambition and diligence brought him by 1889 to the rank of a junior in the accounts department, whence the fortuitous illness of a secretary brought him into the office of Archibald Hood, the chairman of the company. Hood was at that time chairman of a coal-owners' committee which was preparing a case to be presented before Lord Balfour of Burleigh's commission on railway rates. After a disagreement with his colleagues, Hood sent Davies to a meeting in his stead. The terrified young clerk immediately impressed the committee – which included David Davies's father, the chairman of the Ocean Coal Company – with his grasp of the case. A commission to prepare tables for the coal-owners' evidence led to wider opportunities and in the 1890s Joseph Davies was a prosperous commercial statistician, publishing tables of railway rates and acting as consultant to governments and businessmen. He joined the boards of a number of colliery and railway companies, including the Cambrian Railway Company, of which David Davies was a director. Among his business acquaintances was Donald Maclean,[73] later an Asquithian, who encouraged him to enter politics as a Liberal. In December 1910 he was defeated at Hereford City, a Tory stronghold, but this led to his adoption as prospective candidate for Crewe. In late 1916 he was negotiating for the Liberal candidacy at Derby, which in the event went to Sir William Collins,[74] the nominee of the Asquithian whips. He was also chairman of the Lloyd George American Fund, a charity for the relief of distress in Wales set up by Welsh Americans. Although his involvement in public life was extensive, and his commitment to Lloyd George explicit, he did not meet his leader personally until invited to join the

Garden Suburb, and his ambition to enter national politics was apparently limited to a seat in parliament. He was self-effacing, and public spirited, if somewhat narrow in his political vision.[75]

Harmsworth, the latecomer to the Garden Suburb, was the third of the Harmsworth brothers, born in 1869 and junior to Lords North-cliffe and Rothermere. He had been drawn into newspaper publishing by his elder brothers' success and became editor of *Answers*, but his interests lay elsewhere. With his younger brothers Leicester and Hildebrand, he stood in the 1900 election as a Liberal: only Leicester was elected. Cecil and Hildebrand established the *New Liberal Review*, which praised the views of Joseph Chamberlain, and when Cecil entered parliament as member for Droitwich in 1906 he avowed himself a Liberal Imperialist. An extended trip to Africa in 1907 provided material for a book, *Pleasure and Problem in South Africa*, which argued for federal union to allow South Africa to develop as white man's country. After losing his seat in the January 1910 election, Harmsworth was out of parliament until a by-election in July 1911 brought him back as member for Bedfordshire South. In 1914 he became Parliamentary Private Secretary to Runciman at the Board of Trade. In February 1915 he became Parliamentary Secretary at the Home Office under McKenna, and when McKenna moved to the Treasury on the formation of the first wartime coalition in May 1915 Harmsworth relinquished ministerial office to be his Parliamentary Private Secretary. In May 1916 Harmsworth was brought into contact with Lloyd George by Northcliffe, who proposed him as an intermediary to get William Murphy, owner of the influential *Irish Independent*,[76] to lend his support to Lloyd George's proposals for settlement. The events of December 1916 embarrassed Harmsworth deeply. His closest political friends, Runciman and McKenna, left the ministry with the obvious intention of resisting the new government. Harmsworth formed no such intention. To Runciman on 10 December he confessed his fears that the establishment of a Liberal opposition would be a disaster both for the new government and for the Liberal party. He had in addition a private reason for regret in the large part that *The Times*, his brother's newspaper, had played in estranging Asquith from Lloyd George:

...I abstained with my brother Leicester from attending the Reform Club meeting. It is excruciatingly uncomfortable for us to take part in proceedings in connection with the Party of so intimate and domestic a character which arise largely from the action of a member of our family.[77]

During the early months of 1917 his infrequent parliamentary inter-

ventions showed no sign of hostility to the government; but for all his
merits as a link between Lloyd George and the more extreme
Asquithians his temperament did not make him a natural choice for
Chief Whip. Lloyd George later described him as 'shy and reserved',
and his own brother Rothermere regretted that he would 'never cut
much ice in the political world. His failure to make himself felt at
critical moments handicaps him beyond redemption'.[78] Harmsworth's political career, which culminated in a junior post in the
Foreign Office in 1919, was a triumph of diligence and obvious
capacity over his lack of ambition. In his appointment to the Garden
Suburb and his work there, there was little evidence of his own
ambition or, perhaps surprisingly, of an attempt by Lloyd George to
curry favour with his more powerful brothers.

VII

The Garden Suburb was not part of a master plan, an alternative
system of wartime government brought in by Lloyd George. To a
greater extent even than the War Cabinet Secretariat, it owed its
establishment to the opportunistic lobbying of its future members.
Nor was it an important part of a 'Fabian-like Milnerite penetration
of the organised administration': it was as much a monstrous regiment of Welshmen as a nest of Milnerites. Its centre of gravity was
Liberal and progressive, and its role was not to undermine but to
cherish the smooth working of the administrative machine. Though
other considerations inspired its conception and assisted at its birth,
the Garden Suburb was baptised in the rhetoric of administrative
efficiency. Its contribution to the management of wartime administration is the first theme of this study.

2

The new bureaucracy

My general conclusion is that co-ordination is a blessed word like
Mesopotamia which is mouthed by people without practical
experience.

G. N. Barnes, ?12 April 1918.

I

The huge apparatus of government over which Lloyd George
presided, and which the Garden Suburb helped him to rule, was very
largely the product of war and especially of his own premiership.
When war broke out the existing departments had been prepared for
the immediate assumption of new duties by the institution of War
Books at the instigation of the Committee of Imperial Defence.[1]
No machinery had been contemplated for managing a war economy.
At first the war was run as a feverish commercial operation in which
labour and capital took advantage of short supply and intense
demand to exact large profits from the government. Unable to accept
either the financial burden or the delays in production which
resulted, the government resorted to controls over munitions production in the spring of 1915: these were embodied in the Munitions of
War Act of July 1915, and munitions supply was made the responsibility of a single ministry. All extension of government control tended
to follow the principle that effective control could only be achieved if
the whole of each manufacturing process and the supply of raw
materials could be brought under a single authority. The Ministry of
Munitions was the first embodiment of the principle, and the first of
many demonstrations of the difficulty of applying principle in
administrative practice. A pattern of interdepartmental competition
was immediately established by the Admiralty's unwillingness to
relinquish full control over naval munitions, and the conflicting
requirements of industry and the army for men had still to be settled.
Shipping, labour and raw materials had not only to be allocated

between different products and different manufacturers, but between departments. To meet this problem a second stage of planning was entered when Lloyd George, on becoming Prime Minister, set up ministries of Shipping and Labour and a department of National Service. This horizontal integration removed from the producing departments the monopoly power over resources which they had been established to secure. Contradictions were multiplied by the extension of government into agriculture and the food supply by the appointment of a Food Controller and the creation of a Food Production Department within the Board of Agriculture.[2]

Necessity was not the only spur to the extension of control. Every wartime government was under political pressure to appear to be taking action, and the pressure mounted as hopes of a short war receded. While creating an atmosphere favourable to the assumption of control over munitions manufacturers and workers in 1915, Lloyd George tapped a powerful current of opinion in favour of drastic action, which undermined the political foundations of the Liberal Cabinet and contributed to its downfall in May 1915.[3] The manifest success of the Ministry of Munitions under his own leadership sanctified the principle of control, and politics was further polarised by the agitation, once more generated by Lloyd George, which overcame the reluctance of Liberals in the Asquith coalition to impose compulsory military service. After the conscription crisis of April 1916 British politics was conducted as a quarrel between those who favoured control and those who opposed it. Whatever the ideological consequences of this dispute – and it certainly misrepresented the differences between pre-war Conservatism and pre-war Liberalism – it was meaningless in administrative terms. The victory of the 'knock-out blow' and Lloyd George over Asquith and 'Wait and See' said nothing about how control should be organised and the new energy for warmaking harnessed. Two other pressures towards control had more specific effects. Energetic civil servants such as William Beveridge,[4] Hubert Llewellyn Smith[5] and Ulick Wintour[6] found that war justified the exercise of power by an objective administrative state, personified by themselves. In contrast, businessmen who had to deal with civil servants urged that war production could only be organised by other businessmen who understood their problems. Lloyd George's celebrated call in March 1915 for 'a man of push and go'[7] to take charge of munitions, and his subsequent appointment of businessmen to many senior positions in the Ministry of Munitions turned this opinion into a received truth. It was with

widespread parliamentary and public approval that the new ministries of December 1916 were led and staffed by men whose private
business interests lay in areas which they were to manage for the
public good. The three factors of political, business and civil service
interest in the extension of state control combined to produce an
administrative machine which generated tension and suspicion.

Three common variations of this tension were frequently brought
to the Garden Suburb's notice. There were too many departments
with overlapping functions; there was tension between long-estab-
lished departments dominated by civil servants and new departments
dominated by businessmen, and between outsiders and civil servants
in the same department; and throughout the war there was extreme
suspicion on the part of workers and their representatives who
thought, with some colour of reason, that the new bureaucracy was
an instrument specially fashioned for their oppression. It was in the
management of the war economy that most good came of the
Secretariat's facilities to 'secure closer co-operation between departments...to remove as far as possible misunderstandings which had
arisen, to make recommendations which study of a situation naturally
suggests to an onlooker.'[8] They were able to help Lloyd George to
conciliate and to plan, and often the secretaries acted on their own
initiative to solve problems. Their responsibilities evolved gradually.
At the birthday dinner on 18 January Adams took responsibility for
food and labour questions, and Joseph Davies was asked 'to watch
future movements in commodities and shipping'.[9] Since wheat supply
presented the most urgent problems both in commodities and shipping, Adams and Davies worked together for the first month almost
exclusively on food; their work on it then and later is of such importance that it is dealt with in a separate chapter. Adams's work on
labour was confined to reporting without comment on the activities
of Neville Chamberlain as director of National Service.[10] From the
beginning of March the Irish question took up more and more of his
time, and at the end of the month the threat of a railway strike
brought him into contact with the Board of Trade, J. H. Thomas of
the Railway Servants, and the representatives of the railway employers.[11] April added the supply of home-grown timber to his
interests,[12] but Ireland, with food, remained a major call on his time.
When Harmsworth joined the Secretariat at the beginning of May
he took responsibility for labour, which included the task of briefing
Lloyd George on the causes of the engineering strikes and examining
the causes of friction between the director of National Service, the

War Office, and the ministries of Munitions and Labour about the allocation of manpower. Harmsworth also joined Joseph Davies in his work on shipping, watching the merchant shipbuilding programme closely from May 1917 to March 1918 and interesting himself in the shipping of tobacco to England and relief supplies to Belgium.

For clarity, these diverse activities can conveniently be discussed under four headings: shipping, shipbuilding, manpower, and other miscellaneous activities.

II

Shipping questions were the first to occupy the Garden Suburb. In late March Joseph Davies, developing a theme from the food statistics which he had been collecting, entered the debate on the allocation of shipping, arguing with the Food Controller, Lord Devonport,[13] that it was essential to import wheat at the rate of 600,000 tons a month while tonnage was available. Davies's argument, supported by recommendations for curtailing the import of other commodities, was circulated on 11 April:[14] on 15 April the War Cabinet accepted his view, pressing the Shipping Controller, Sir Joseph Maclay,[15] to increase the rate of shipment from the United States.[16] Davies later recalled that a number of departments had telephoned to complain that he was interfering in their business: an indication, as he wrote, of 'the usefulness of a secretariat such as ours in getting at the best plan from data emanating from various sources'.[17] From then until the 1917 harvest was gathered the Secretariat gave Lloyd George regular reports of cereal stocks and rates of importation. These comparisons culminated in a detailed report sent in by Davies at the beginning of September, showing the relationship between cereal stocks, available tonnage for import, expected shipping losses, and the shipbuilding programme.[18] No other agency could have made these comparisons.

An important constraint on imports was the time taken to unload ships. Traditional restrictive practices in the docks, and wartime shortages of labour, were countered in November 1915 by the establishment of the Port and Transit Executive Committee, a body of shipowners, port employers and trade-union representatives which regulated labour conditions in the docks through local consultative committees. After the imposition of conscription, Port Labour Committees were created to decide which dockers were doing essential work and should be exempted. Acute labour shortages in 1916 led to the use of Transport Labour Battalions, which were sent to ports where the supply of civilian dockers was insufficient. The system was typical of the *ad hoc* arrangements by which control over vital economic functions was exercised, and in July 1917 it created an urgent problem which Joseph Davies was called upon to solve. On 28 July Harry Gosling,[19] secretary of the National Transport Workers' Federation and the senior labour representative on the P.T.E.C., wrote to Sir Frederick Dumayne,[20] the chairman, to complain that 'men have been released by Port Labour Committees, have been drafted into the Transport Workers' Battalions, and later, have been sent back to do the work they did in civilian life, but under military discipline'.[21] Gosling and his fellow trade unionists withdrew from the Port and Transit Executive Committee and from all its local advisory committees, thereby bringing its constructive work to a halt. The action was taken more in sorrow than in anger, and the other members of the committee informed the Prime Minister that

...civilian labour regards, and is fully warranted in regarding, such action as in breach of the principle underlying the Transport Workers' Battalion scheme: but neither the Port and Transit Executive Committee nor its local Consultative Committee have, as matters stand, any control over the action of the Port Labour Committee.[22]

Lloyd George remitted the problem directly to Joseph Davies, who brought together at Downing Street the representatives of the War Office, the Admiralty, the Ministry of Shipping, the port employers and the trade unions.[23] After a number of meetings he secured an agreement, ratified by the War Cabinet on 18 October, by which all members of local Port and Transit Committees were to be members of local Port Labour Committees, and labour representation on the national Port and Transit Executive Committee was strengthened.[24] This simple reconstruction, which lasted without friction until the end of the war, was notable first for the number of interests involved, and second for the contrast between its simplicity and the administrative confusion which had preceded it.

An administrative failing of another sort was occupying Harmsworth's attention at the same time. The tobacco question was a small part of the enormous problem of tonnage allocation imposed on the government by the success of the German submarine campaign. The balance between the necessities of war and the necessities of life was preserved by a system of licences. In August the Imperial Tobacco Company and the Tobacco Controller, L. G. H. Smith,[25] warned the government that there would be a tobacco famine in late

1918 unless licences were immediately granted for the import of
larger quantities than the 20,000 tons then envisaged. Harmsworth
investigated on the Prime Minister's behalf and reported his findings
on 26 September.[26] Lloyd George took no notice and when Harmsworth discovered that Smith had failed to persuade the President of
the Board of Trade to find tonnage for 50,000 tons of tobacco, the
Prime Minister was away in France. Harmsworth wrote instead to
Bonar Law, warning him that unless steps were taken soon the supply
of tobacco favoured by the working classes would run out in March
and not be recouped for some months. 'I cannot imagine anything
better calculated to foment discontent or bring the government into
disrepute.'[27] He repeated the point to the Prime Minister when he
returned,[28] but it was with Bonar Law that he conducted the rest of
the correspondence. In January he warned that the arrangements
made by the War Cabinet to put tobacco on the list of goods to which
tonnage must be assigned would not in itself solve the problem;[29]
later reports from the Tobacco and Matches Control Board suggest
this was because the allocation of space for tobacco did not mean that
the Shipping Controller would be able to find that space when the
tobacco, marketed seasonally, was available for shipping.[30] Harmsworth then dropped out of the affair, but when in March the Control
Board reported that stocks were so low that consumption must be
restricted, they were able to take their problems directly to Bonar
Law who sponsored them in the War Cabinet. Harmsworth had
merely offered a temporary alternative to the normal channels of
communication.

Another neglected commodity became a considerable charge on
Harmsworth's time in March 1918, when he was given responsibility
for finding shipping to carry food to Belgium for the Commission for
the Relief of Belgium. The Commission was an international organisation with a unique status which was responsible for providing
food and medical supplies to the civilian population of Belgium.[31]
The administration was American and American money bought the
supplies. Britain and France found the shipping through the Allied
Maritime Transport Council. This humanitarian work imposed a
further burden on a shipping stock already so depleted that tonnage
restrictions, mentioned briefly above in connection with tobacco,
affected even basic foodstuffs and vital raw materials and munitions.
The most acute difficulties were caused by goods requiring long
voyages: the cross-channel journeys made on behalf of the Commission occupied a relatively small tonnage for a relatively short time.

Nevertheless, the administrative effort of arranging those journeys, with their attendant port-handling and customs supervision, was considerable. The British Shipping Ministry bore most of the burden on behalf of the Allied Maritime Transport Council, but the blockade department of the Foreign Office was responsible for ensuring that essential materials did not pass to Germany through the activities of the Commission.

In early 1918 the Commission was having difficulty in obtaining the needed shipping from the Shipping Controller. W. B. Poland,[32] the European director of the Commission for the Relief of Belgium, found it difficult to get authoritative information about British intentions, and appealed to W. H. Page,[33] the American Ambassador, who sought the help of Astor on 1 March.[34] On 26 March, Poland was able to report to Herbert Hoover, the American head of the C.R.B.:

I have been called on today by Mr. Cecil Harmsworth M.P., one of Mr. Lloyd George's secretaries, to be put in touch with the real situation of the Relief. I found him most intelligent and apparently able to appreciate, not only statistics but the broader aspects of the question from the standpoints of military strategy and Inter-Allied politics.[35]

Harmsworth recommended that Poland await the answer of the Ministry of Shipping and ask for an interview with Lord Robert Cecil and a Treasury representative if the answer was not satisfactory.[36] Poland did what was suggested, but found that Cecil would only refer him to the Ministry of Shipping and that the only hope for the C.R.B. was to deal with the Allied Maritime Transport Council. He asked Harmsworth to ask Lloyd George to state that the provision of shipping for the C.R.B. was the wish of the British government.[37] Harmsworth both warned the Prime Minister of the problem and contacted the Ministry of Food, who intervened with the Ministry of Shipping and took the matter to the War Cabinet, which settled it in the Commission's favour.[38] Meanwhile, as a result of telegrams from Hoover to Lloyd George and a meeting between Poland and the Prime Minister, Smuts[39] was appointed to oversee the relations between the British government and the C.R.B.[40]

The effect of the appointment was that Harmsworth continued his work of co-ordination with somewhat greater authority in that he began to act on Smuts's behalf as an agent of the War Cabinet. Soon he came into conflict with the Foreign Office. After a conference at which the Admiralty, the Ministry of Shipping, the Ministry of Food, and the Wheat Commission were also represented, Harmsworth wrote on 17 June to the blockade department of the Foreign Office, asking for 'any information that comes your way' about the problems. The department was discomfited:

> The Imperial War Cabinet, apparently finding the time hanging heavy on their hands, have turned to Belgian Relief as a diversion: it seems to have occurred to them only as an afterthought, however, that the Foreign Office might also have some slight interest in this question. We are not informed what question in connection with Belgian Relief the Conference was kind enough to discuss; in the absence of such information it is difficult to see what steps had best be taken to ensure the minimum of interference from the Cabinet in a question which, so far as I can see, does not concern them even remotely.
>
> Would they, for instance, be interested in the question of the export of enemas for the C.R.B., a matter which has engaged our attention recently?
>
> It is certainly annoying that the Foreign Office is first entirely left out of the discussion, and then asked to furnish full information to an unknown gentleman at 10, Downing St.[41]

A meeting was arranged between Harmsworth and Cecil,[42] and Harmsworth received a memorandum from the Foreign Office explaining the diplomatic problems posed by the C.R.B. and urging him to prevent the government from committing itself in any way without first consulting the Foreign Office. Cecil, unlike his subordinates, was not reluctant to give up some of the responsibility to another part of the government.[43] Formal co-operation was thus secured, though Harmsworth still trod lightly. He wrote on 12 July:

> Lord Robert understands, I think, that I am an involuntary – I will not say an unwilling – participant in this work of Belgian Relief. For the time being I act, as it were, in a secretarial relation to General Smuts, convening informal conferences and informing General Smuts from time to time of the position of affairs.[44]

The blockade department replied in the same spirit, accepting his invitation to conferences, but decided not to inform him that Poland had been granted an interview with Cecil about clothing shipments, in which Harmsworth had expressed an interest.[45] Harmsworth continued to convene conferences at Downing Street until at least October, making it easier for the C.R.B. to explain its needs to the multitude of departments with which it had to deal.[46]

The various shipping questions with which the Secretariat had to deal illustrate the role of the outsider in wartime government. Joseph Davies in particular, with his understanding of commodity statistics, was able to challenge the bureaucracy on its own ground. Yet the Garden Suburb's importance did not depend solely on expert knowledge. Even after the multiplication of ministries in December

1916, the new bureaucracy found it difficult to solve problems which demanded interdepartmental co-operation; from its central position the Garden Suburb could work *ad hoc* to foster that co-operation, acting as a substitute for 'proper channels' which did not exist.

III

Joseph Davies first became concerned with shipbuilding when he accompanied J. H. Thomas and the Labour Mission to the United States as an adviser. Lloyd George's permission for the excursion was given on condition that Davies brought back a report on American shipbuilding capacity. The mission, whose main purpose was to inspire American trade unionists to support the war which America had just entered, left England on 23 April and returned on 16 June.[47] Davies's shipbuilding report deprecated the more extravagant claims of the U.S. Government, and made predictions of the total production for 1918 which were accurate to within 100,000 tons in a total of 3 million.[48] He returned to London to find Harmsworth 'struggling to convince the Admiralty that new construction of merchant ships is now of greater importance than making additions to the navy'.[49] Thus began almost a year's involvement in a classic problem of administrative and industrial co-ordination.

Until May 1917 naval shipbuilding had been commissioned by the Admiralty and merchant shipbuilding left essentially to private enterprise. Since the Admiralty had powers to requisition materials under the Defence of the Realm Act, merchant ships had a low priority and Maclay, the newly appointed Shipping Controller, could not easily recoup the depredations caused by submarines. On 11 May, as part of the attempt to improve the efficiency of the Admiralty occasioned by fear of the submarine campaign, the War Cabinet appointed Eric Geddes[50] as Controller of the Navy to manage naval shipbuilding and naval dockyards, and added the construction of merchant ships to his responsibilities. It was an example of the horizontal integration which found favour when pressure on resources became severe. Maclay was upset,[51] and the shipbuilders continued to resent the intrusion of officials from the Navy Controller's department into their merchant work. Geddes's department inspired little confidence. In July he produced an estimate of future building promising one million tons over the rest of the year and 3 million in 1918.[52] Davies disputed the figures and urged Lloyd George not to send them to the United States lest they create undue complacency.[53] The War

Cabinet on 10 July accepted Geddes's report 'in principle as a matter of extreme importance and urgency' but referred the problem to a committee and resolved that a letter drafted by Davies for Lloyd George to send to President Wilson should be substituted for the letter which Geddes had proposed to send to the British War Mission.[54]

Despite Davies's scepticism, the merchant shipbuilding programme started with high hopes. Maclay insisted that 'the programme now under discussion must...be regarded as a minimum and nothing should be permitted to interfere with its due execution',[55] and the committee on resources, sitting under Curzon, began its work.[56] Nonetheless, momentum was soon lost. On 17 July Carson was 'kicked upstairs' to the War Cabinet and Geddes promoted to replace him as First Lord of the Admiralty. Sir Alan Anderson,[57] capable but lacking Geddes's ruthlessness, became Controller. The Curzon Committee uttered a new list of priorities, diverting steel from shells to ships, on 3 August;[58] but it depended on the Ministry of Munitions for its execution and Churchill, the new Minister, was already losing patience with the Admiralty's claim to 'a super priority upon all supplies'.[59] General Collard,[60] the Deputy Controller for Auxiliary Shipping, who was responsible under Anderson for merchant shipbuilding, failed to win the confidence of shipbuilders. In September Harmsworth warned Lloyd George of imminent trouble,[61] and in early October joined Davies in advising the Prime Minister to convene a meeting between shipbuilders and the Controller's department.[62] The meeting, on 12 October, revealed that the shipbuilders were still short of steel plates and were losing labour to shipyards directly under Admiralty control.[63] To meet the steel shortage, Harmsworth and Davies recommended that Churchill should be directly involved as chairman of a committee to allocate supplies.[64]

For a few months the new procedures were tried out, and the Garden Suburb monitored output on Lloyd George's behalf. Parliamentary disquiet at the apparently low figures grew until on 14 March Harmsworth reported that only a complete change in the administration of shipbuilding would satisfy the critics.[65] With Davies he had already put forward a scheme under which control would remain with the Admiralty, to avoid the embarrassment of moving it elsewhere less than a year after the great centralising scheme of May 1917, but a powerful executive director would be appointed under a board chaired by a minister of Cabinet rank.[66] Lloyd George took the unusual step of sending Harmsworth's highly critical memorandum directly to Geddes,[67] and soon afterwards Lord Pirrie,[68] chairman of Harland and Wolff and an extremely successful shipbuilder in his own right, was appointed Controller of merchant shipbuilding. The appointment put an end to argument about shipbuilding administration, but did not solve all the problems of production. Although Churchill's committee had improved the supply of raw materials, increased production was still restricted by labour difficulties. In November 1917, at the suggestion of Harmsworth and Davies, Lloyd George had met shipbuilders and workers' representatives who jointly proposed a reorganisation of labour relations to restore freedom to settle conditions directly at the shipyards.[69] The War Cabinet had only partly accepted the scheme,[70] and on 1 March a deputation of shipbuilders told Lloyd George that five separate departments interfered in their labour relations.[71] G. N. Barnes, as the senior Labour politician in the government, investigated the situation and reported that 'My general conclusion is that co-ordination is a blessed word like Mesopotamia which is mouthed by people without practical experience.'[72] Nevertheless for the months of March and April Davies records Harmsworth 'concentrating on finding a solution [through] a number of meetings with representatives of all the interests. Backed by the commanding influence of the Prime Minister, he has succeeded in overcoming obstacles and ironing out friction, rendering useful help to Lord Pirrie'.[73] Harmsworth also had to follow up the War Cabinet's decision to release skilled men from the Home Army for shipbuilding, reminding Lloyd George on 22 March that 'of the 20,000 ordered to be released from the army, only 1800 had so far come forward'.[74] Anderson, to whom this was communicated, replied that the army's demands for men 'show a complete lack of sense of proportion' and, in an extraordinary example of the difficulties of interdepartmental communication, that the best way to find out how many skilled shipwrights were serving in the Home Army would not be to ask the War Office, but to advertise in shipbuilding towns for information from wives and union officials.[75]

Davies toured the shipyards in April 1918, investigating the state of production and particularly the attitude of the shipyard workers; he submitted his report on 3 May. Although he noted irritation with the new Controller, shortages of components, and a need for propaganda to keep the workers hard at work, his report lacked the sense of urgency which had hitherto characterised the secretaries' work on shipbuilding.[76] The same optimism was not felt by Harmsworth, who sent his analysis of the figures to Lloyd George on 26 April.

The shipbuilding figures continue to be most unsatisfactory and disquieting. There is at present no sign whatever of a large progressive increase. Three weeks only of the first sixteen weeks of the year show encouraging returns and in regard to these three weeks I cannot avoid a suspicion that the figures have been sophisticated. I mean that it looks to me as if whenever it was desired to make a good impression tonnage was slipped suddenly into the water in all stages of incompletion.[77]

In view of this continuing concern, it is surprising that no further interest in shipbuilding is recorded, either by Davies or in the secretaries' papers. One reason might be that, for all Harmsworth's disquiet, the projections he reported for British shipbuilding – 1,086,500 tons in 1918 – would, when added to the projections from the United States, even as modified by Davies's report of June 1917, and to expected transfers of requisitioned neutral shipping, approximate to the expected loss of Allied shipping in the year: a state of affairs not satisfactory, but not disastrous.

IV

Manpower occupied the attention of more departments and sub-departments during the last two years of the war than any other commodity. The problem was simply stated: to allocate men between the army and civilian occupations, and within civilian occupations between munitions, agriculture, transport, and other vital economic functions, and to do all this with the substantial consent of the workers themselves. To achieve this end the War Office was armed with compulsory powers to recruit; the Admiralty and the Ministry of Munitions had labour departments, with less comprehensive legal powers, to promote the efficient use of labour in munitions production; and in December 1916 a Ministry of Labour was established to take charge of Labour Exchanges and labour conditions, and a Director of National Service appointed to allocate labour between all requirements, military and civilian. The powers and responsibilities of these offices overlapped, and no department could give orders to the others. The internecine bureaucratic tensions thus created were compounded with political difficulties to make labour a constant source of anxiety to the government. The needs of the army had a symbolic importance which could not be ignored; but conscription had strained the loyalty of large and militant sections of the working populations, and too many men could not be taken without risk of crippling strikes or worse. The compulsory direction of civilian labour was too inflammatory to mention in public.[78] Lloyd George needed political antennae of the highest sensitivity to enable him to remain in control of the situation: his Secretariat helped to provide them.

One of Harmsworth's first tasks was to brief the Prime Minister on the establishment of the Commission of Enquiry on Industrial Unrest. The Commission was established to identify the causes of industrial friction which might give revolutionaries their opportunity. It was a response to discontent over 'dilution' of skilled by unskilled labour and over the operation of the Military Service Acts, both of which had contributed to the Amalgamated Society of Engineers' national strike in May 1917 and, more fundamentally, to the growth of the shop-steward movement which was threatening to wrest the leadership of labour from the national officials of the trade unions.[79] After the settlement of the A.S.E. strike Addison took up the idea of a commission, which had first been mooted by Henderson. Harmsworth, who had first been brought into the business by Adams, accompanying him to meetings with Ministry of Labour officials on 9 and 10 May,[80] attended a preliminary meeting about the Commission on 30 May. He reported to the Prime Minister that eight panels had been set up to cover the country and that the more restless elements in the labour movement would be included. He also briefed Lloyd George for the meeting on 12 June at which the Commission was inaugurated.

His brief, written before any local enquiries were made, shows a considerable understanding of the distrust of employers felt by industrial workers. His analysis of the causes of industrial unrest, drawn presumably in part from his experience at the Board of Trade, contained all the elements of the final report of the Commission except for the conclusion that the operation of the Military Service Acts was causing trouble.

I believe that the main causes of industrial unrest are these:

(1) fatigue and overstrain
(2) high prices and 'profiteering' or the belief that 'profiteering' is rampant.
(3) The clumsy handling of labour difficulties
(4) Uncertainty as to the future position of Trade Unionism
Pacifism I should put a bad fifth. It derives the greater part of such strength as it possesses, I am sure, from the irritation caused by (1) (2) and (4).

The belief that 'profiteering' is on a huge scale becomes more general every day and I fully share the belief myself. The Labour press rings with denunciations. . .[81]

He pointed out that the problem was not insoluble. As he remarked, even Bonar Law was an inadvertent profiteer,[82] and many in a like position would welcome strong action by the government to limit profits. A strong Food Controller could control prices. The range of the document is evidence of the extent to which the conclusions of the Commission of Enquiry were known in advance in government circles. The government knew what was wrong, and even knew what had to be done to put it right. It was prepared to deal with prices, and make pledges about trade-union rights after the war, but it would not or could not deal with the structural problems of British industry which were eroding the position of skilled engineering workers. The Commission's contribution to policy was, if anything, to satisfy demands for immediate action, to identify minor regional variations, and to provide respectable support for some of the government's ameliorative measures, such as Whitley Councils and a post-war housing programme. Harmsworth had already distilled for the Prime Minister the common wisdom which was to form the basis of policy.

Another labour question which Harmsworth addressed was the performance of the National Service Department. Again, his contribution was not to make original and influential suggestions, but to communicate commonly held opinions to Lloyd George in a useful form. Neville Chamberlain, who was appointed Director of National Service in December 1916, was hampered from the first because it was assumed when his duties were defined that the government would take compulsory powers to direct civilian labour. When it was decided not to take these powers, Chamberlain was left with the responsibility of matching men to jobs without powers either over the men or the employing departments. Even after the promulgation of an uneasy truce with the departments – of whom the largest and most obstructive was the Ministry of Munitions under Addison[83] – Chamberlain proved unable to co-ordinate National Service volunteers with vacant jobs, and thereby to release men from munitions work to the army. He pressed for an end to the policy of exemption from military service by occupational category and for the introduction of a block release to the armed forces of a quota from each occupational category, regardless of badging or any other protective scheme. He wanted control of the Labour Exchanges, whose co-operation had been promised but had never been given.[84] On 22 June he submitted a report reiterating his recommendations and proposing that unless his conditions could be met his department should be abolished and that responsibility for labour supply should revert to those departments which had made it impossible for him to carry out his appointed task.[85] Lloyd George had not liked Chamberlain from the start and he was not disposed to support him against other departments; yet he was as always reluctant to countenance the departure of anyone from a prominent position associated with the government.

Harmsworth had not intervened in the debate about recruiting methods and the control of labour, which was fought out at a high level. When Chamberlain submitted his report, however, he found it sufficiently alarming to deserve attention. On 28 June he wrote to the Prime Minister:

I have been reading the Director-General's 10th Report dated June 22nd 1917. In this he expresses a doubt as to whether the department ought to continue to exist unless certain conditions are realised...His position is difficult and embarrassing, but there are important reasons why he should not be allowed to shut down his department.

...If the National Service Department were absorbed or merged in the Ministry of Labour we should be thrown on the uncovenanted mercies of the Labour Exchanges and I will say in confidence that in my considered judgment they are amongst the most ambitious and least competent of the departments of state...we may yet need an employment department which is not fatally unpopular with capital and labour...the National Service Department *with a free hand* should be made responsible for the job.

...The suppression of the National Service Ministry would be very hurtful to the Government; I need not develop the point.[86]

His views had been formed in conversation with Cecil Beck M.P.,[87] a loyal Lloyd Georgian Liberal who stood to the National Service Department much as Kennedy Jones M.P.,[88] stood to the Food Ministry: as Chamberlain's Parliamentary Secretary he was the Prime Minister's envoy to a malfunctioning department.[89] On 26 July Beck sent Harmsworth the results of his correspondence with John Hodge, the Minister of Labour, about Labour Exchanges, which had begun with a memorandum written by Beck in early July traversing the same ground as did Harmsworth's memorandum quoted above. Hodge replied scathingly on 12 July, and Beck passed the matter to Harmsworth in the hope that he would 'proceed to prepare a memorandum'.[90] No such memorandum has been found, though it is evident from its form that Beck's original memorandum was sent for the Prime Minister's attention.

Chamberlain finally resigned on 8 August. Feiling, the authorised biographer, assigns as a reason Derby's suggestion to a commons select committee on 24 July that the National Service Department should undertake military recruiting.[91] Chamberlain's letter of resignation referred also to the lack of co-operation from other departments and the absence of support from the War Cabinet.[92] He was replaced by Auckland Geddes,[93] who had a seat in the commons and the responsibility for military recruiting. Besides the seat, which Chamberlain believed to be the most important attribute of a successful administrator,[94] Geddes had the powers over Labour Exchanges that Chamberlain, Harmsworth and Beck had recommended.

V

Lloyd George's ultimate political responsibility for subordinate areas of administration led his secretaries to many obscure corners which defy categorisation. The work they did can appropriately be illustrated by an extended example: Harmsworth's handling of air-raid insurance. An air raid on London on 7 July 1917 had caused considerable damage and loss of life. Public morale had suffered both from the effects of the raid and from the impression gained that British opposition had not been effective. The War Cabinet discovered that the squadrons of aircraft available for the defence of London had recently been depleted by the sending of machines to France and that only thirty-six 'first-class fighting machines' had actually been sent up to attack the enemy bombers.[95] Harmsworth, who had only ten days previously sent in a memorandum calling for aircraft production to be managed with 'the same fiery energy, the same disposition to multiply and multiply again the demands of the military advisers, that you brought to bear on the Munitions situation in 1915',[96] drew the Prime Minister's attention to an article in the *Westminster Gazette* emphasising the importance of London to the Entente. He argued, following the paper's war correspondent, that London was not only the most important munitions centre but also the effective political centre of the alliance. If the Germans made a few more successful air raids the government might find itself 'in the midst of an inflamed and unmanageable populace'. To prevent this breakdown of morale he urged the Prime Minister to insist on priority for London over any of the battlefronts in the allocation of defensive military aircraft.[97]

The War Cabinet Committee on Air Organisation and Home Defence against Air Raids, which was set up on 11 July, echoed

Harmsworth's analysis of the importance of London but not his assessment of priorities; it did, however, recommend a substantial increase in the force available to defend the capital.[98] The government was committed to bombardment insurance by an ambiguous remark made by the Prime Minister to a deputation led by the Lord Mayor of London on 13 July.[99] The deputation, understandably, had played on the threat to morale posed by the fear of uncompensated damage to property and Lloyd George, no doubt afraid that the Lord Mayor and his friends might become 'inflamed and unmanageable', promised to extend the existing government insurance scheme. He did not make it clear whether he intended the extension to be provided free to all property owners or just to small householders. Harmsworth was given the job of minimising the cost. On 27 July he reported to Lloyd George that officials of the Treasury and the Board of Trade were anxious for an interpretation of the Prime Minister's words.[100] After further discussion he reported that the Treasury had arranged a joint conference with the Lord Mayor to discuss a scheme under which the government would provide free compensation up to 'a certain moderate limit' beyond which people would have to pay for insurance within the existing government scheme.[101] Negotiations on that basis were conducted with Stanley Baldwin[102] leading for the Treasury. The Lord Mayor would not budge from his interpretation of Lloyd George's words, even after Harmsworth had conveyed to Baldwin the Prime Minister's message that he had not meant to promise free, unlimited insurance. When the Lord Mayor refused to deal with the Treasury and demanded to see Lloyd George again, Harmsworth asked Baldwin to put him off such an idea.

Are not the Lord Mayor and his friends taking too much on themselves when they presume to speak as if they represent the nation at large? Perhaps we have fostered the notion by treating them as if they had representative character.

If the Prime Minister restates his intention I hope he will convey the impression, clearly but quite firmly, that this is a national matter and that if the Lord Mayor, etc. will not continue in conference with the Government Departments concerned the Government will nevertheless proceed to the establishment of a national scheme on their own lines.[103]

Harmsworth had not in fact talked to the Prime Minister about the question since first eliciting his intentions. With Baldwin's agreement the course of action he suggested became government policy; Lloyd George signed a letter to Baldwin stating his views and the Treasury worked out a scheme which was presented to the War Cabinet on

29 October, following a formal War Cabinet decision on 4 October.[104] For the rest of the war the government compensated owners of property for loss of up to £500 as a result of air raids, provided that the balance of the value of the property was insured under the government scheme.

VI

The activities of the Garden Suburb described above in four separate sections have common features which should not be overlooked. The secretaries had no executive power, but their existence was essential to the proper discharge of Lloyd George's executive responsibility. Their job was not to innovate, nor to control, but to warn of imminent administrative breakdown. They relied not only on expert knowledge, but also on their central position which enabled them to understand the different needs and bargaining positions of the different departments. Their role was political, in the sense that they were particularly concerned with areas where the administrative performance of the government was of political consequence: labour, shipping and shipbuilding were of vital importance to a belligerent country heavily dependent on imports, but public approval for the government's handling of them was no less essential to its power to govern. These points are valid also for the food-supply questions discussed in the next chapter.

The Secretariat's function as a gatherer of administrative intelligence was largely, if not completely, confined to 1917. This might be explained in part by the appointment in September 1917 of the War Priorities Committee of the War Cabinet, under Smuts, which gradually evolved an elaborate system of sub-committees to allocate materials, and, after considerable argument and delay, labour, between competing departments. It is interesting that such an arrangement was foreshadowed by David Davies shortly before his resignation from the Garden Suburb in June 1917. Writing to Smuts after a conversation on the subject, he complained that no one had authority to decide between the competing claims of departments, and that the fighting services received an undue priority:

Nor is the difficulty overcome by the appointment of numerous ad hoc committees under the chairmanship of a Cabinet Minister.

To ensure continuity of policy and a thorough investigation into the circumstances of each particular case it is submitted that there should be a standing committee for the allocation of all materials and supplies. Further, that the committee should be vested by the Cabinet with executive powers and the fullest authority to deal with disputes which may arise between the Government departments. That the committee shall only refer to the War Cabinet questions of policy. That it shall meet continuously and devote its whole time and attention to the study of the problem involved.[105]

To a very limited extent the Garden Suburb in 1917 attempted to discharge the function of co-ordination which was eventually put on a proper footing by the War Priorities Committee. Its work provides examples not of the typical performance of wartime administration – for when it was functioning properly the machine could generally look after itself – but of the typical form which breakdowns might take. Therein lies one starting point for a study of wartime administrative history.

3

Food and agriculture

I

Since the 1880s, when cheap North American wheat had captured the English market, British farmers had given up the attempt to feed the nation. Millions of acres of arable land, first broken up in the early nineteenth century to feed a growing industrial population, had been returned to pasture. Hundreds of thousands of men had left the land. Good grassland, created at great expense, was the principal capital asset of many farms. Store-cattle bought from Ireland or Scotland or the English and Welsh hill-pastures could be fattened with a minimum of labour and sold at a good profit to the towns. In many areas of England grains were only grown as animal feed, and other areas depended even for their feeding stuffs upon imported cereals.

The coming of war upset this equilibrium. The destruction of British shipping threatened the supply of imported grains. To avoid serious food shortages, and the demoralisation which would inevitably follow, it became necessary to alter the balance of British agricultural production. An abnormally good harvest in 1915 postponed the problem until 1916, when a poor harvest coincided with serious losses of shipping. As Lloyd George's coalition came to power stocks of food were rapidly diminishing. R. E. Prothero, the new President of the Board of Agriculture, prophesied political disaster unless the matter was taken in hand.[1] The War Cabinet, following plans tentatively laid by the previous administration, decided to regulate consumption to make the most economical use of shipping and to encourage the production of food in Great Britain to make an absolute reduction in the amount of tonnage required. The extension of planning brought its own difficulties. The responsibilities of the newly established Ministry of Food overlapped with those of the Food Production Department, newly created within the Board of Agriculture, and caused friction between the responsible ministers.

The Board also came into conflict with the War Office over the conscription of skilled agricultural workers. These administrative disagreements were given a personal flavour by the fact that Lord Derby, who as Secretary of State for War was hungry for recruits, was a large landowner and a strong opponent of the Board's policy of ploughing up pasture land.[2]

Both the Board of Agriculture and the Ministry of Food based their policy on contemporary scientific wisdom, expressed by the Royal Society's Food (War) Committee. For the purpose of war, the most important part of the human diet was held to be that which gave energy, usually starch in the form of bread.[3] The Ministry of Food developed the 'Breadstuffs Policy': there would be no rationing of bread and priority in shipping would go to grain.[4] The Board, observing that a pound of meat cost much more in energy than it gave to the man who ate it, decided that pastures should be put under the plough. To overcome the natural opposition of farmers to this destruction of their capital, the Board had a stick, in the Defence of the Realm Act, and a carrot, in the form of a guaranteed price policy which was later elaborated in the Corn Production Act. Under DoRA local Agricultural Executive Committees could, on behalf of the Board, issue instructions to farmers to break up their pastures. Farmers would typically respond that these instructions were impossible to obey, since their skilled workers were in the army, and because they lacked fertiliser, petrol, horses and transport facilities. To meet the objections the Board had to petition the government departments concerned for the release of men, shipping, petrol or railway facilities for the farmers. In spite of frustration and delay enough was achieved to win the co-operation of the farmers, and the tillage campaign was a notable success. Its first real achievement, however, was the harvest of 1918, too late to have much effect on the war.

The Corn Production Act had even less real effect. By fixing minimum prices for grain (Part I) and restricting the increase of agricultural rents (Part III), it was intended to provide in the Act a charter under which effective cultivation (Part IV) could be enforced without injustice to the farmer. The Act also provided for a minimum wage of twenty-five shillings a week to be paid to agricultural labourers (Part II). The minimum price was effectively superseded by the Food Controller's minimum price, which was higher.[5] Scarcity of labour did more for the farm worker's economic security than any Act of Parliament could. The teeth of the Act – Part IV, which enabled the Board of Agriculture to order changes in cultivation methods and in the crops grown, and in the last resort to take over the management of inefficient holdings – were never used because the Board preferred the wider powers available under the Defence of the Realm Act. The political achievement of the Corn Production Act was more remarkable than its impact on the production of food. 'Conservatives (though not all) were prepared to plough their pastures, while Liberals and Labour members (again not all) were prepared to harrow their economic principles, if only they could mend the food situation.'[6] In passing the Corn Production Act the government could claim that it had been prepared to sacrifice the selfish interests of the majority of its supporters to the common good.

The regulation of consumption would have been a more difficult business even if it had been undertaken with the same determination as the Board of Agriculture showed towards production. The Food Ministry's most important decision, in the eyes of its own historian, was a decision not to regulate consumption: the Breadstuffs Policy. Devonport, the first Food Controller, was an unfortunate choice; Beveridge observed with some justice that in his relations with the public he 'appeared to be unable to avoid the lure of the trivial. Attacks on flaunting displays in shop windows went hand in hand with orders about...the construction of buns.'[7] The Ministry's loss of public esteem damned it in Lloyd George's eyes and eventually in those of the War Cabinet. Before the end of March 1917 Kennedy Jones, M.P., was appointed by the Prime Minister to the Ministry, ostensibly to take charge of the Food Economy campaign. It was generally accepted that he was a personal agent of the Prime Minister, sent especially to watch over Devonport.[8] When Devonport finally did produce a rationing scheme (for sugar) it was:

discussed and re-discussed at conferences with Lord Milner, Mr. Arthur Henderson, Mr. Cecil Harmsworth, and other representatives of the War Cabinet who visited the Ministry of Food for this purpose...It was rumoured that some at least of the distinguished visitors desired to inform their minds less about rationing than about the personnel and organisation of the ministry, which by this time [May 1917] had lost most of its credit with the public.[9]

The Ministry did little of any value until May 1917, when Devonport, who had providentially fallen sick, at last resigned. He was succeeded by Lord Rhondda. The new Controller, unlike the first, was not a wholesale grocer and did not feel obliged to apply his own expertise to every one of the Ministry's problems. Under his supervision the Ministry committed itself more heavily to rationing schemes, especially after the appearance of meat queues in the winter of 1917–18. Local monitoring committees were set up, which anticipated or at least reported local failures of supply or abuses of the regulations, and the Post Office co-operated by issuing ration cards. The most important achievement, however, was the transformation of the Ministry into an enormous trading agency, controlling supplies and prices through a near-monopoly of home-grown and imported foodstuffs. Rhondda died of overwork in June 1918, and was succeeded by J. R. Clynes.[10]

II

The Garden Suburb was most active in its attention to food questions in the first few months of 1917. As in the other war-production matters already discussed, the secretaries assisted Lloyd George by standing outside the newly created bureaucracy and commenting critically on the information coming to the Prime Minister and the War Cabinet. As the first steps were taken towards an agricultural policy, Adams and Joseph Davies briefed Lloyd George and the War Cabinet and helped to modify the Corn Production Act. When Milner was delegated by the War Cabinet to investigate the Ministry of Food, Adams and Harmsworth, who had been keeping Lloyd George informed of its performance, acted for him in collecting and explaining information about its activities. When the agricultural policy had been established and the Ministry of Food had restored its reputation, the secretaries withdrew to their vantage point in Downing Street and confined themselves to summarising food statistics with the minimum of comment. The policies which concerned them were laid down in outline before the Garden Suburb was set up.

On 13 December the War Cabinet decided to continue the policy of fixed prices for the 1917 crop. The labour problem was recognised; Derby and Prothero were asked to come to an arrangement about the use of reservists on the farms.[11] On the other side, the appointment of a Food Controller was in itself a commitment to the policy of rationalising and reducing consumption. Discussions within the government quickly took on an alarmist tone. On 11 January Devonport circulated a pessimistic report about the supply of bread and sugar.[12] The next day Neville Chamberlain presented his first report on National Service to the War Cabinet, making it clear that the agricultural labour situation could not improve.[13]

Adams attended his first War Cabinet meeting on 19 January.[14] It was a huge affair, with twenty-seven ministers and officials present besides four members of the War Cabinet. The occasion was Neville Chamberlain's presentation of his revised man-power report, which had already been referred back to him once. For our purposes the most important aspect of the report was that it made no specific estimate of the number of men who would be called up from agriculture. Thus it was without any prompting from the National Service department that the War Cabinet decided on a figure of 30,000 men to be released from the land by the end of January. Both Derby and Prothero attended the meeting: the minute bears the marks of a compromise between them. Prothero was able to make the stipulation that the figure of 30,000 would not be exceeded without fresh authority, and that men certified as indispensable by their local War Agricultural Committees would not be called; but Derby made this conditional on the provision of an adequate substitute from agriculture within seven days.

The strain of wartime government seems to have encouraged a ruthless attitude to compromise agreements. On the 22nd Lloyd George wrote to Derby to ask him to slow down the call-up of farmworkers, because he was receiving 'representations' about the shortage of food and the danger of submarines.[15] The War Cabinet, clearly at Prothero's prompting, called a conference of Prothero, Derby, Chamberlain and Lord French[16] under Walter Long's chairmanship to go over the whole problem again. As Long reported on the 23rd, the military held their ground; but Prothero extracted the further concession that Home Defence units would provide 15,000 substitutes and that the War Office would find a further 15,000 from its own surplus.[17] Even this was not to be the end of the matter. This encounter between two departments competing for the same resources illustrated the urgent need of a detailed and constructive agricultural policy to be set against the needs of the army.

Adams's first task was to follow up the provision of agricultural labour from the army and the arrangements made by Neville Chamberlain.[18] Lloyd George's repeated requests for information reflect his suspicion of Chamberlain's competence and of the capacity of the War Office to recognise that, for agriculture as for shipbuilding or munitions manufacture, a skilled man at home was worth more to the war effort than the same man in a trench in France. Adams continued to watch the transfer of labour until late May, when matters became so bad that the War Cabinet appointed Milner to take charge of the agricultural programme and order the departments concerned to co-operate.[19] War conditions had also disrupted the supply of artificial fertilisers, which were partly imported and partly manufactured as by-products by the peacetime chemical industry. Shortage of shipping and the change to munitions production coincided with an increased demand for artificials as the tillage programme brought marginal land back into arable production. Adams, by keeping in touch with civil servants in various interested ministries, was able to inform the Prime Minister about fertiliser supply:[20] but his more constructive effort was to conceive and organise a Fertilisers Committee, which began to meet in January 1917, bringing together civil servants from the Board of Agriculture with representatives of the chemical manufacturers to co-ordinate supply and demand and arrange the transport of fertilisers from the chemical works.[21] He also interested himself in the supply of tractors, which were essential if much new land was to be broken up.[22]

While Adams watched the Board of Agriculture, with the help of other departments, trying to increase food production for 1917, he was also concerned in the making of longer term policy on which efforts for 1918 and afterwards would be based. In the evolution of the policy which became embodied in the Corn Production Act both Adams and Joseph Davies furnished information and insight to the War Cabinet. The policy upon which the Act was based was elaborated by Prothero in a letter sent to Lloyd George at Adams's request at the end of January. The letter stated the position in stark terms: agriculture was 'politically. . .the most assailable point of the Government's position'. There was only one solution: 'A system of guaranteed prices lasting over a series of years seems to me to be the only possible means which would restore confidence to the farmer and encourage him to embark on increased production with its attendant outlay and risk.'[23] Prothero's idea was to guarantee a minimum price for wheat, oats and potatoes by undertaking to reimburse the farmer if the market price dropped below the guaranteed figure; he also proposed that the government set a minimum for commandeering commodities (in the case of wheat, 10s. a quarter higher than the guaranteed price). He insisted that a long period of price supports should be accompanied by legislation setting a standard agricultural wage and compelling the landowner to cultivate 'in the national interest'. Adams was entirely in sympathy with agricultural regeneration, which he had helped to foster in Ireland in his work for the Department of Agriculture and Technical Instruction, and he welcomed the decision to assist it by deliberate governmental action. To him, as to Prothero, the exigencies of war gave an opportunity to reverse the decline of British farming. Commenting to Lloyd George on food imports in March 1917, he observed:

There have been, I am glad to say, improvements in our herding and feeding of livestock, and in our cultivation and yield of crops. But when we take a broad view of the shrinkage of the tillage area, and of the enormous growth of our food and feeding stuff imports [since 1875], we cannot but realise how necessary it is to get ourselves to improve this state of affairs. . . The exodus from the land is in itself an indication of the decreased employment and the under-production which is going on in rural Britain.[24]

The success of Prothero's scheme would depend on details, such as methods of support and the levels at which prices were fixed. The government's decision to purchase the whole harvest at contract prices in 1917, which implied an intention to do the same each year for the duration of the war, circumvented the market and thus made the guaranteed minimum price irrelevant. Prothero himself thought that even if the contract system were not renewed the market price would never fall so low that the government would have to spend money on supporting the prices.[25] The problem was to be expected when the war was over; to encourage capital investment in preparing the land the guarantees had to be promised for a number of years, but the future of the market was difficult to predict. Any price set in 1917 might be too low to interest a farmer, and therefore ineffective in encouraging production, or so high that the government would be involved in enormous expense for the support of a glutted market.

These arguments were rehearsed at a War Cabinet meeting on 14 February.[26] Prothero's suggestions were supported by Selborne, and his scheme adopted to the last figure.[27] The Prime Minister undertook to announce the policy in parliament. As though at a signal, opponents of the scheme, hitherto silent, emerged to contest it at a meeting on 17 February.[28] The minutes indicate that all present at this second meeting spoke in favour of the policy of a guaranteed wage and minimum prices. It is curious, then, to note that the minimum-wage decision was suspended as a result of the discussion.[29] Evidence given by experts from the Ministry of Food also impelled the War Cabinet to give up the idea of undertaking not to commandeer below fixed prices.

With the policy in a state of flux, Joseph Davies now entered the argument with a comment on the prices themselves. He was particularly concerned about the prospect of a post-war glut. He estimated

the free-market price of wheat in the year after the end of the war as
43s. 6d. per quarter, against the 55s. proposed minimum price.
On this basis he estimated the likely cost to the Treasury for the
wheat subsidy alone at 85 million pounds.[30] His criticisms provoked
a reply from A. D. Hall[31] of the Board of Agriculture, one of the
co-authors of Prothero's original memorandum. Hall described
Davies's report as embodying 'the worst fear of the farmer'. His view
was that neither the fall in prices nor the increase in production
would be as great as Davies feared.[32] Both of these reports were
presented to the Prime Minister who implicitly accepted Hall's argument by ignoring the problem. Davies was more successful in an
attempt to persuade Lloyd George that the farmers' *morale* needed
direct attention. He drafted a letter for the Prime Minister to sign,
which was sent to every farmer to encourage him to produce more
with the resources at his disposal.[33]

Adams now intervened to defend the position that a guaranteed
price should be paid only for crops sold in the market. The Selborne
Committee[34] had recommended that the farmer be paid a sum calculated on his whole production of grain. Adams was sure that this
would be both difficult and expensive; he said so in a note to Lloyd
George on 20 February, two days before the Prime Minister's major
house of commons speech on the new agricultural policy. He was
particularly insistent that, whichever way the government determined
to pay the subsidy, the policy should be clearly stated in the house.[35]
Lloyd George, who had had a brief prepared by Adams and Kerr for
the occasion, departed from his text and in particular failed to make
clear which basis would be used.[36] This was all the more unfortunate
since the War Cabinet had in fact decided on the 21st to pay on
marketed produce.[37] The ambiguity of the parliamentary statement
allowed the question to come to the surface again when the bill had
been drafted.

Drafting occupied the latter part of February and the greater part
of March. In the initial draft the question was left in doubt, and
Adams commented in a letter to Bonar Law 'I have come much more
strongly to the view that marketing – and not production – is the only
workable basis.' He also suggested that the state should purchase any
grain which could not be sold above the minimum price, instead of
proclaiming a cumbersome system of subsidies based on the average
Gazette price which would favour producers who had good luck in
the market.[38] These arguments he repeated in a note to Lloyd George
on 31 March.[39] In defence of both these proposals Adams collected

memoranda from the Department of Agriculture and Technical Instruction and the Board of Agriculture.[40] The matter came before the War Cabinet on 3 April. The subsidy system was left in the bill, apparently without discussion. The other question provoked much disagreement but was finally settled in favour of Adams's proposal.[41] Thomas Jones noted in his diary, 'There was much diversity among the experts as to whether the guarantee should be for corn *produced* or corn *marketed and sold*. Ultimately the latter carried. A memorandum from Adams to the P.M. (which the P.M. digested) contributed not a little to the result.'[42] With the Garden Suburb's mark upon it, the Corn Production Act was offered to parliament.

III

The Garden Suburb also helped Lloyd George to intervene in the administration of food control when Devonport's inadequacies became too obvious to ignore. In March the War Cabinet held a number of meetings to allow the Food Controller to state his plans for dealing with the alarming decrease in stocks. For the meeting of 15 March 1917, Adams prepared for circulation a long memorandum on current stocks and prices.[43] The paper was moderately optimistic, but noted weaknesses in the supply of oats and of sugar, and observed that the price of food, especially of cheap food, had increased more rapidly than the cost of living. The War Cabinet postponed its decisions, and Adams was able to return to the charge with a brief for Lloyd George for the War Cabinet on 20 March.[44] He criticised Devonport for laxity in handling the sugar shortage and for insisting on the policy of 'meatless days', which were positively dangerous because meat was plentiful and cereals, the obvious substitute, in short supply. These points were brought out in the War Cabinet,[45] presumably by Lloyd George, and found support among ministers. Charles Bathurst M.P., Devonport's Parliamentary Under-Secretary,[46] was in any case on the point of resignation over the meatless days, which he later described as 'nothing less than insane'.[47] Addison, sensitive to the needs of his working-class constituents in Hoxton, complained to the Prime Minister on 21 March of Devonport's failure to guarantee the supply of sugar to the poor.[48]

On 24 March Adams amplified his earlier criticisms, telling the Prime Minister that Addison's protests were justified and repeating his own words of the 17th. 'The Food Controller has been much too considerate of the confectionery interests, and a great deal of popular indignation has been rightly aroused over the display of confectionery which is still to be seen.'[49] Meanwhile Sutherland had been talking casually to food importers who had told him that Devonport's price-fixing policies discouraged them from placing orders abroad: they had therefore not felt confident enough to order sufficient to feed the country. Sutherland informed Lloyd George, adding the recommendation that 'we' should ask the Ministry what steps it was taking.[50] Lloyd George took the unusual step of instructing Sutherland to send Adams's report to the Food Minister. Hitherto the Garden Suburb's reports had either been used exclusively by the Prime Minister or had been circulated as Cabinet papers. This new procedure, making obvious the potential of the private Secretariat as an intelligence organisation, disconcerted the Food Controller. He had already smarted under criticism from the War Cabinet and from the press; now another source of criticism threatened. His reply to Lloyd George revealed his insecurity.

The enclosed documents have been forwarded to me from 10 Downing Street, I understand at your request and asking for the comments of my department thereon.
 I do not propose to make any observations on the detailed criticisms on the working of my department which they contain. If you have any doubts in your own mind as to any decision or action taken for which I assume full responsibility – I will always gladly discuss them with you – but it would be simply intolerable for a running comment or criticism to be supplied to you as to the working of my department and for such to be passed to me for reply. To be perfectly frank and I need scarcely say in no way wishing to be discourteous I cannot submit to such methods. I am sure you have only to place yourself in my position to realise how hopeless it would be to attempt to carry on under such conditions.[51]

Lloyd George ignored the complaint. His dissatisfaction with Devonport's management of food supplies soon led him to appoint Kennedy Jones to a position in the Food Ministry. More than two weeks after the sugar incident, the Prime Minister sent Devonport two brusque enquiries on disorganisation in wheat supplies and in supplies of sugar beet, remarking in the latter:

I did not reply to the letter which you sent me in reply to my previous memorandum because I thought on reflection you would realise it as an impossible attitude to take up. When complaints come to me I am bound to investigate them as the public hold me responsible if anything goes wrong.
 As for your suggestion that I could send for you to come and talk these matters over with me, it is quite impossible for either you or me to find time to do so on every occasion when these letters arrive.[52]

Although the experiment of sending his criticisms to Devonport was not repeated, Adams himself continued to be interested in food matters. The emphasis shifted somewhat, from the Ministry of Food to the wider area of food importing, involving the Shipping Controller. Both Joseph Davies and Harmsworth took part in this activity. Devonport's response to the problems raised at the War Cabinet meeting of 15 March on food stocks was slow. On 5 April he circulated proposals for limiting the price of home-grown wheat, which was increasing rapidly due to the shortage.[53] His proposals were accepted by the Board of Agriculture and the War Cabinet,[54] but the fact remained that, whatever the price, the total quantity of wheat in the country was diminishing rapidly. On 11 April Davies circulated a detailed and cogent plea for increasing the quantity of wheat imported at the expense of other commodities, notably American cotton and Australian wool.[55] Although he drew on figures supplied by Carson on shipping and Devonport on wheat, his recommendations differed from theirs and were the ones adopted by the War Cabinet on 18 April.[56]

In May the Food Controller put forward his plans for compulsory rationing. He told the War Cabinet on 7 May that although stocks would probably be adequate until the 1917 harvest, he was concerned for the next year and wished to get a scheme under way before September.[57] He was asking the War Cabinet for a decision of principle; but the War Cabinet coyly declined to give one, and instead appointed Milner, Henderson and Devonport to investigate the question with expert help. It was decided that parliament should not be told the state of supplies and that the government's attitude would be that compulsory rationing was an evil which it was hoped could be avoided. Milner, who had obviously been expecting this decision, had consulted Adams about food statistics two days earlier,[58] and on the 7th Adams sent him a copy of some rationing estimates prepared in the Garden Suburb.[59] It would appear that Milner felt the need of an outside expert to support him in his discussions with the Food Ministry's officials.

During May the conferences which Beveridge saw as political reconnaissance took place at the Ministry of Food. After one such meeting, Milner tersely recorded in his diary: 'no conclusions'.[60] After a private discussion with Adams and Harmsworth on the 12th he concluded that the control of food was 'in a very unsatisfactory state'.[61] The most striking shortcoming was in sugar. Home-grown sugar supplied an insignificant part of the country's consumption.

Imports, as Adams had noted before, had been insufficient to maintain stocks; and in the first weeks of May sugar had been unobtainable in some areas. The Food Ministry had been dealing with the problem by regulating distribution to different areas of the country. It was now proposing to ration individuals. This was a policy which Adams could not accept.

This opinion he pressed on Milner in a letter on 21 May. He had collected figures from the Sugar Commission to support his view. Part of the note was devoted to showing that the prediction he had made in March about sugar stocks had been vindicated. With this established he went on to argue that until adequate stocks had been built up nothing further could be done:

The moral of the tale is that urgent priority is needed for sugar imports, in fact I think their claim comes before wheat – physiologically and psychologically!...

It would not seem, to me at least, wise to start rationing sugar without a better reserve in hand. The prospect of not being able to honour the tickets, no matter how good the excuse, would be an even worse condition than the inequalities and hardships which exist under the present state of affairs.

I therefore urge that the building up of a reserve is the immediate practical question as regards sugar. Harmsworth concurs.[62]

The committee on Compulsory Rationing recommended on 30 May that any scheme of general rationing would be premature. Despite Adams's advice Milner recommended that arrangements be made to ration sugar, though it is clear from his criticisms of the extant distribution arrangements that he did not expect them to come into force very soon. Underlying the scheme was the feeling that sugar rationing could be elaborated into general rationing at short notice.[63] Besides a note to Milner, who clearly preferred Adams's information about food to that of the Ministry of Food, this was almost the last example of the Garden Suburb's positive intervention into the distribution of food, and it is significant that it coincided with the resignation of Devonport. After the Ministry of Food had been put in the competent hands of Rhondda, only details of policy raised the same passions and risk of public disapproval. It was to be expected, therefore, that Lloyd George would be represented by Harmsworth and Adams at a conference at the Ministry of Food on 17 July which had been convened to set the prices which the Ministry would pay to farmers for beef and wheat.[64] Harmsworth protested to Lloyd George at the level of prices agreed because they seemed to him to make it impossible to charge reasonable prices in the shops, but the Prime Minister ignored his objection and the War Cabinet ratified the proposals of the conference.[65]

IV

With the completion of the plans for the 1917 Agricultural Programme and the Corn Production Act, and the inauguration of Rhondda's 'Heroic Age'[66] at the Ministry of Food, the Secretariat's activity in matters of food and agriculture lost urgency. Adams and his colleagues took no part in the tremendous struggles between Derby and Prothero over the release and exemption of agricultural labourers from the army, which went on long after Milner had ordered the War Office very peremptorily to carry out the wishes of the War Cabinet. The Garden Suburb played a significant part in the negotiations which led to the elaboration of policy both for food control and food production, but they had little to do with the equally important negotiations which continued throughout the war to keep the policies going. Their early activity can most plausibly be explained by the lack of an orderly administration or a settled policy in either the Ministry of Food or the Board of Agriculture. The problems were clearly important enough to warrant close attention from the Prime Minister, and neither department had an information staff sufficiently developed, nor a view of policy sufficiently comprehensive, to present the facts about food supply in an integrated and convincing form. When policies were settled and departments better organised there was less reason for outsiders to concern themselves with details. Beveridge has described in great detail the improvement of the Food Ministry's organisation after Rhondda's succession. Agricultural problems were taken firmly in hand by Milner and an expanded Food Production Department. Although the food supply was never as large nor as secure as could have been hoped, there was less reason to believe as time went on that administrative breakdown in the responsible ministries was causing shortages. There was consequently less need for Lloyd George to be concerned, and less need of a central Secretariat to provide information which no other source could collate. The withdrawal of the Garden Suburb from this area of policy took place when the purpose of intervention disappeared. Despite Devonport's objections, the Garden Suburb was not ejected by angry departments; it left of its own accord when the job was done.

Food supply and production furnish an extended and informative illustration of the role of the Garden Suburb in wartime administration. It is difficult to see how the government's control of food supply, with its associated political and economic problems, could have been managed without the central direction of the Prime Minister or the War Cabinet: the interpenetration of food supply with other sectors of the economy was too great, and the pressure on resources common to other forms of production too severe, for either the Ministry of Food or the Board of Agriculture to carry out their responsibilities in isolation. At the same time the problems raised were often technical and therefore difficult for a busy Prime Minister or War Cabinet to assimilate. The expert knowledge at Lloyd George's disposal through his private secretaries was invaluable in disposing of these problems and maintaining an effective and plausible food policy. The Prime Minister's ability to preserve public morale was essential to the war effort. His Secretariat enabled him to bear the burden which he could not and would not delegate to Devonport: 'the public hold me responsible if anything goes wrong'.[67]

4

Foreign affairs

From the end of 1916. . .I was almost as close to the center of
world affairs as it was possible for a man to be.

Philip Kerr in *The Prevention of War* (New Haven, 1923), p. 8.

The real issue we are going to have to decide in the next few weeks
is whether we are going to stand by Serbia or throw her to the
wolves.

Philip Kerr, 1 June 1917.

I think you are all mad.

Lord Robert Cecil's reply, 1 June 1917.

I

Of all its activities, the Garden Suburb's intervention in foreign
affairs has been the most misunderstood. This is largely because Kerr,
after the end of the war and after the dissolution of the Secretariat,
accompanied Lloyd George to the Paris Peace Conference and
became associated thereafter, in the minds of affronted contemporaries, with his master's personal and controversial style of diplomacy. During the war, however, Lloyd George's entourage did not
contain a second Foreign Office, and there is no justification for
attributing to the Garden Suburb part of the responsibility for the
erosion of Foreign Office influence over foreign policy during the
war.[1] Instead, the Garden Suburb was concerned with foreign affairs
in two ways: Kerr developed an interpretation of the diplomacy of
war which was used in Lloyd George's public speeches, and Kerr and
David Davies took an episodic but pertinacious interest in certain
aspects of foreign affairs which resembles in style and purpose the
work done by their colleagues in domestic matters. Kerr's analysis of
the meaning of the war is more properly examined in chapter 7
below, with the Garden Suburb's other contributions to propaganda.
The present chapter describes his work with David Davies in support
of the Serbian cause and the 'eastern strategy'; their interest in

maintaining the war-making power of Russia; and Kerr's excursions
to meet enemy diplomats in December 1917 and March 1918.

II

The Allied expedition to Salonika, in Greece on the Aegean, had
begun in October 1915 in an unsuccessful attempt to bring Greece
and Bulgaria into the war on the Entente side. [2] (See map on p. viii.)
In 1916 British, French, Italian and Russian troops on the Salonika
front were joined by the Serbian army, driven from its homeland by
the Bulgarian army when Bulgaria entered the war on the German
side, and by Greek contingents loyal to the exiled former Prime
Minister, Eleutherios Venizelos,[3] who had launched an insurrection
against the government of King Constantine of Greece.[4] Throughout
1916 the British General Staff, dominated by the C.I.G.S., Sir
William Robertson,[5] opposed any extension of the Salonika expedition, while the Foreign Office lamented the strengthening of French
influence in the Balkans. In France the military authorities wanted to
fight Constantine, who was pro-German and likely to use his troops
against the Entente flank; they had the support of the Assembly, for
whom Sarrail,[6] the French commander and the only Republican
among French generals, was a hero and Venizelos, a white-haired
former revolutionary, was almost a saint. Lloyd George's accession to
power altered the balance of strategic thinking in Britain. His confidence in the 'eastern' policy of attacking Germany's weaker allies
was unshaken even by the Dardanelles episode; his power *vis-à-vis*
Robertson was greater as Prime Minister than as Secretary for War;
and his immediate strategic intentions were to organise a further
attack somewhere in the east for the start of the campaigning season,
and to find an alternative in the west to the bloody and ineffective
methods of the Somme campaign.[7]

The new War Cabinet in December 1916 had to face the military
and diplomatic problems created by the existence of an Allied force
at Salonika, while deciding whether it should remain in place, be
extended, or be withdrawn. Any action had to be concerted with
unhelpful allies and untrustworthy neutrals. The scene was set by a
skirmish between Greek and Entente troops in early December which
led to the imposition of a blockade with the triple purpose of forcing
Constantine to join the Entente, to make concessions to the Venizelists, and to withdraw his troops from Thessaly, where they
menaced the Salonika force.[8] This policy came under attack from

two directions: the Italian government, fearing a Greek Republican *revanche* under French influence, insisted on guarantees against a Venizelist invasion of Greece, while Sarrail wanted stronger political terms and threatened to secure his flank by attacking Greece.[9] These local problems in Salonika coloured the discussion at the Anglo-French military conference in London on 26 and 27 December 1916, at which the French proposed to extend the Salonika expedition by sending two further divisions.[10] The War Cabinet, anxious about Sarrail's intentions, were driven to support Robertson, who was determined to stop the diversion of resources from the Western Front.[11] It was an uneasy co-operation. Hankey remarked that the War Cabinet 'don't believe in Robertson's "Western Front" policy, but they will never find a soldier to carry out their "Salonika" policy'.[12] Their suspicion of Sarrail merely strengthened Robertson's hand for the next military conference in Rome on 5–7 January 1917. While Lloyd George expounded in formal sessions his own strategy of attacking the Austrians on the Italian front, Robertson sabotaged it in private interviews with Cadorna,[13] the Italian commander.[14] Meanwhile the French, reluctant to reinforce Italy, brought up evidence of Greek plans against the Salonika force to justify an attack on Greece by Sarrail. Lloyd George consented to this course being taken if Greece refused demands contained in an Allied note drafted at the conference.[15] Robertson had thus succeeded in keeping troops on the Western Front by defeating eastern plans one after another; but the diplomatic cost of leaving the initiative in the Balkans to France had still to be met.

The War Cabinet soon regretted the concession to France as it became obvious that French ambitions in the Balkans were large.[16] As a result of British pressure, an Inter-Allied military conference at Calais on 27 February resolved that:

for the present, the decisive defeat of the Bulgarian army is not a practical objective, and that the mission of the Allied forces at Salonica is to keep on their front the enemy forces now there, and to take advantage of striking the enemy if the opportunity offers.[17]

It was thought imprudent to press the French to clarify their intentions. The British government differed both from the Italians, who were anti-Venizelist and anti-French, and from the French, who now seemed determined to overthrow the Greek monarchy. There was little prospect of winning assent to the British policy of installing Venizelos as Prime Minister in a constitutional monarchy.[18] In explaining this for King George's benefit Arthur Balfour,[19] the Foreign Secretary, did not go on to explain that British influence was unlikely to prevail so long as British military participation at Salonika was kept to a minimum. As the campaigning season drew nearer the strategic debate within the British government began to widen. Sarrail, prevented by the Calais decision from mounting a major attack, put forward a scheme to drive the Greek army out of Thessaly. When British consent was denied, he suggested a minor attack on the Bulgarians.[20] In London both the Admiralty and the War Office objected to any further commitment of resources; but new voices were to be heard calling for a reconsideration.

David Davies was among the first to express a hankering for action. On 5 April he urged Lloyd George to ask for an American expeditionary force to be sent to Dedeagach, on the coast east of Salonika. His letter is interesting not for its strategic suggestions, for Davies made no claim to have examined American capacity to mount an expedition, but for its criticism of the direction of British and French policy in the Balkans.

The C.I.G.S. wants you to abandon the Salonika expedition. This would mean abandoning Venizelos and the Serbs to the tender mercies of Ferdie and Tino. . .[21]
You should insist on getting rid of Sarrail – dethroning Tino – play up to Venizelos – improve his stature by giving him a military mission – help the Serbs in the same way. . .this is a glorious opportunity which should not be missed of giving a fresh chance to Salonika. Otherwise you will be blamed for a policy of 'wait and see':- the westerners will blame you for immobilising 200,000 British troops.[22]

By pressing for the dismissal of Sarrail, Davies undercut Robertson's powerful debating point that increased activity at Salonika necessarily implied support for an untrustworthy commander; by reminding Lloyd George about the Serbs he challenged the Foreign Office view that the diplomatic problem posed by the expedition lay entirely in the competition between the Allies for influence in Greece. In this he was supported by Admiral Troubridge,[23] a personal friend of the Crown Prince of Serbia, who had spent some time with the Serbian army. On 3 April Troubridge wrote to Carson from Salonika, warning that the Serbs were discontented, and might soon refuse to make further efforts for the Entente. Disaffection was aggravated by the behaviour of the French towards the Serbian army. Troubridge recommended that a British force be attached to the Serbs. 'The Serbians as a whole look to England for their salvation, recognising that any assistance we give them is disinterested as regards their country.'[24]

For the moment problems of supply inhibited British thinking about the Serbs or any other policy for Salonika. Distrust of Sarrail simmered in the War Cabinet, and Lloyd George was moved to ask Painlevé, the French Minister for War, to send out another commander. He received a discouraging reply, accompanied by a request for a further offensive at Salonika. Balfour drew an apt moral from the exchange:

...from a political point of view, there was something to be said for leaving General Sarrail in supreme command at Salonika, because we do not wish to be left in charge of a campaign which is in an unsatisfactory state, and which might eventually have to be abandoned on account of transport difficulties.[25]

However, Sarrail's removal was the only policy upon which the British government could wholeheartedly agree, and even that was impossible to achieve because of disagreements about related matters. The shipping crisis, arising from the Admiralty's failure to control the German submarine campaign, combined with Robertson's strictures to force an anxious War Cabinet to ask for a reduction of the British force at the Inter-Allied conference at St Jean de Maurienne on 19 April.[26] The reduction, finally agreed in Paris on 5 May, was obtained in return for British agreement to a peaceful occupation by Sarrail of Thessaly, with the aim of seizing the harvest, improving the efficacy of the blockade of Greece, and consolidating the tactical position of the Salonika force against the Greek army.[27] This was unwelcome both to the War Office and the Foreign Office. British weakness at the two conferences had been exploited by the agreement between the French and Italian governments, which became obvious at St Jean de Maurienne, whereby the Italians abandoned their objection to French activity in Greece in return for large post-war concessions in Asia Minor.[28] The British government had lost the initiative in the Near East because the only policy it could settle on was to reduce its own influence. A Foreign Office official commented in March that:

So long as the French are in Naval and Military command in the E. Mediterranean, it is not reasonable to expect them to play a minor role.[29]

Lord Robert Cecil[30] drew the same moral from the meeting at St Jean de Maurienne:

...Robertson and Jellicoe are clamouring for a withdrawal from Salonica on the score of tonnage leaving the French in undisputed possession to defend Salonica. That I think will hardly do. However we are to have one more blow at the Bulgars anyhow.[31]

While international conferences witnessed the bankruptcy of British policy, the return to London of Troubridge and his now defunct mission to the Serbian army gave the Garden Suburb an occasion to intervene. David Davies reported to Kerr on 18 April what he had learned of the liaison arrangements between the British and Serbian forces.

The British Liaison Officer is our sole representative at Serbian G.H.Q. This gentleman cannot speak Serbian and before the war was a parson. On the other hand the French mission consists of 5 officers...In handing over the Serbs to the tender mercies of the French we are identifying ourselves with their policy which does not always appear to coincide with Serbian interests.

On 20 April Kerr passed this on to the Foreign Office with a second recommendation derived from Troubridge's mission, that a proper survey should be made of racial and international boundaries in the Balkans:

Major David Davies...thinks that if the Foreign Office puts some pressure on the War Office, they might be willing to re-establish a mission with the Serbian army, a course which would appear to have nothing but beneficial results, from the point of view of past pledges to Serbia and the settlement at the end of the war.

G. R. Clerk[32] in the War Department of the Foreign Office, received these schemes unfavourably, minuting to Cecil on 23 April:

As possibly schemes founded on such suggestions may be sprung upon you at the War Cabinet, I send them for your inspection...

Cecil responded more indulgently that the proposed mission, though probably fruitless, could do no harm; and Clerk consequently suggested to Kerr that although the boundary survey was a waste of time the proposed mission should be suggested to the War Office.[33]

In view of Davies's unhappy relations with the War Office, this was an unprofitable course.[34] Kerr, who was afraid that the Entente war effort would be seen abroad to be losing its moral significance, became concerned at the withdrawal of troops from Salonika. In early May he urged Lloyd George to consider the wider consequences:

If we are going to withdraw any troops at all, I think it is vital that at the moment when the withdrawal begins there should be a new and emphatic declaration that we shall not make peace until Serbia is restored. The withdrawal, even of a regiment, is bound to be made use of by German propagandists and is almost certain to be misinterpreted by the Serbian army which is already very disaffected.[35]

Soon afterwards Kerr learned from Ronald Burrows,[36] principal of King's College London and a partisan of Venizelos, that a Greek army corps, which had the previous year deserted in a body to the Bulgarians, had reappeared on the Balkan front. These troops were widely assumed to have deserted under orders from Constantine and his General Staff. Kerr underlined Constantine's unreliability in a minute to Lloyd George on 18 May.

...Our policy in Greece still appears to be based on the assumption that it is possible to reconcile Tino and Venizelos. This policy has had a pretty useful run for its money and the results so far achieved have not brought any success to the cause of the Allies. It is a policy which is not understood in this country and is certain to be a source of weakness to the Government as time goes on.

Has not the moment come when the Allies should definitely plump for Venizelos and insist on the exit of Tino?[37]

By now the Garden Suburb was openly recommending a policy which had been rejected by the War Cabinet: that Britain should not only consent to a forward policy in the Balkans, but also wrest the initiative from France.

On 18 May, when Kerr's minute was going to the Prime Minister, Robertson and Jellicoe,[38] the First Sea Lord, sent in concerted notes to the War Cabinet insisting that, whatever the political consequences, the troop withdrawals from Salonika should go ahead.[39] On 22 May the War Cabinet met to discuss those consequences, and was forced to admit that, in the words of an unnamed member

we ought to make it clear to the French Government that, though we had agreed to their taking a leading *role* in Greece, the policy for the carrying out of which they would be responsible would be an Allied policy and not a purely French policy.[40]

It was too late to carry out this excellent intention with any hope of success. On 23 May Lord Derby, the Secretary of State for War, brought news that the French wanted Sarrail to take pre-emptive action, marching on Athens after the occupation of Thessaly, deposing Constantine and establishing a Venizelist government. This was said to be both a safe way to deal with the military problem at Salonika and a necessary condition for the survival of the French administration. Cecil remarked that the French were 'inspired by a

desire to achieve a cheap military success for purely political purposes'; the War Cabinet accepted advice from Robertson that British
troops should not participate; but the fear that British public opinion
would not accept a policy which appeared to buttress Constantine
prevented a firm decision to oppose a French invasion of Greece.
The problem was adjourned for discussion at an Anglo-French conference.[41]

Once again the Serbian question had been submerged by the desire
to have the best of both worlds in Salonika. Kerr reiterated his
recommendation that a military mission should be attached to the
Serbian army.[42] Although the War Cabinet had demonstrated its
attitude to Serbia by deciding to withhold information about its plans
from the Serbian government, Davies optimistically sent Lloyd
George a shopping list of strategic demands to be made of the French
at the forthcoming conference which paid special attention to Serbia:

...(2) Press for the withdrawal of Sarrail – and get the French to consent
to a British Military Mission with the Serbian army. This is now
blocked by Col. Buckley in the W.O. The Serbs want a British
mission but will not ask for it officially unless they know we are
prepared to send one, for afraid [sic] of irritating the French people.

(3) Can't you get the French to agree to the appointment of Missitch as
commander in chief.

(4) If the Russian offensive is likely to come off – cannot the withdrawal
of our troops be postponed? – all these points are part and parcel of
the whole problem. They all hinge on Sarrail – unless he goes you
may as well chuck it. I should sack Milne too – he has been there
too long – Pitt would have outed him long ago...[43]

In the discussions, which Kerr and Davies did not attend, Lloyd
George and Milner led the War Cabinet in presenting a policy which
was internally consistent if not very attractive in the light of past
British aspirations. Under instructions, Cecil drafted a proposal that
the Allies should seize the harvest in Thessaly, then inform Constantine that his régime was unconstitutional and invoke the 1863 Treaty
of Guarantee to insist, on pain of blockade, that he abdicate in favour
of one of his sons, who would be required to appoint Venizelos as
Prime Minister. The French insisted that the Isthmus of Corinth
should be occupied by Allied troops and that the British contingent at
Salonika should not be run down until the new régime was installed
in Athens. Over the objections of Robertson, Jellicoe and Cecil, this
was accepted. Lloyd George and Milner persuaded the French that
British troops under British commanders should seize the harvest.
Cecil welcomed the idea as the only way to ensure a peaceful

operation, but Derby and Robertson vetoed it, thus ensuring that the only concession won from the French was that, instead of landing at Corinth, Sarrail would merely make all necessary preparations, landing only if Constantine took military action.[44] Dissent was widespread. Cecil disliked 'even the very qualified and conditional assent which we gave to military operations in Old Greece'.[45] The Serbians had already protested that the withdrawal of a French division for operations in Thessaly exposed their lines of communication.[46] The Italian commander at Salonika protested at the loss of his artillery, and won his government's support for a plea that Sarrail be replaced.[47] Worst of all Venizelos, the supposed beneficiary of the French scheme, protested to the French government against any Allied military action in Old Greece.[48]

Venizelos had grounds for his suspicion of Allied motives. British policy since the insurrection of August 1916 had been to work for a reconciliation between Venizelos and Constantine. That purpose, with Italian objections to a Venizelist *revanche*, led to the guarantees against a Venizelist invasion offered to Constantine in January. In April the Foreign Office, alarmed to hear of French intentions to withdraw the guarantee, put pressure on Venizelos to come to terms with Constantine.[49] Further alarmed by the withdrawal, at St Jean de Maurienne, of Italian objections to French intervention, the British insisted at Paris in early May that Venizelos should not be allowed to use his troops independently to seize the Thessalian harvest. Venizelos thus had large grievances against Britain. French policy, though directed against Constantine, was seen by Venizelos as manifestly self-serving. While encouraging Venizelists in Old Greece, the French were supporting Royalists in the islands, where Venizelos was strong.[50] French leaders made no secret of their indifference to the Venizelist cause, except as it served French interests or bore on French domestic politics.[51] With such friends as these, Venizelos decided to do the job himself, offering to force Constantine to abdicate within two months, and promising twelve divisions for the Salonika front within three months. If this was refused, he threatened to come in person to Britain and France to rouse public opinion against the governments which had so mistreated him. His message to Lloyd George was transmitted by Ronald Burrows through the willing agency of David Davies.[52]

Burrows's report, with other information already in his possession, gave Davies the material for a comprehensive indictment of Allied policy in the Balkans, in which he was supported by Kerr. He was reinforced in his view that Serbian interests were being neglected for the sake of Anglo-French squabbling over Greece.

> If the Serbs are left in the lurch – Goodbye to the strategy of cutting the Sophia–Constantinople Railway – goodbye to the idea of a powerful Jugo-Slav state as a barrier to the expansion of Germany towards the East – goodbye to the policy of closing the back door by an effective blockade and encircling the central powers with a band of steel...Then there is the political aspect. If Serbia goes out of the War it will be one of the severest blows for the cause of the Allies. It may well be that Russia and Roumania will follow suit. In this country there is certain to be a storm which will shake the government to its foundation and probably wreck it. I do not think that it would be possible to shelter behind the French for we are equally responsible with them.

In an interview with one of Troubridge's staff, Davies had also confirmed his own belief that the Serbian army was on the verge of mass desertion, that Sarrail was mischievous, that Milne was demoralised, that Misitch was the only competent general at Salonika, and that Venizelos should be allowed to manage the Thessalian expedition on his own.[53]

Kerr made many of the same points in two memoranda commenting on Troubridge's final report on Serbia.

> I think we are drifting into a Balkan situation which will end either in the success or failure of the whole allied cause and the success or downfall of your government. Our Greek and Salonika policy ought really to be subordinate to our Serbia policy, and the real issue in the next few weeks is whether we are going to stand to Serbia or throw her to the wolves.[54]

In a second memorandum he argued that to withdraw from the Balkans, leaving the Serbians to the mercy of the French, the Greeks, the Bulgarians, and the Germans, would be 'an act of cowardice and treachery without parallel in our history'. He also prophesied that if Serbia capitulated the Central Powers were quite likely to offer peace with the condition that they would restore Russia, recognise Poland, evacuate Belgium and France, and recognise Alsace-Lorraine as French territory.

> Germany would be left overlord of a number of willing subordinates stretching from Belgium to Baghdad...and we should have thrown away the strongest moral justification for continuing the war, the liberty of small nations calling for liberation.
>
> The independence of Serbia is the key to the victory of the Allied Cause.[55]

Cecil, invited to comment on Kerr's hyperbolic memoranda, remarked that 'you are all mad'.[56] His opinion is defensible: Serbia did not necessarily have the pivotal significance in German calculations which Kerr attributed to it. Yet although indifference to Serbia had been predominant in British thinking the War Cabinet was awakening to the need to do something for Serbia, if only to replace Sarrail. The strategic suggestions made by Kerr, Davies, and Troubridge were incompatible both with the 'western' strategy favoured by the War Office and with the 'Italian front' strategy preferred by Lloyd George. To that extent their energetic arguments were purposeless, since there was little possibility of agreement on their scheme, and in any case their opinion as strategists carried little weight. The value of their reasoning was rather to emphasise that the Salonika expedition had an importance in its own right, arising from the delicate position of Serbia as a *casus belli*, and that it was therefore important to make it an effective part of the war effort, and not just to hope that by stubborn resistance to anything suggested by the French the problem could be made to go away. It was a corrective to the calculations which had impelled Robertson and Derby to refuse to use British troops in Thessaly. Troubridge's report, in particular, was acknowledged in the War Cabinet's reopening of the Salonika question on 5 June. As in the previous December, agreement was reached through a decision to seek the dismissal of Sarrail, which Robertson, who had recently learned that Sarrail had thrown away 'an opportunity to deal a heavy blow at the enemy'[57] could support. David Davies was chosen to carry the message to the French government.[58]

The new direction in British policy was not to last long. Davies delivered his message on 7 June. Sir Henry Norman,[59] a Liberal M.P. who was formally attached to the British military mission in Paris while acting as Lloyd George's confidential informant, accompanied him: 'D.D. put his case as strongly and well as it could possibly be put, so any decision is not due in any way to any weakness of statement on his part.'[60] Norman's letter prepared the Prime Minister for the news that because of domestic political conditions and the recent mutiny of French troops on the western front, Sarrail could not be replaced until the operation in Thessaly was complete. On 11 June an anxious War Cabinet considered that reply, which it felt obliged to accept, and contemplated the preparations being made by Sarrail for the invasion of Old Greece. Both Robertson and Cecil regarded them as excessive,[61] but nothing could be done before 12 June, when Sarrail was suddenly vindicated by Constantine's decision to step down in favour of his second son, who accepted Venizelos as Prime

Minister. The Greek question which had divided the British and French governments had ceased to exist. Now that its political ends in Greece were achieved, the French government muted its objections to British troop withdrawals; the War Cabinet averted its attention from the Balkans now that the Greek question no longer threatened to consume military resources. Although the Venizelist government promised military support to the Entente, the Balkan front had no significant part in the war until late 1918. The Salonika force was reduced to a defensive role, and the Serbs, who had relied on their allies to restore them to their country, were forced to wait until the war was won in the west.

Within the British government this change of atmosphere represented a defeat for the Foreign Office, which had emphasised resistance to French political incursions in the Balkans, and a victory for Robertson, who was enabled to prevent further distractions from the western front. The policies favoured in the Garden Suburb, of supporting Serbia as a symbol of the moral superiority of the Entente and of maintaining military pressure in the east, were both defeated. Davies, disgruntled for other reasons with the direction of higher policy, delivered himself of a strong protest on 23 June, which precipitated his departure from the Garden Suburb.

The Serbs are averting their gaze from the west, has the last ray of hope disappeared? has the British Prime Minister in whom they trusted – the champion of the small nations – has he really been guilty of the great betrayal? Perish the thought – but the vigil has been so long – the days drag on – Sarrail is still in command – is there no hope, must it be surrender after all? please don't say 'rot' just imagine yourself a Serbian soldier – try and feel what he feels and can you blame him if, his patience exhausted he succumbs to Austrian promises and blandishments however insincere these may be?[62]

III

The affairs of Russia gave the Garden Suburb yet more opportunity to disagree with the proper authorities about strategy, diplomacy, and military liaison. Again, it was David Davies who raised the subject as one of strategic importance, and Kerr who took it over as part of his larger interest in fighting a just war. Davies's interest in Russia had been aroused in January 1917 when he was searching, with evident frustration, for some serious work. On 17 January he talked to General Sir Henry Wilson,[63] who was about to leave for Russia as senior military member of an Inter-Allied mission led by

Milner. The mission was to examine the Russian war effort and estimate Russia's need for munitions. On 19 January Davies was on a train to Scotland as a supernumerary and somewhat unexpected member of the party.[64] Without specific duties, he spent his time in Russia talking to Russians outside the higher circles of government, and visited the Riga front and the White Sea ports where munitions were shipped to Russia from the western Allies. When the mission returned many of the members wrote reports on the discussions each had had with politicians, soldiers, or officials. Davies, denied these contacts, wrote an heretical report on the basis of his observations.

The heresy of Davies's report lay partly in its conclusions, partly in the tone of its recommendations. The British members of the mission were not unaware of the parlous state of Russia. Sir George Clerk,[65] the senior Foreign Office representative, reported that the mission was 'kept in a sort of ring fence and prevented from hearing any defence or serious explanation of the Emperor's policy', and noted that he himself was in a minority in believing that there would be no revolution before the end of the war.[66] Milner remarked on the 'chaotic way in which public business is at present conducted in Russia',[67] and discussed Russia's internal affairs with Prince Lvov,[68] who had worked for a liberalisation of the régime for many years. Yet, as Milner put it to Lvov:

They were not here to discuss the internal affairs of Russia but the conduct of the war, and it was only in so far as the conduct of the war was adversely affected by the internal conditions that the Allied representatives could even indirectly approach a political problem.[69]

Davies rejected this approach and tried to give an account of Russian conditions which would go beyond the narrow purpose of improving the war effort in detail. The theme of his comments was set down on the first page of his lengthy report.[70]

The truth is that the broad aims and objects of the Allies in the war are incompatible with the ideas underlying the present system of government in Russia.

He identified three groups – pro-German, pro-Ally, and outright Nationalist – in the Russian élite, and recommended first that some effort be made to win the Nationalist group more firmly to the Entente side. The mass of the population, he believed, was 'inarticulate' but anxious to win the war. He warned that after the war the ambitions of the peasantry for more land would precipitate great changes.

Davies then turned to the shortages of food and fuel which were creating discontent. He was alone among members of the mission in relating the inadequacy of the Russian transport system to the likelihood of revolution. Milner, Clerk and Wilson had urged that the government must be reorganised so that munitions could get through: Davies argued that the survival of organised government depended on a complete change of régime. He observed that the army and the civilian population were giving their support more and more to the Duma, while the government was likely to resist the Duma's recent demand that the police structure should be liberalised. He concluded that a dangerous conflict could scarcely be avoided.

It is true that the old revolutionary societies, the Nihilists and the Anarchists, no longer exist, and it is not believed that a popular uprising would have any chance of success. What may happen is a palace Revolution, ending in the removal of the Emperor and Empress.

He backed this up with concrete proposals for British policy:

1. To endeavour to persuade the Empress by all possible means to leave Russia and to remain as a guest in one of the Allied countries until the conclusion of the war.
2. To watch closely the course of events and be ready to make proposals for the carrying on of Government if a Revolution takes place.
3. To keep in closest touch with the leaders of the Duma and the Zemstvos, in order to win their confidence and direct their activities into the proper channels.
4. Under the present régime to insist as far as possible upon security of tenure in office of capable and loyal ministers, who have proved their devotion to the cause of the Allies.
5. To conciliate the present Government officials, and to spend money when necessary to enlist their active co-operation in the carrying on of the war.

Most of the report examined supply, which had been the mission's principal business. A few examples will indicate Davies's approach. He criticised the Russian government for siting munitions plants, built with Allied money, hundreds of miles from their supplies of raw material, simply so that they could be turned into textile plants after the war. He observed that Russian railways were jammed with passengers, and that congestion could therefore be relieved by raising fares. He pointed out that every shipper in Russia bribed railway officials to move his goods faster, but that no one offered bribes on the government's behalf. He dealt in simple and informative terms with the capacities of the ports, and suggested which sorts of munitions could best be sent to Russia. Little of this was controversial in Britain, since all the persons and organisations criticised were Russian.

He went on to describe the organisation Wilson had suggested for the military liaison staff, under which the gathering of intelligence would be separated from the supervision of supplies, then turned his attention to the naval staff, which he discussed under three heads.

1. Commodore Kemp, who is described as the *Director of the Naval Defence of the White Sea.* This officer is stationed at Archangel, and apparently does not confine his activities to the duties which have been entrusted to him, but has also assumed the supervision of the naval transport arrangements at Archangel, and has consequently developed unpleasant relations with...
2. Captain Bevan, who is described as the *Naval Transport Officer* for the port of Archangel. This officer has under his control, during the navigation season, a large staff of about twenty-five naval officers who are charged with expediting the unloading of vessels at the port, and with keeping the Admiralty informed as to these operations. It appears that almost all these officers are unable to speak Russian, consequently their efficiency is impaired.
3. The naval transport officers at Kola, Vladivostock, and later on at Kem; also a senior officer at Kola, who is in command of H.M.S. Glory.

Davies drew no immediate conclusion from this information, but elsewhere in the report suggested that an army officer should undertake the supervision of all munitions transport, whether by sea or land. He also criticised the lack of Russian-speaking officers.

It is perfectly obvious that we cannot expect the Russians to pay attention to our demands if they are being harassed by a crowd of officers who cannot speak Russian and who have no clearly defined duties.

Davies finished his memorandum on 10 March and sent it to be printed. The abdication of the Tsar five days later cut across the political section of the report: his predictions were old news before they were circulated, and the urgent need to establish relations with the provisional government was obvious. This enabled Lloyd George to remark later that Davies 'sent home more useful and accurate information than any other member of the party. He foreshadowed revolution, whereas Milner and the others were of opinion that nothing was likely to happen'.[71] However, the report could have no influence over the development of policy. Instead the political themes were taken up by Kerr as part of his developing analysis of the morality of the war. Where Davies had remarked that the old régime in Russia was incompatible with the aims of the Entente, Kerr now saw the new Russia as a valuable moral asset.[72] This benevolent optimism persisted long after Lloyd George and the War Cabinet had recognised that the provisional government was either unwilling or unable to contribute to the war effort, and that the Russian revolution might therefore force the Allies to sue for peace.[73] It was not until late May that Kerr realised that the Russians wished only 'that the war should end so that they may get on with their own internal revolution'.[74] Hitherto he had taken Russian politics for granted and made no suggestion about British political intervention: afterwards he was inclined to give Russia up for lost.

The military sections of Davies's report had a more direct effect. In mid-April the Admiralty awoke to his subversive suggestion that soldiers should take over traditional naval duties. Much internal correspondence was generated on the rather half-hearted theme that 'as regards any friction that may have existed in the past, this was infinitessimal [sic], and any possible causes of this have, it is hoped, been removed'.[75] This tacit admission of past difficulties was removed from the Fourth Sea Lord's[76] memorandum of 18 April, which defended the principle that 'the line of demarcation between the respective responsibilities of the navy and the army should be high water mark or ships' side'. The suggestion that central control for Russian supply should be transferred to Petrograd was also resisted.[77] In the end it was apparently decided not to carry the complaint to the War Cabinet. Davies's memorandum had exposed a source of considerable embarrassment to the Admiralty, which had a thick file on mismanagement and friction between naval officers in Russia.[78]

After Davies's departure from the secretariat, Kerr took the major responsibility for commenting on Russian questions. His information came from the Political Intelligence Department of the Foreign Office and from the Ministry of Information, with occasional help from academic visitors to Russia who sent information through Adams.[79] His conviction that Russia, especially Bolshevik Russia, was hopelessly lost to the cause of the Entente limited his interest in the subject: in January 1918 he lamented that 'the Russian soul is partly Bolshevik'.[80] His attention was directed to Russian internal affairs again in June 1918, when Alexander Kerensky,[81] the former leader of the deposed provisional government, arrived in England privately and asked for an interview with Lloyd George. Kerr was sent to make preliminary enquiries, and discovered after cautious questioning that Kerensky had come to seek Entente support against the Bolsheviks but would not make any public statement of his purpose.[82] This gave Lloyd George a chance to escape from embarrassment. On 24 June the Prime Minister saw Kerensky and explained his difficulties: although the Entente would wish to stand by Russian democracy to the end 'the de facto Government in Russia was apparently as hostile to the Allies as it was to Germany.'[83] Kerr interviewed Kerensky the next day to clarify points of detail. These conversations were not 'negotiations'.[84] Kerensky had nothing to offer except information and both Kerr and Lloyd George were sceptical of its value. Kerr, who had made the record of the meeting on 24 June, repeated in his own interview Lloyd George's insistence that Entente intervention would be an act of war against the *de facto* government and could not therefore be contemplated. Although the War Cabinet was engaged in confused attempts to arrange military intervention in Siberia, the nature, purpose, and limits of this intervention were still a matter of argument when Kerensky was seen. Lloyd George was less anxious than some of his colleagues to intervene without reference to the Bolsheviks, or to appear to be making war on them.[85] However both he and Kerr exaggerated this reluctance in their conversations with Kerensky, probably because it was feared that Kerensky would jeopardise delicate negotiations with the United States and Japan by speaking out in public. This was justified when Kerensky, despite his assurances to Kerr, addressed the Labour party conference on 27 June.[86] In a 'Memorandum on Points to be made clear to Mr Kerensky' drafted on 28 June Kerr indicated that the Allies were prepared to give military and economic help to 'the Russian people' to 'restore an Eastern Front against Germany', but warned that in 'making their intervention the Allies take no sides either for or against the Bolsheviks or for or against Kerensky and his associates'.[87] This position reflected precisely the opinions of British political and military leaders making decisions about Russia; as Kerensky and later historians realised, it was quite impossible to maintain in practice.[88]

Kerr was thus drawn into the question of Allied intervention in Siberia. On 19 July he suggested to Eric Drummond[89] at the Foreign Office that to protect all interests in the Siberian expedition, political leadership should be conceded to the United States and military leadership to Japan.[90] On 21 July he drafted, under supervision, the British reply to President Wilson's rejection of the plan to intervene in Siberia.[91] On 4 August, a Sunday, he acted as secretary to an emergency War Cabinet which considered the plight of the Czechoslovak forces in Siberia.[92] In all these activities his concern was more with words than actions, more with the form of policy than with its substance. Although he was drawn closer to the centre of events, his contribution to those events diminished in significance.

IV

Kerr's two missions to Switzerland, in December 1917 and March 1918, must be seen in the context of frequent and extensive covert diplomatic contacts between the belligerent powers.[93] A landmark in this secret diplomacy was a letter from the Austrian emperor to a cousin serving in the French army, Prince Sixte of Bourbon, in March 1917, written in terms which suggested that Austria might be detached from her German alliance. This possibility came to dominate Anglo-French efforts to end the war by diplomatic means. Negotiations initiated by the Sixte letter foundered because Italian interests were ignored in the Austrian proposals, but in late November a further invitation to discuss terms came from Austria, and Smuts was sent to meet Albrecht Mensdorff, formerly Ambassador to Britain,[94] in Switzerland. Kerr accompanied him. Discussions were inconclusive, but a hint of flexibility in Mensdorff's attitude induced the War Cabinet to send Kerr back in March to interview Alexander Skrzynski, the counsellor of the Austrian legation in Berne,[95] to discuss a possible renewal of talks. On both expeditions Kerr also discussed, with a neutral intermediary, the possibility of detaching Turkey. Negotiations with Turkey traditionally differed from Austrian negotiations in that they were not limited on the British side by the assumption that Turks were honourable men. In early 1917 Lloyd George had casually allowed a bankrupt railway contractor, John Pilling, to open negotiations with Turkish intermediaries in Switzerland; and in a more organised effort the next winter, Sir Basil Zaharoff, a freelance arms salesman employed by Vickers Ltd, was authorised to offer 10 million dollars to leading members of the Turkish government to agree to open the straits of Constantinople to the Entente.[96] Left ignorant of these efforts, the Foreign Office hoped, more conventionally, that the Turks could be persuaded to grant *de facto* independence, under the description of 'autonomy', to the parts of the Turkish empire conquered by Britain, and pursued the idea through its own intermediaries, though not without contemplating large bribes where necessary. In late 1917 hints transmitted through the British legation in Athens suggested that Turkish leaders might be prepared to accept these terms.

Switzerland, a salubrious and conveniently placed neutral country with a discreet banking system, was a natural forum for such dealings. Its principal disadvantage was that, with frontiers to four belligerents, it pullulated with spies; and the British Minister, Sir Horace Rumbold,[97] therefore made a determined effort to keep clandestine contacts with the enemy under his supervision, but out of direct touch with the Berne legation. His favoured intermediary was Dr Parodi,[98] head of an Egyptian student-welfare organisation in Geneva, and it was through Parodi that the Smuts–Mensdorff meeting was arranged. When the Austrian message was received, the Foreign Office was initially reluctant to take action. Lloyd George, with the approval of the Allied governments gained at a convenient Supreme War Council meeting at the end of November, overwhelmed this resistance, and Smuts was delegated to meet the Austrian envoy. Kerr accompanied him, apparently because as an unknown figure he could travel more freely in Switzerland and thus visit Parodi and Rumbold in Berne. Last minute objections from Balfour against the whole mission were set aside.[99]

Smuts met Mensdorff in a Geneva suburb on 18 December 1917 and put to him the British proposal, developed during 1917, that Austria could be left intact in a peace settlement to act as a counterweight to Germany in central Europe. Mensdorff accepted this gratefully as preferable to the dismemberment of Austria–Hungary in the interests of the subordinate nationalities, which had been suggested by the Entente reply to President Wilson's Peace Note in December 1916.[100] He nevertheless insisted that nothing could persuade Austria to desert the German alliance. Smuts firmly resisted any attempt to discuss a general peace, and the only results of his three amicable interviews with Mensdorff were a suggestion from the Austrian that conversations should be renewed, and an impression in Smuts's mind that Austria would urge Germany to moderate her war aims.[101] Meanwhile Kerr travelled to Berne to interview Parodi about what he had learned of the Ententophil opposition in Turkey from contacts with the Turkish Red Cross Mission, which was in Switzerland discussing prisoner-of-war questions. Kerr's report confirmed what the Foreign Office had learned from other sources: a significant minority in the ruling Committee for Union and Progress would consider a settlement in which Arabia was given complete independence, Syria, Mesopotamia and Palestine given autonomy under nominal Turkish suzerainty, Armenia left at the disposal of the Entente powers, and the straits neutralised with Constantinople left as capital of Turkey. The Turkish war debt would also have to be discharged, and economic support given by the Entente after the war.

After discussions with Rumbold and Smuts, Kerr drafted a statement to be communicated by Parodi to Moukhtar Bey, the head of the Turkish Red Cross Mission.[102] The document, which was left with Rumbold to be passed on if authorised by telegram from London, reflected the reported desires of the Ententophil Turks, except that the discharge of debt was limited to the areas removed from direct Turkish control. Kerr and Smuts returned to England on 19 December, and Kerr submitted his lengthy report on his conversations with Parodi and the document which arose from them.[103] The Foreign Office, learning of Parodi's information by telegram from Rumbold, authorised him on 21 December to communicate to Moukhtar the terms which had been worked out for communication *via* the Athens legation: neutralisation of the straits leaving Constantinople in Turkish hands, autonomy for Syria and Palestine, and complete independence for Armenia, Arabia and Mesopotamia.[104] When Rumbold informed the Office, by return, that Smuts and Kerr had left a memorandum offering different terms, there was a moment of confusion. Ronald Graham,[105] the official principally concerned with Middle Eastern affairs, preferred Mesopotamia to be independent of Turkey, as in the terms already prepared. He was even more insistent that Palestine should not be under the Turkish flag, for the sake of British prestige among Moslems in Egypt and India, and out of consideration for Zionist sentiment. The Foreign Office, on Cecil's authority, confirmed on 24 December that the memorandum left with Rumbold could be communicated to the Turks at the first opportunity, with the amendment that Palestine, as well as Armenia and Arabia, would have to be wholly independent of Turkey.[106] The proposal as finally authorised corresponded closely to Kerr's original intentions. In May 1917 he had been in touch with Graham, supporting a cautious British declaration in favour of Zionism as a means to bolster the enthusiasm of Russian and American Jews for the war;[107] furthermore, he was probably aware of the part played by his friends Milner and Amery in drafting the Balfour Declaration of 2 November 1917, which sought to use Zionism as a bridgehead for British interests in the Middle East.[108] In Switzerland, he had at first listed Palestine among the areas to be separated completely from Turkey, only to have it returned to the Turkish flag by Smuts, who had otherwise left his draft untouched.[109] The practical difference would have been small, since all the former Turkish empire except for Syria was likely to be incorporated *de facto* in the British empire, but the symbolic importance was believed by contemporaries to be considerable. As a result of Graham's intervention, the British peace proposals for Turkey after 24 December were very largely Kerr's handiwork.

After Kerr and Smuts returned to England the possibility of renewing conversations with Austria was urgently discussed. The War Cabinet, apparently at the prompting of Lloyd George and Milner, confirmed on 2 January 1918 that Smuts should return to Switzerland.[110] On 8 January Smuts himself suggested a postponement until the effect of Lloyd George's major war-aims speech on 5 January should be known.[111] For the next six weeks the Foreign Office conducted a campaign of obstruction under the leadership of Cecil and Balfour. When a message from Skrzynski suggested that the Austrian Foreign Minister, Czernin, might wish to meet Lloyd George, Cecil warned that it might be a diplomatic smoke-screen to cover an assault on Italy, or an attempt to separate Italy from the Entente.[112] On 18 January the War Cabinet decided to offer Smuts instead, but Balfour delayed the telegram until Italy could be consulted. By the time the War Cabinet discovered the delay on 28 January, Balfour could urge that Czernin's offer to meet an American representative was a reason for further delay.[113] The War Cabinet resolved to send a telegram to President Wilson, but Balfour did not send it until 6 February.[114] He decided, eventually, that the Americans ought to conduct any negotiations with Austria, and recommended this both to Wilson and to the War Cabinet meeting of 1 March.[115] By the beginning of March Milner and Bonar Law were losing patience with the Foreign Office.[116] In the meeting on 1 March concern was expressed that the Americans might run away with the negotiations, and it was pointed out that Skrzynski had offered proofs of Czernin's sincerity. Balfour was overruled, and instructed to seek further details from the Austrians. When Skrzynski replied that Czernin wished to know if Britain would enter negotiations if the Austrians gave assurances that they were interested only in a separate peace, the War Cabinet decided to send Kerr to investigate Austrian intentions in greater depth, despite a rearguard action by the Foreign Office, which argued that American negotiations were going so well that Kerr had better stay at home.[117]

Meanwhile Turkish negotiations had proceeded slowly. Although Lord Newton,[118] the chief British negotiator at the prisoner-of-war conference, had remained alert for signs, nothing appeared until the end of January, when Moukhtar promised to obtain his government's permission to engage in negotiations. The Foreign Office tended to accept Newton's estimate of Moukhtar as thoroughly untrustworthy and corrupt, and the received opinion did not change when he returned in February, asking for a bribe from the British government in return for his agreeing to talk.[119] Nevertheless it was important to examine any chance of detaching Turkey, and Kerr was instructed to find out if Moukhtar was authorised to negotiate.[120] Conversations with Parodi convinced him that the Turks knew the British terms and were in no hurry to negotiate. He reported that British attention was turning to the north and east and that she would be happy to leave the Middle East to the Entente. With this knowledge, which was not entirely welcome in Britain, he had to remain content.[121]

Most of Kerr's second mission to Switzerland, which lasted from 9 to 19 March 1918, was occupied with the Austrian question. On his arrival he had extensive conversations with Rumbold and Parodi, on the basis of which he telegraphed to London that Skrzynski appeared to be genuine in his claims to speak for Czernin. His report was described in the Foreign Office as 'not very convincing,'[122] but Lloyd George was impressed by Kerr's opinion that conversations could lead either to a separate peace or to such disruption among the enemy that the Entente could only gain. He therefore authorised his secretary to meet Skrzynski and arrange for Smuts to meet Czernin. The meeting took place, but failed completely in its purpose. Even before Kerr arrived in Berne, Skrzynski had been ordered by his government to withdraw from contact with the British because the Entente appeared to be acting insincerely.[123] When Kerr, accompanied by Parodi as an interpreter, penetrated to Skrzynski's hotel room in Montreux 'by an escalier de service, so far as I could judge entirely unobserved', he found his interlocutor polite but unaccommodating. Skrzynski protested gently that the behaviour of the Allied governments suggested that they were interested not in a genuine settlement with Austria, but in isolating Germany the better to defeat her, and that Czernin had decided therefore not to proceed with any meeting. Recognising that his principal task could not succeed, Kerr delivered a speech whose main theme was that war was caused by injustice and that lasting peace must be based on a just settlement. He earnestly reported to Lloyd George on his return that Skrzynski had found it most interesting. No dialogue between the two men was possible because Kerr had been ordered to explore the possibility of a separate peace and Skrzynski had been ordered specifically not to do so.[124]

Two scholars, in examining Kerr's interpretation of his interview with Skrzynski, have criticised him respectively as 'obtuse' and 'slow in realizing that there was a new situation'.[125] Their contention is based on his recommendation, even after Czernin's refusal to go further, that preparations be made to present a complete set of peace terms to Austria, in case the Austrians were merely temporising, and his failure to take full account of the fact that Austria was now counting on a military victory by Germany in the west. This is to ignore the evidence contained in the full text of Kerr's report. Although he did not commit himself to an explanation of the sudden change of attitude, he did consider explicitly the possibility that Czernin was looking to military success. His recommendation was not merely that the Entente should prepare peace terms, but that it should do so as part of a military–diplomatic offensive which might persuade the Austrians that they could at any time choose to give in and seek terms. Thus the Entente could still hope to separate Austria from Germany, without letting up the military pressure. He realised that there was a new situation: he differed from the Foreign Office, which had always been costive about negotiations with Austria, in declining to give up hope immediately. His decision not to break off conversation immediately Skrzynski's position was clear was an optimistic one, but it did no harm and the desire not to waste entirely the opportunities provided by back-stairs diplomacy in a Swiss hotel was an understandable self-indulgence.

Kerr returned to England on 19 March 1918, two days before the opening of the German western offensive. Like German successes in the east in 1917, the early victories of German arms undercut any attempt to make a negotiated peace. Kerr's effort had failed, through no fault of his, and it marked the end of attempts to end the war diplomatically before the military and economic collapse of Germany. In his two visits to Switzerland he had borne a great responsibility – greater on the second occasion, when he had not been under the guidance and instruction of Smuts – for understanding the proposals put forward by enemy diplomats, making an immediate response which would protect British interests, and reporting constructively to those in Britain who would ultimately make political decisions. Though the Foreign Office had doubts, the War Cabinet trusted his judgement, and expressed its satisfaction at his work.[126]

5

Ireland

Ireland, though inconstant, is never dull!

Midleton to Adams, 1 March 1918.

I

The Irish question, like many areas of policy examined in this book, was never far from crisis during the war. In 1914 Asquith had achieved a temporary settlement of the Ulster crisis by putting Home Rule on the Statute Book and suspending the Act for the duration of hostilities. Sir Edward Carson had acquiesced on behalf of Ulster, promising his followers that suspension meant that Home Rule would never be applied to the six counties. Ulstermen volunteered in large numbers, and their regiments were allowed to fight under the Red Hand of Ulster. No corresponding generosity was shown to the Irish Volunteers, whose services were declined when offered to the War Office by John Redmond, the leader of the Irish Nationalist Party.[1] The Nationalists were discredited in Ireland by Redmond's acquiescence in the compromise over the Home Rule Act, and by his decision to accept a moratorium on the discussion of Irish constitutional matters for the duration of the war. The rising in Dublin at Easter 1916 was a direct consequence of Irish loss of confidence in parliamentary means of achieving a satisfactory political settlement. For all that, it was the work of a minority, and its historical importance as a representation of Irish political aspirations was established only by the Dublin Castle government, whose policy of executions, 'a fresh batch every morning for breakfast',[2] made heroes of the rebel leaders and blackened the already tarnished name of English rule. In the aftermath Lloyd George on behalf of the British government contrived an agreement between the Nationalists and Ulster leaders, providing for the immediate introduction of Home Rule with Ulster temporarily excluded. This was vetoed by a combination of English Conservatives and Southern Unionists. The only course apparently available to the government was once again to close the question until the end of the war. This second moratorium was, in its way, a victory for the Unionist parties, especially the Southern Unionists, and consequently the Unionist movement, though frightened, was at the end of 1916 in a fairly strong position. The change of government brought many stalwarts of the Ulster crisis into high office: Milner and Bonar Law in the War Cabinet, Carson at the Admiralty, and Balfour at the Foreign Office. Lord Midleton, the Southern Unionist leader, no longer had the standing he had enjoyed in English politics as Secretary of State for War in Balfour's Cabinet,[3] but his party's interests were regarded sympathetically by Curzon and Long. By contrast the Liberal partisans of Home Rule had for the most part either followed Asquith out of government or fallen away before December 1916. On becoming Prime Minister Lloyd George promised Redmond that he would not consent to conscription in Ireland without the introduction of Home Rule,[4] but his Unionist colleagues extracted a pledge that he was 'under no obligation' to the Nationalists, although 'no pledge could be given that Home Rule might not come on the tapis again at a later date'.[5]

Ireland did indeed arrive on the 'tapis' within a few months. The immediate cause was the parliamentary activity of the Nationalist leaders, who feared that governmental obduracy and the growing strength of the Sinn Fein movement would destroy their party's position. Dissatisfied with the vague promises made in Lloyd George's early statements, the party put down a motion for the beginning of the new parliamentary session in February, calling upon the government to 'confer upon Ireland the free institutions long promised her'. The motion was apparently calculated to enrage Unionist members and waste scarce parliamentary time; it was a warning that the Nationalists might revert to their tried tactics of parliamentary obstruction. To anticipate trouble, the government reluctantly began to consider terms for a constitutional settlement. The attempt was thwarted by Nationalist objections to any settlement which excluded Ulster, and Ulster Unionist objections to any which did not. In May 1917 the War Cabinet therefore resorted to the idea of a constitutional convention of representative Irishmen; and after delicate negotiations the Irish Convention began its work in Dublin in July. The Convention was hauled back from the brink of disaster in December 1917, but its final report in April 1918 was opposed by 29 of the 73 members voting, including all the Ulster Unionists and the

more extreme Nationalists. The political problem was handed back
to the British government, in circumstances even less auspicious than
those which had attended the birth of the Convention. Public order
in Ireland had deteriorated steadily as Sinn Fein, which had refused
to join the Convention, strengthened its hold on Irish opinion.
Antagonisms were sharpened by the announcement in April 1918 of
the extension of conscription to Ireland. The Nationalist party split
and John Dillon,⁶ who had succeeded as leader on the death of
Redmond, led many into co-operation with Sinn Fein to resist conscription. Despite the appointment of Lord French as a strong
Viceroy in May, and the arrest of 150 leading Sinn Feiners on the
pretext of a 'German plot', British political supremacy in Ireland
began to crumble. Further attempts to reach a constitutional settlement by consent foundered in the summer of 1918. In December
Sinn Fein won an overwhelming victory in the general election, and
1919 saw the beginning of the armed rebellion which was to bring
about the recognition of the Irish Free State by the British government in December 1921.

The Garden Suburb took more responsibility for the substance of
Irish policy than it did with respect to any other subject. It was able
to do so because the Convention removed the Irish constitutional
question from Westminster politics for almost ten months; during
that time the principal link between the Convention and the British
government was the correspondence between the chairman, Sir
Horace Plunkett, and his old friend and former colleague, Adams.
Adams supported the idea of a constitutional convention as early as
February 1917. When it was taken up by the government in May he
helped to negotiate the terms on which the Irish Nationalists would
join. He advised Plunkett when the Convention was approaching
deadlock in October 1917, and from December 1917 to February
1918 he orchestrated the government's policy towards the Convention in an attempt to prevent its collapse. His policy suffered a set-
back when the War Cabinet decided on conscription – a policy to
which Kerr, on the other hand, gave strong support. Adams soon
became secretary to the War Cabinet committee which drafted a new
Home Rule Bill. The committee never had much hope of seeing its
bill pass into law, but Adams was convinced that the bill it produced
would help to determine the conditions under which any future Irish
settlement was made, and he worked with some success to influence its
form. During his last months in Downing Street he was critical of the
harsh policy favoured by the Dublin Government, and disappointed

by the Westminster government's apparent indifference to the long-term fate of Ireland.

In the Garden Suburb opinion and knowledge of the Irish question varied from secretary to secretary. Harmsworth, who had been educated at Trinity College, Dublin, and came of Irish stock, was sympathetic to Home Rule and opposed to coercion. Astor, who had no direct knowledge of the country, derived his views in favour of conscription for Ireland and a settlement in the form of federal devolution for the whole of the United Kingdom from his associates in Milner's circle. Adams, who was the secretary most involved, was a moderate Home Ruler, with leanings to federalism, and an optimist. His years in Ireland had convinced him that the Irish economy, whose decline had exacerbated many political problems, could be revived. He was acknowledged an expert on Irish public finance, and had served on the Primrose committee which in 1911 had recommended that a future Irish government should be given full control over Irish taxation and spending.[7] He favoured federal devolution as a cure for legislative and administrative congestion in the United Kingdom, and 'Home Rule All Round' therefore appealed to him as a neat and rational scheme which would benefit both Ireland and Great Britain. He was opposed to partition, describing it in 1914 as having 'nothing to commend it but solely the hope that it will avert serious civil disturbance'.[8] His leaders in the *Political Quarterly* were marked by an optimism amounting sometimes to perversity, as he discussed 'approaches towards a common understanding'[9] in February 1914 and 'a real advance in the sense of responsibility about the Irish question'[10] in May of the same year. After the breakdown of negotiations in 1916 he found hope in the knowledge that partition had been rejected and that it had at the same time been recognised that no progress could be made without Ulster's consent.[11] His conviction that an agreed constitutional settlement for the whole island would be achieved, despite the chaos of recent Irish history, led him to insist that the Irish administrative structure should remain intact.[12] In broad outline Kerr held similar views. He too believed in federal devolution, which had been promoted by the Round Table group in 1913 and 1914.[13] He believed that Irish political problems could be solved, given goodwill. He differed from Adams in believing that the country would respond to strong government, and the difference over this overwhelmed any similarities in the two men's points of view. It arose partly from temperament, partly from contrasting careers. Kerr was preoccupied with moral analysis, and he attached a special value to his belief that the state had the right to command its citizens; he had also rejected the Catholic Church, and his attitude to the religion of the majority of Irishmen was such that Plunkett, a tolerant observer, feared that he was incapable of dispassionate judgement in Irish matters.[14] His opinions on Ireland were shaped by his imperial philosophy. Not only did he reject Ireland's separation from the Empire as 'not only suicidal but impossible',[15] but for reasons of defence he declined to contemplate an Ireland which stood in the same relation to the United Kingdom as the self-governing white colonies. He regarded Ireland's political future as subordinate to British interests. While Adams, who had spent formative years in Ireland, recognised and respected the frustration felt by many Irishmen at the slow and partial response of the British government to Irish needs, Kerr was inclined to regard it as the product of subversive agitation. Yet distance lent a certain clarity to his thoughts. When in January 1917 Lloyd George wanted a telegram to reassure the Australian Prime Minister, William Hughes,[16] of the new government's sincerity towards Ireland, Kerr delivered a draft based on four explicit assumptions: that the Home Rule Act should be brought into operation, that Ulster should be allowed to opt out at the end of three years, that conscription should be imposed immediately, and that an Irish general election should be held as soon as possible.[17] This was a neat compromise, but it was weighted heavily against the Nationalists, who were asked to accept conscription in return for a united Ireland from which Ulster was free to withdraw. Kerr adhered to his prescription until the end of the war.

II

The Nationalist challenge at the opening of the parliamentary session came at a moment when legislation was urgently needed to confirm the establishment of the new ministries on which the government's new policies were founded. Conscious of the perils of obstruction, the War Cabinet held a 'preliminary discussion on the question of Ireland' on 10 February.[18] Lloyd George was then left to find a solution which would satisfy all the conflicting parties in the government, in parliament, and in the unfortunate country itself. The parliamentary debate was finally set for 7 March, and the Garden Suburb was set to work to provide a brief both for the debate and for the negotiations which were to precede it. Adams submitted a comprehensive paper in the early days of March, arguing that the time had now come for the government to take the initiative in an 'exceedingly critical situation'. Sinn Fein was gaining sympathy, the Nationalists were in decline, and there was 'a hardening of opinion in Ulster since the Dublin rising and a stiffer determination that they will not submit to a settlement imposed on them'. Adams's solution was for the government to 'state plainly that the settlement of the Irish question depends on the Irish themselves, and that what Irishmen will agree on England and the Empire will accept'. Following on an earlier memorandum by L. S. Amery,[19] he suggested a constitutional conference of representative Irishmen, to meet in Ireland and draw up a settlement.

Adams saw no reason, save certain vital British interests, to restrict the nature of the constitution which the conference might suggest, but he followed Amery as well as his own inclination in proposing federal devolution to soothe Ulster's fears. He linked his political advice with a policy of economic regeneration. The tone of his memorandum reveals considerable sympathy with the ideals of Sinn Fein, and he was prepared to use the spirit of 'We Ourselves' to promote, with government cultivation, the renaissance of Irish life and Irish industry which he believed to be necessary. On the other hand, he was conventionally critical of revolutionary activity, and he noted the advantages in the immediate political situation of shifting responsibility for the Irish settlement from the government to the Irish themselves.[20]

Lloyd George met Bonar Law and Carson to discuss the Irish question on 2 March.[21] After suggesting that the Dominion Prime Ministers, soon to arrive in England for the Imperial War Conference, might sit on a commission to draw up a settlement, he handed over Adams's paper. Carson studied the proposals in consultation with his Ulster Unionist colleagues, and wrote the next day that he could not accept the commission because Ulster would see it as a device to evade the promise of separate treatment. Instead he suggested that Lloyd George should state that the government would pass agreed legislation but was pledged not to raise controversial issues during the war. He added:

Of course it would be open to you, if you thought on consideration that it was the necessary course to take, to throw out views of the convention as suggested by Professor Adams, though I do not believe myself that that would lead to any useful result, as the moment the convention was started it would be found that the persons nominated were not really able to bind their followers in any way.

As though in passing, he mentioned that if the government's proposals were misconstrued in Ulster his own position would be undermined: a clear hint that he was prepared to resign.[22] Kerr was then despatched to Carson. He returned with the outlines of a speech which had received the Ulster leader's 'general agreement'. The draft avoided definite proposals; its avowed purpose was to create an atmosphere in which a conference or convention might succeed, without actually proposing a conference. It promised a bright economic future for an Ireland closely linked with Great Britain, made much of the importance of 'a united Ireland, in a United Kingdom, in a united Empire', and concluded that the government could not accept a settlement without general consent.[23]

Lloyd George then turned to the Nationalists, and worked out with T. P. O'Connor,[24] the member in whose name the Nationalist motion stood, a scheme for a staged debate which would cushion the blow to Nationalist aspirations and leave scope for further negotiation. O'Connor warned that a speech on the lines proposed by Kerr and Carson would invite only derision from the Irish benches.[25] Meanwhile the Garden Suburb prepared the ground further. Adams, required to produce something optimistic about the Irish economy, suggested handing over to a new Irish government the mortgages taken out under the land purchase scheme; beyond that he could only recommend a safe reference to the rise in agricultural prices.[26] He consulted Dillon through C. P. Scott,[27] apparently to find out whether he could be used as a lever against Redmond or Joseph Devlin,[28] the third member of the Nationalist leading group. The response was not encouraging: after dismissing Sinn Fein as 'an atmosphere, not a party', Dillon described the situation as 'so bad and hopeless that almost any reasonable solution might be accepted if put forward in the proper manner', and suggested a tribunal of Dominion Prime Ministers to design a compromise which all Irish leaders might accept if they did not have to take responsibility for suggesting it. Nevertheless he warned that without an encouraging offer from the government in the forthcoming debate, the Nationalists would adopt a 'permanently antagonistic attitude', and he indicated that he would not act independently of Redmond and Devlin.[29] In sharp contrast, Astor consulted F. S. Oliver, whose letter recommending that Dillon, 'cold, hating, drunken, intensely jealous, very timid of responsibility (for all his clamours) and yet more nearly, as far as I can judge, the leader of the Irish people than any other', should be treated 'even as Rasputin was treated', would have reached

Lloyd George on the same day as Dillon's views. As was to be expected from his long association with the Round Table and his seminal part in the group's proposals for a federal solution before the war, Oliver proposed that Ireland should be allowed to manage her own affairs without separation from the United Kingdom. He also supported conscription and persuasion, not coercion, of Ulster.[30] Though his views were firm, he admitted ignorance of the immediate situation, and Astor also looked for enlightenment in the mood of the house of commons. He found members friendly to the government because of the recent agriculture debate, and impatient with the obstructive attitude of the Nationalists; but, he warned, Dillon was forming a nucleus of members who might be a source of trouble in the future.[31] Astor convened a meeting of two Nationalists, two Liberals, and two Unionists, who concluded that the Nationalists would not make difficulties about the powers granted to an Irish parliament, provided only that Ireland was united, but would not hear a refusal of Home Rule without violent protest.[32]

The War Cabinet met on the afternoon of 7 March and agreed on the terms of Lloyd George's speech to the commons. The conclusion was determined by Carson's position; the speech ended with an amendment to O'Connor's motion, welcoming any suggestion for a settlement on which both Ulster and the South could agree. Its terms were similar to those put forward in Kerr's draft.[33] In the house this brusque rebuff to the Nationalists led to a breakdown of debate. Lloyd George made the concession of accepting the idea of a conference, but his speech was frequently interrupted, and after a short but bitter reply Redmond led his party from the chamber.[34] Soon afterwards the Irish members sent an angry public protest to the President of the United States.[35] The debate marked the failure of the new government's first attempt to deal with the Irish question. The next day Adams, Astor and Kerr submitted to Lloyd George a plan for the government to take the initiative and so relieve the Nationalists of the burden of making all the sacrifices necessary for a peaceful settlement. They endorsed the speeches of those Irish members who blamed the government for driving Ireland into the arms of Sinn Fein, and emphasised the importance of maintaining the Nationalist party in being. The government should 'refuse to be distracted by the theatrical conduct of the Irish, and announce their intention of putting their proposals to a thorough test by introducing a bill for the establishment of Home Rule in the twenty-six counties at once'. Following Dillon's arguments, they recommended that the

Nationalists should not be asked to take responsibility for partition, since the negotiations in 1916 had shown that they could not do so.

We believe that the condition of a settlement is now a move by Ulster... If Ulster is now prepared to come forward and say that she is prepared for the sake of the war and the unity of the Empire to enter into a convention with the nationalists to draw up a settlement on the basis of Irish unity, we believe that the Irish question would be solved...[36]

This was an ingenious proposal to exploit Ulster's fear of an extremist victory in the South, English Unionists' impatience with Ulster, and Redmond's urgent need of support against Sinn Fein. By talking to Devlin and James Craig,[37] a leading Ulster Unionist, Astor discovered that the Nationalists would 'give any safeguards – reduced legislative powers or extra representation to Ulster for a united Ireland', and Craig feared that without immediate action by the government Redmond would be replaced by Dillon, which would be 'calamitous'. Craig would not be coerced into the first All-Ireland parliament, but he might 'construct bridges over which [Ulster] can cross into the Parliament later'. Astor suggested that Lloyd George see Craig for 'This looks like the beginning of a move from Ulster but I don't think that they will go very far unless helped or appealed to.'[38] In the event Craig's hints were followed up by Carson, who sent the Prime Minister a memorandum through Kerr on 20 March, observing that 'At the present moment I do not believe Ulster would agree to come in on any conditions; but I think the conditions which could be offered to her should be ascertained and should be included in any amending Bill, so as to leave it open to Ulster at some later period to accept these terms.' He suggested that until the settlement was finally made a 'consultative assembly' composed of a delegation from the Dublin parliament and the Ulster M.P.s at Westminster should meet regularly to harmonise legislation.[39] This suggestion was taken to the War Cabinet, which approved of it after first trying without success to get Dominion Prime Ministers to serve on a commission.[40] As before, Lloyd George took the proposal to O'Connor and Devlin, who rejected it and told him that for once he ought to defy Ulster.[41] At this point sympathy between the government and the Nationalist party was at a low point. O'Connor reported to the Nationalist leaders that Lloyd George seemed determined on exclusion, and the War Cabinet took fright lest the Irish members would obstruct the bill to extend the life of parliament. Yet the future was not altogether hopeless. O'Connor also reported his suspicion that Lloyd George was 'playing a deep game for the purpose of compelling the Orangemen into county option'; the Nationalists were not in fact determined to obstruct the parliament bill;[42] and the War Cabinet's discussion did produce some proposals. The question was discussed on 17 April. Adams had prepared a summary of his opinions for the Prime Minister. He had no doubt that the government should propose a settlement, otherwise 'the situation in Ireland will grow more difficult and the position of the Government will be weakened not only in Ireland but in Great Britain'. His recommendations were a synthesis of Carson's memorandum and the Garden Suburb's letter to Lloyd George of 8 March. He suggested that it was impossible either to bring Ulster into a Home Rule parliament or to arrange for exclusion under the 'county option' plan, whereby each county was to vote separately on inclusion in the Home Rule area. Instead he suggested temporary exclusion of the six counties *en bloc*, with final constitutional arrangements to be left to the end of the war. Meanwhile the Irish administrative structure should be retained as far as possible intact; a committee should be appointed to consider federal devolution for the whole United Kingdom; and Ireland should continue to be represented at Westminster.[43] This proposal, in essence to postpone the most difficult decision until the end of the war, while solving the immediate problem by introducing as much Home Rule as possible without coercing Ulster, was raised in the War Cabinet but rejected on the grounds that the Unionists saw it as too great a risk and the Nationalists as 'an expedient to exclude Tyrone and Fermanagh' because it was proposed to demand the support of 55 per cent of the voters for inclusion. The plan of a commission was abandoned because the Dominion Prime Ministers were reluctant to serve. Failing agreement on a scheme which could be presented directly to both sides as a compromise settlement, the War Cabinet decided to introduce a bill, take it to the Second Reading, then submit it to a conference of Irishmen for amending before the committee stage. Thus it was hoped to avoid confrontation with the Nationalists. Curzon, Addison, and Henry Duke, the Chief Secretary for Ireland, were appointed as a committee, with Adams as secretary, to draft the government's bill providing for immediate exclusion by county option, with 55 per cent of voters required to support inclusion, a joint council of Northern and Southern delegates to consider harmonising legislation, and the opportunity for further plebiscites to consider incorporating excluded counties in the Home Rule area.[44] The Nationalists made only a token resistance to the parliament bill, but the information which began to reach them about the government's intentions hardened their determination to resist the government's settlement, as Astor found out as early as 21 April.[45] In the War Cabinet on 17 April Carson had registered dissent from the county option element of the government bill, and Lloyd George and the drafting committee reverted to the idea of a 'clean cut' of the six counties until three years after the end of the war, rather as Adams had first suggested. This suggestion was transmitted through C. P. Scott to O'Connor, Devlin and Dillon on 3 May.[46] All three rejected it, but the final form of the bill conceded only that a plebiscite in the excluded area would be taken in each county 'shortly after the termination of the war'.[47] Adams, who drafted the letter explaining the bill's provisions to Redmond, criticised the bill for unnecessary details likely to offend the Nationalists,[48] and said in private, in Plunkett's words, that Lloyd George had 'thrown himself in with the Carson group'.[49] He was further dismayed when Lloyd George seemed to take the defeat of the Nationalist candidate in the South Longford bye-election as a justification for delay. Protesting that 'the Government should proceed, despite what has happened of late', he pointed out that the draft bill could be defended because it was not simple partition, but insisted that 'the Government bill should make as good an offer as possible' by making all concessions possible to the Nationalists within the limits set by Ulster objections.[50] Parliamentary pressure from both sides was increasing, and Astor reported that 'the same people who last summer, ran the movement in the Commons and Lords against a settlement of the Irish question during the war, are getting busy in both Houses. We are, however, organising a memorial to show the extent of Unionist support for a reasonable and immediate settlement.'[51] Yet the draft bill remained the government's only policy, and the Nationalists still hoped for county option.[52]

In this troubled atmosphere the idea of a convention, which had dropped out of negotiations, was revived by T. P. Gill,[53] a former colleague of Adams in the Department of Agriculture and Technical Instruction, who had a long connection with the Nationalist party. On 11 May he wrote to Adams, with whom he was in frequent contact about Irish agriculture, remarking that he had heard that the government planned to deal with Ireland by:

Forming at once a Constitutional Assembly; stating (by resolution or otherwise) the *amount* of power to be given to an Irish constitution; and leaving the Constituent Assembly to fabricate the Constitution; final effect

to be given to the Constitution when the C.A. has decided on a scheme. . .
It is, in my opinion, in all the existing and especially the new circumstances
(a) the best way out of the present dilemma for the P.M. and (b) intrin-
sically the best solution.

Adams asked for more details and on 15 May received an elaborate
scheme of representation requiring 120 members, 80 to be nominated
by representative institutions, mostly local authorities, and 40 nominated by the government.[54] Gill also sent a copy of his scheme to
Redmond.[55] It embodied the principle, if not the detail, of the Irish
Convention as it was finally established at the end of May.

Adams submitted this correspondence to Lloyd George on 15
May.[56] Late that afternoon Scott called at 10 Downing Street. In a
few minutes snatched between 'almost continuous War Cabinets' the
Prime Minister told Scott that Asquith would not contribute positively to a settlement, and Scott reported that Dillon had told him
that day that partition was unacceptable and that the best solution
was a free conference. Lloyd George then said that the letter to
Redmond, explaining the government's proposals, was not ready.
When Scott returned half an hour later:

he sd. draft of letter was no good & and he had sent for another. he hd. it
appears commissioned more than one draft & this one was I think he said
prepared by Professor Adams. It was a formal and stuffy document not at
all to his mind.

Lloyd George then ordered Kerr to produce a draft, which he com-
pleted in time for the War Cabinet to consider by 8 p.m. Then Kerr
and Scott worked together until ten amending the War Cabinet's
version. Scott described Kerr's drafting as 'very rapid and a little
slapdash', but he was pleased with the result, which emphasised the
provisional nature of the arrangement, 'one of the vital parts for the
Nationalists'.[57] Scott's notes suggest that Lloyd George had read very
little of the papers on Ireland until the last minute, and it would
seem that the Prime Minister first heard of the idea of a convention
as a way out of the difficulty not from Gill through Adams, but from
Redmond through Lord Crewe.[58] Crewe learned from Redmond on
the evening of 15 May that the Nationalists would accept a convention if the government suggested one, and he called on Lloyd George
late that evening, returning to Redmond in the morning to get
proposals in writing.[59] Also on 16 May Adams submitted another
batch of correspondence from Gill, including a plan for a reduced
convention of 80 members.[60] The War Cabinet met at 11.30 a.m. on

16 May to discuss the letter to Redmond. Carson confirmed his insistence that the excluded area should be defined as a 'clean cut' of
the six counties, including, that is, Tyrone and Fermanagh where
the Protestants were in a minority of 45 per cent.[61] At a further
meeting in the afternoon a draft was approved which incorporated,
as an afterthought, the convention proposal; the letter was sent to
Redmond, Sir John Lonsdale,[62] a leading Ulster back-bencher,
Midleton, and William O'Brien[63] and Tim Healy,[64] the joint
leaders of a small 'Independent Nationalist' group of M.P.s. The
last paragraph saved the situation. Redmond, though 'irreconcileably
opposed' to the bill, accepted the convention,[65] and O'Brien took the
same view 'subject to the discussion of details'.[66] Lonsdale accepted
either bill or convention, but made it clear that Ulster Unionists
would not accept amendments to the bill changing the excluded
area or altering the powers of the Irish Council which was to
harmonise legislation.[67] Midleton accepted the convention.[68] Neither
the Nationalists nor the Ulster Unionists had serious illusions about the
convention's prospects, since both had sworn dreadful oaths never to
accept a settlement on the lines favoured by the other. The Southern
Unionists had something to gain from it, since although they preferred
to leave the question closed, they were painfully aware that Ulster
might abandon them to Home Rule in order to secure exclusion for
the Northern counties. No party to the Irish dispute gained as much
from the decision to hold the convention as did the government itself,
which won the certainty of a breathing space. Within a week of Gill's
suggestion to Adams and Redmond, the convention proposal had
transformed the immediate outlook for Irish settlement and offered
hope, albeit slim hope, for a final solution.

It was recognised that the ultimate success of the convention
would depend on the details of its composition. A convention had to
be designed in which each of the major Irish political parties –
Nationalist, Ulster Unionist, and Southern Unionist – felt that it had
adequate numerical representation, and in which key minorities and
interests such as business, the trade unions, and the churches were
also represented. Adams, who was largely responsible for the final
form of the Irish Convention, pressed for a small body based on the
schemes suggested by Gill, in preference to the scheme for 171
members proposed by Redmond. On 21 May the War Cabinet,
using arguments from other constitutional conventions supplied to
Lloyd George by Adams,[69] rejected Redmond's scheme and sent
Duke to discover the Nationalists' minimum conditions;[70] the next

day 'the greater part of the meeting was occupied in an endeavour to frame a smaller convention in which the various interests suggested by Mr Redmond should be adequately represented.'[71] Duke was then asked to follow the Nationalist leaders to Ireland, where they had gone after their meeting with him on 21 May, to present a plan for 70 or 80 members. Though Devlin accepted the principle of a smaller convention, Redmond and Dillon continued to insist on a comprehensive body where Nationalist sentiment would predominate, and Duke therefore returned empty-handed.[72] At this anxious moment Adams intervened with new ideas and new *dramatis personae*. Insisting in his frequent minutes to Lloyd George on the importance of a small convention from which an efficient drafting committee could be drawn, he held long discussions with Dr Denis Kelly, the Catholic Bishop of Ross,[73] an experienced administrator and politician whom he had met through the Department of Agriculture and Technical Instruction. Adams and Kelly, who feared that Redmond's proposal to include nominees of professional groups such as teachers would lead to endless claims for representation, preferred to follow Gill's original plan in confining rights of nomination to parliamentary parties and statutory bodies such as local authorities, leaving the government to nominate a balanced representation from the rest of the community. On this basis they hoped to reduce the size of the convention to 60 or less, and Adams advised Lloyd George of their conclusions.[74] They drafted a scheme for 60, of whom fewer than 20 were to be M.P.s, and submitted it to Duke and to the War Cabinet, who endorsed it on 24 May.[75] Later that day it was presented to Irish leaders at a meeting attended by Lloyd George, Duke, Curzon, Adams, T. P. O'Connor (the senior Nationalist politician left in London), and James Craig.[76]

The response was not at first encouraging. O'Connor baulked at the small number, and even Duke was doubtful. O'Connor telegraphed the offer to Redmond, Dillon and Devlin.[77] The two latter rejected it: Dillon protested that 'if we attempted to defend such a body we should be charged reasonably with having betrayed the country',[78] and that 'there is a regular conspiracy on foot to pack the Convention so as to put the Unionists practically in control'.[79] Redmond was temporarily out of reach. O'Connor apologised for Adams as 'a clever man and a friend, but of course not a trained politician'.[80] Behind these protestations the Nationalists were ready to compromise. Redmond's original scheme had been produced without reference to his colleagues, and Devlin and Dillon accepted without demur that nomination should be confined to political parties, statutory bodies, and the government. Within that framework, which was the essence of the Kelly–Adams proposal, they were prepared to bargain about numbers. Redmond, Dillon and Devlin met on 25 May and as a result Dillon conveyed to O'Connor that Sinn Fein should be allowed the same representation as the Nationalist and Unionist parties and that all 33 county councils should be represented by their chairmen instead of the 8 to be nominated under the Kelly scheme;[81] but Devlin was content to add one Ulster liberal to the Kelly scheme to represent Ulster Nationalism, and O'Connor had an intermediate plan of his own, apparently based on Redmond's principle of nomination by interest groups.[82] Meanwhile, to O'Connor's dismay, Lloyd George was pressing for an immediate decision and Redmond for an immediate announcement.[83] Much of the confusion was dissolved by Gill, who after consultation with Adams, Duke and Kelly visited Redmond at his home in County Wicklow and elicited a statement of Nationalist desires which was the same as Dillon had suggested to O'Connor. Gill reported his conversation to Adams and advised that the government should accept the terms, with a consequent increase to about 100 members. He concluded:

Ring up T.P.O.C. and read him this. I am posting him a letter from J.E.R. which he should read by the light of this. Further, R. says let Duke come over here if he cannot fix it up over there. I think T.P., Duke and you can get it right if you try.[84]

O'Connor reacted by sending in a scheme for 114 members, which he expected to be submitted to the War Cabinet and Carson,[85] but Adams responded with a version of the Kelly–Adams scheme, extended to 101 members to include all the county-council chairmen and more government nominees, and allowing nomination by Trades Councils and Chambers of Commerce, but reducing the direct representation of political parties to 5 each.[86] O'Connor telegraphed it to Dillon and Redmond, who agreed,[87] and Adams was able to report his success to the War Cabinet on 31 May.[88] This settled the composition of the convention, which was then conveyed to other parties so that they might decide whether or not to come in. Two factors had contributed to the achievement of a convention of moderate size based on the Kelly–Adams scheme: Adams's long and confidential acquaintance with Kelly and Gill, who were invaluable as advisers and intermediaries, and the earnest desire of the Nation-

alist leaders to relinquish to the government any responsibility for
the composition of the convention.

The War Cabinet, on learning of the Nationalists' assent, proceeded to consider the questions which Adams, after consultation
with Duke, had prepared for it.[89] It settled on church and labour
representatives, and decided to invite the Speaker[90] to be chairman
and Sir Francis Hopwood, who was shortly to retire from the
Admiralty,[91] to be secretary.[92] Details of the scheme were sent to
Lonsdale and Midleton, who persuaded their followers to take part.
The general council of the Irish Unionist Association (the Southern
Unionists) agreed to come in on 1 June, without agreeing on the
purpose of their joining;[93] the Ulster Council, more obviously reluctant, decided on 8 June to send a delegation which was to be
chaperoned by an advisory committee of diehards to ensure that it
did not forget its *non possumus* manners.[94] Sinn Fein was a tougher
problem. Its co-operation was essential to the ultimate success of the
convention. If war had not prevented local elections, Sinn Feiners
would probably have overturned many of the county-council chairmen who had been included in the convention as staunch Nationalists; furthermore, the release of Easter Rising prisoners had permitted the party to organise.[95] Its leaders had come out against the
convention shortly after it was announced,[96] but Duke was confident
that someone representing extreme views could be persuaded to
participate,[97] and Adams's connections enabled negotiations to be
opened.

Through Lord Monteagle, a former colleague in the Irish Agri-
cultural Organisation Society,[98] Adams arranged to meet George
Gavan Duffy,[99] with whom he discussed the possibility of virtual
representation of Sinn Fein through the National League and the
Gaelic League, two organisations devoted to the cultural renaissance
of Ireland. On 1 June Monteagle crossed to Ireland and met the
'Mansion House Committee' which led Sinn Fein. He reported to
Adams:

...1) that the moderates...wd be satisfied with Dominion status 2) wd
some of them act on a Convention, given amnesty and a really representative constitution of Convn. – 3) will none of them look at it without both
the 2 conditions.[100]

Plunkett, who had recently returned to the United Kingdom from
a period of illness in America, was also in touch with Adams
and active in promoting the convention among extreme parties:
Monteagle feared that neither he nor Duke realised the importance

of meeting Sinn Fein's two conditions. On 7 June Adams reported
to Lloyd George that Sinn Fein could be brought in, either directly
or through the National League, but emphasised the importance of
amnesty for Sinn Fein prisoners.[101] On the weekend of 10 June
Adams persuaded Plunkett to write to Lloyd George asking for
amnesty,[102] and the resulting letter was considered by the War
Cabinet on 14 June, together with a memorandum to the same effect
by Duke.[103] A general amnesty was announced in parliament the
next day. Even this gesture was not enough, since the representative
nature of the convention was in doubt. Duffy, who had been encouraged by his meeting with Adams, emerged less hopeful from an
interview with Duke, who talked about Ulster's 'inexpugnable
position' and even raised doubts about amnesty. Newspaper reports
of ill-treatment of Irish prisoners made matters worse.[104] When the
Irish press gave a poor impression of the amnesty proposal, Plunkett
wrote to Adams that he now felt that Sinn Fein's official position
would not change, though individuals might find it easier to come
in.[105] Nothing was to come of this. Late in July Adams and Duke
discussed a proposal to invite three Sinn Feiners, but Duke, after
helping to draft the letter, backed down because of Sinn Fein disorder.[106] In the event neither Sinn Fein, nor the National League,
nor the Gaelic League sent representatives.

William O'Brien's group and other independent Nationalists
offered the possibility of another bridge to Sinn Fein. O'Brien feared
that Redmond, once in the convention, might accept partition; he
therefore demanded a referendum on any decision by the convention. Plunkett, in his enthusiasm for the convention idea, spoke
warmly of a referendum in public at Dundalk on 25 June, and provoked a public correspondence with O'Brien.[107] Plunkett then asked
Adams to get the War Cabinet to promise a referendum officially,[108]
but Adams, while supporting the principle in a note to the War
Cabinet,[109] rebuked his friend for making it public and perhaps
giving Ulster an excuse to back out. Duke despatched the proposal
in a hostile memorandum,[110] and independent Nationalism was
brought in through the government's nomination of W. M. Murphy,
George Russell,[111] and Edward MacLysaght.[112] O'Brien and Healy
both refused.

In 1918 Adams looked back on these several negotiations as one of
the Garden Suburb's most important contributions to the operation
of wartime government. His success was achieved by private negotiation through personal acquaintances; it was irrelevant to the

negotiations with the Unionist parties, who dealt directly with Duke and Lloyd George, and to Labour which was also managed by Duke.[113] Adams could meet the Nationalists and other separatist parties through common friends who shared his own earnest commitment to the convention. He was not to blame for the obvious inadequacies of representation in the convention, and he deserves considerable credit for its acceptance by the Nationalists.

III

The Irish Convention, representing at least some of the great interests in Irish life and politics, opened in Dublin on 25 July in a troubled atmosphere. On 10 July Eamon De Valera[114] had defeated the Nationalist candidate by a majority of 3000 in East Clare, the seat left vacant by the death in action of John Redmond's younger brother, William. The result was doubly alarming: it emphasised the weakness of Nationalism and the strength of Sinn Fein, a party which stood aloof from the Convention, and it lent support to Unionist leaders who were pressing for harsher measures of law enforcement in Ireland,[115] which could only embarrass the Convention. Sir Bryan Mahon, the Commander-in-Chief in Ireland, wanted to take severe measures, as did Lord Wimborne, the Viceroy.[116] Adams, in a memorandum to Lloyd George, objected that the government had to decide between making arrests for sedition and inflammatory speeches, and a more limited policy of keeping warlike stores out of the hands of Sinn Fein. If Sinn Feiners were arrested:

Thousands of young Sinn Feiners will covet the distinction of going to prison; it will be a cheap D.S.O....It is probably what the Sinn Fein leaders wish the government to do. It will be represented as the government's taking revenge for the Clare election...to begin a policy of arrests for seditious language, the end of which we cannot see, is probably to deal a death blow to the Convention.[117]

Duke shared these doubts, but feared that Sinn Fein would co-operate with the Germans: he therefore advised that newspapers which printed seditious speeches should be seized and that although no arrests should be made for seditious speeches *per se*, the regulations against drilling and processions should be strictly enforced.[118] The logic of his policy led the military authorities to arrest Sinn Fein leaders, not for sedition, but for inciting crowds to assemble unlawfully. Public justification was inadequate, and the political cost was immediately felt in the Convention. Plunkett, who had been elected chairman after the Speaker declined the position, wrote to Adams in August after he had persuaded the Irish government to release De Valera in order to keep the Lord Mayor of Dublin in the Convention, 'I am rather hanging on by my eyelids, but I think I have got all the difficult people to agree not to forsake the Convention without first coming to see me'.[119] Such difficulties beset the Convention throughout its life. Its internal conflicts were important on their own, and its progress towards settlement was further hampered by external developments both in Ireland and Westminster.

The first months of the Convention's work were strongly influenced by the personal style of the chairman. Plunkett had been nominated to the Convention by the government as an influential Irishman who was not representative of anything except himself. Although he had been a Unionist M.P., his influence in Ireland was based on his work for agricultural organisation, his hereditary membership of the Irish social and political élite, and the fact that he knew everybody who mattered. He was chosen as chairman in preference to Hopwood, the nominee of a selection committee, as a result of pressure by Redmond and Russell. He was not a good chairman in the ordinary sense; a poor speaker, he did not think quickly on his feet. He believed, however, that the Convention did not need an ordinary chairman. He preferred to allow conflict to dissipate in talk before serious matters were reached, and the first three weeks of the Convention were spent on procedural questions. He then circulated a plan for a 'Grand Committee' to work out solutions for the various problems and present them for ratification to the whole assembly. The Convention worked under this scheme until October. The first months clarified the points of disagreement without producing solutions. The Ulster Unionists procrastinated, apparently content to let the Home Rulers try to prove the necessity for change.[120] Besides exasperating the Nationalists, this strategy upset the Southern Unionists, who wanted to make the Convention a success in order to avoid a repetition of 1916 in which Ulster had offered to sacrifice Unionists in the South for the sake of partition.[121]

In October Plunkett crossed to England to discuss the state of the Convention with the government. His visit marked the beginning of the end of the Convention. The occasion was an incipient dispute over the 'fiscal question', which had troubled the authors of every Home Rule bill, but which had been overshadowed in 1914 by the Ulster crisis. The Nationalists wanted the Irish parliament to fix and collect all Irish taxation; the Unionists, Northern and Southern, feared the economic and fiscal effects of separation from the United Kingdom. To colour the dispute, control of Customs and Excise was a matter of pride to the Nationalists, while the Unionists, especially in Ulster, professed to fear the malevolence and incompetence of a Nationalist commercial policy. The technicalities were complicated, and few members of the Convention could have understood them: but few were inhibited from holding strong views. Under Plunkett's loose reign, the Convention had begun by early October to lose impetus and chafe at unsettled questions. On 13 October, at the insistence of the Ulster Unionists, a sub-committee of the Grand Committee, consisting of Midleton, three Ulstermen and five Nationalists, was set up to discuss the outstanding questions of the Irish parliament and Customs and Excise. After a fortnight's adjournment, the sub-committee resumed their discussions in London, and settled the parliament question by a craftsmanlike gerrymander in which Unionists were to get a bare majority of both Irish houses voting together. Then, in early November, the Nationalist demand for 'fiscal autonomy' was put forward by the Bishop of Raphoe,[122] and negotiations came to a standstill. Plunkett had anticipated the difficulty, and when in London had been introduced by Adams to A. C. Pigou, the Cambridge economist,[123] who was interested in the financial settlement. Shortly afterwards Pigou visited Plunkett in Ireland and together they worked out an 'examination paper' which was submitted to members of the sub-committee to clarify the points of difference. The Nationalists replied with a statement of doctrine; the Ulstermen, who had as usual waited for their opponents to commit themselves, replied in insulting terms.[124]

The Convention was now threatened by collapse. Adams, impatient with both sides, wrote to Plunkett:

This fiscal controversy is in danger of getting entirely out of proportion. The first and greatest thing is to get one Irish Parliament...It should never be forgotten that an agreement on the part of the North to come into a Parliament is such a big concession that they should be met by a considerable concession on the other side.

Tariff powers would be incompatible with the development of federal relations within the United Kingdom, which is the true and proper line of solution.[125]

After the breakdown of the sub-committee's discussions, he argued that the Nationalists should not

leave Ulster alone and try to get an agreement with the other Unionists. This sort of policy to me simply spells failure.[126]

Instead he thought that since both parties had taken up positions more extreme than those of 1914, both had room for manoeuvre, and he urged Plunkett to get the Nationalists to see that representation at Westminster was the crux for Ulster. Plunkett disagreed, seeing no difficulty in persuading Nationalists to accept continuing representation at Westminster, but no obvious solution to the 'fiscal crux'. He saw hope only in the offer by Londonderry, an Ulster Unionist peer,[127] to introduce a federal-devolution plan based on a pamphlet by Selborne and F. S. Oliver which had recently been circulated.[128] When the Ulster chaperone committee refused to let the scheme go forward – Plunkett thought because it meant the substance if not the appearance of Home Rule[129] – the Convention had nowhere to turn, and on 22 November Duke told the War Cabinet that breakdown was imminent. Representatives of the Convention were summoned to meet Lloyd George when he returned from a conference in Paris.[130]

Adams now began to take a direct part in the discussions. On 28 November he arrived in Ireland and met an Ulster delegate, Hugh Pollock.[131] The next evening he heard the fiscal autonomy case from the Bishop of Raphoe. After a full day of discussions with Plunkett and the Convention Secretariat,[132] he returned to London to submit a fairly optimistic report to Lloyd George: 'The Irish Convention is not *in extremis*. The situation is critical but hopeful; critical because the situation is one which demands immediate action.' He explained that on the day of his arrival Midleton had tabled a compromise resolution calling for a diminished Irish representation at Westminster with a compulsory contribution to imperial expenditure made up of the Irish Customs revenue, which would be Ireland's only financial obligation to the United Kingdom. He approved of this scheme and urged Lloyd George that it was 'now very important that you should see at the earliest possible moment the various parties'.[133] Submitting a note by Midleton on 4 December he pressed the point: 'The Nationalists must give up their demand for fiscal autonomy...It is felt strongly that you alone can bring home the necessity and urgency of a settlement, and that now is the moment...'[134] On 5 December he reminded the Prime Minister that the Southern Unionists were prepared to give the Irish parliament far wider powers than were given by the 1914 Act, and he suggested that Lloyd George should give them the chance to state their views on the protection of minorities and the idea of an Ulster Provincial Council.[135] Even Kerr added his mite, urging Lloyd

George to take action to quash the belief 'that the Government is not really sincere about the Irish Convention, in the sense that it regards it chiefly as a useful method of keeping Ireland quiet during the war'. The government should take the initiative. 'But I don't believe that anybody can exert pressure to bring moderate Ulstermen and moderate nationalists together, save yourself as Prime Minister.'[136]

The Prime Minister's interview with Convention delegates took place on 5 December, but did no material good.[137] The Nationalists were apparently afraid of W. M. Murphy, who was threatening to denounce any compromise.[138] Plunkett learned that they would give up Customs only if they were assured of Ulster's agreement;[139] but Ulster was even more cautious, and the advisory committee repudiated Midleton's initiative.[140] Faced with such sullen attitudes, Midleton insisted that the issue must be faced before he would agree to talk about anything else, and that he could make no further concessions.[141]

Adams now tried to bring about an initiative from the government. On 10 December he suggested to Lloyd George that Ulster should be encouraged to take up Midleton's proposal, lest the Convention should break up, leaving the Nationalists committed irrevocably to fiscal autonomy and opposed to the government. In the latter event he suggested that the government should proceed with a compromise on its own responsibility.[142] Pursuing this line of thought, he talked to Londonderry, who fell back on the argument that the Ulstermen were only delegates who could not accept any Nationalist or Southern Unionist scheme on their own responsibility, but would have to consider their position if the government offered a solution. Londonderry had entirely given up hope of an agreed settlement and wanted the government to impose a settlement, govern firmly, and bring in conscription.[143] Lloyd George was opposed to immediate intervention if it was avoidable, but Adams suggested to Southborough (Hopwood, recently ennobled) that if the Convention failed to agree it should appoint spokesmen to the government and thus force the War Cabinet to put forward its own plan.[144] It was not a propitious time for government action. The War Cabinet was in acute difficulties over the Manpower question, and Adams found Lloyd George busy and elusive.[145] Redmond, without whom the Nationalists would certainly not consider a compromise, had been conducting an impassioned correspondence with the Prime Minister, begging him to bring Ulster round,[146] and he was in no mood to trust the government. When Plunkett assured him that

Lloyd George would put the Southern Unionist scheme into operation if the Convention accepted it, he replied merely that 'from his
experience negotiating with him nothing was of the least value unless
it was in writing'.[147] Even this was perhaps optimistic, since although
Lloyd George had written a vague but encouraging letter to Redmond about the scheme,[148] the most that Adams could extract from
him in private was that he saw it as a line of settlement which he
would discuss with the War Cabinet.[149]

Since the War Cabinet was busy, the Convention, in full session
again after two months of committee and sub-committee discussions,
was left to its own devices. Midleton announced on 11 December
that he would introduce his resolution at the next meeting, and
furious debate ensued within the various groups. The Ulstermen
decided almost immediately to go one step further than refusal by
moving first an amendment that both Customs and Excise should be
reserved, then another affirming the right of the imperial parliament
to impose conscription.[150] Plunkett thought that they were 'trying to
build a bridge over which British opinion will approve of their
breaking with the Convention'.[151] Among the Nationalists, the
Bishop of Raphoe emerged as spokesman of a faction which held
that 'any compromise that is not with the North is no good, for an
agreed scheme at least',[152] while to one side of him the independent
Nationalists rejected any sort of compromise and to the other side
Stephen Gwynn, M.P.,[153] tried to persuade his party to accept the
Midleton plan. Both Midleton and Gwynn tried through Adams to
get the government to give a written undertaking to accept the
scheme if the Convention agreed upon it, but Adams replied that
the government would have to know what measure of agreement any
scheme represented.[154] The suspense lasted until 15 January 1918.
Midleton wanted to press his motion to a division; Plunkett and
Adams, afraid of the wrath of an unpersuaded Ulster, tried to postpone it. Redmond decided that there was a secret agreement
between Ulster and the government.[155] He therefore prepared an
amendment accepting the proposals subject to ratification by the
government, and wrote to Lloyd George asking for his agreement.[156]
At the same time Londonderry put down a conscription resolution.
In a moment of alcoholic confidentiality a Belfast Labour representative told the Viceroy's private secretary that 'Me and Londonderry's going to wreck the Convention on conscription'.[157] To avoid
direct clashes, Plunkett tried to spin out discussion by bringing up
land purchase and other technical questions. Meanwhile Adams was

trying with little success to get the Prime Minister to pay attention to the Convention's problems. At last on 11 January he was able to urge him in a private conversation 'to go right through with the recommendations of the Convention...without getting entangled in fresh compromising negotiations [and] to be willing to contemplate the departure of Carson from the Cabinet'.[158] On 14 January Lloyd George and Adams had private discussions with Bonar Law, who had been putting pressure on the Ulster delegation through H. T. Barrie.[159]

On 15 January the situation took a new turn. The Bishop of Raphoe, strongly influenced by the independent Nationalist Russell, gathered the Catholic bishops around him and in exasperation at the delay and doubt 'ran amok' and persuaded Devlin to join them in withdrawing support from the compromise.[160] Many county-council chairmen followed. Redmond's influence was destroyed; he refused to move his amendment when Midleton's scheme was introduced,[161] and hopes of an immediate settlement were dashed. Plunkett and Southborough experimented with plans to grant Customs to Ireland after a period of years, but the Southern Unionists did not respond.[162] Finally on 17 January Lord Macdonnell,[163] a former Irish official who sat in the Convention as a government nominee, introduced an amendment giving control of Customs to the United Kingdom parliament throughout the war and thereafter until a Royal Commission could consider the question. Midleton refused to make any further concession.[164] The Convention adjourned on 17 January. The next day Plunkett explained the position to Lloyd George and Milner, who agreed that delegates from the Convention should once again see the Prime Minister.[165] Lloyd George's letter of invitation was cautious, apparently because he was anxious to help Carson, who resigned from the War Cabinet on 21 January, to bring the Ulster members round to a compromise; Adams had to explain for Redmond's benefit that the government could go no further.[166] Adams also asked the Convention Secretariat to encourage Unionists to vote to accept the invitation.[167] On 25 January Plunkett read the Prime Minister's letter, and after a long debate the Convention accepted the invitation and adjourned.

While Lloyd George was away at the Supreme War Council in Versailles, Adams tried to devise a policy statement which would be widely acceptable. Because the Convention had failed to reach full agreement, the detailed agreements reached by the Grand Committee were void, and even the Irish parliament had to be considered afresh. On 28 January he saw Barrie, who suggested setting up an Ulster Committee, with full powers of initiative, in the Irish parliament, and establishing some government departments in Belfast. This was a considerable advance on Ulster's previous position, and Adams was encouraged.[168] Adams next saw Carson, who promised that he would try to deal with Ulster's *non possumus* attitude and said that he had been considering two Irish houses of commons, with periodic joint sittings. Adams thought this was the most important part of the conversation 'showing how his mind was moving', but another subject was to loom larger in the future: Carson declared in favour of a federal solution for the whole United Kingdom and referred Adams to F. S. Oliver.[169] Adams found that Oliver had not considered that Ulster's fears were concerned with internal Irish policies which the federal solution would not affect; Oliver responded to this criticism by suggesting four provincial committees within Ireland so that Ulster would not be marked out. Adams strongly disagreed, arguing that Ulster's position was peculiar and that it was undesirable to encourage provincialism in the Irish parliament. Oliver rejoined that it was time to consider anew the question of devolution within the United Kingdom.[170]

Adams now had some idea of what was acceptable to Ulster and of what might be desirable. On 31 January he returned to Carson and persuaded him that federalism alone was not a solution. He then suggested that the Irish representatives at Westminster should be elected directly, and not be delegates of the Irish parliament as Sinn Fein and the extreme Nationalists wanted. Carson readily agreed. Adams then explained his own conclusions, that the Nationalists would rather leave things as they were than accept two houses of commons. He suggested instead a single parliament with a statutory Ulster Committee with a veto over administrative appointments and the application of certain legislation to Ulster; the house of commons to sit alternately in Dublin and Belfast; and the commercial and industrial departments of government to be sited in Belfast. Of the statutory committee 'Sir Edward Carson seemed to think that such a proposal was reasonable and that in practice it might not involve, if things worked out fairly, any serious amount of independent action by the Ulster Committee.' He was more enthusiastic about the other two elements of Adams's plan, though he concluded that 'while he thought these were all useful points, there underlay them all the question of whether they would accept the idea of an Irish Parliament'.[171] This was a qualified success, achieved by putting

Barrie's ideas to Carson, but it had not touched the immediately
pressing question of Customs and Excise. Adams reported his interviews to Lloyd George and sent him a note from R. J. H. Shaw,[172]
a member of the Convention Secretariat who had been secretary of
the Irish Unionist Alliance, elaborating what was to emerge as the
Adams–Plunkett–Shaw solution to the crisis: a plan to throw the
moral weight of the government behind the Midleton scheme and
rely on public opinion to bring Ulster in without coercion.[173]

During the next few days Adams, Plunkett and Shaw discussed
tactics for the conferences which were due to begin on 6 February.
From their discussions sprang a series of memoranda from Adams to
Lloyd George. For the Southern Unionists he advised gentleness:
'They are rather sore at the twist things have taken and are inclined
to close the Convention.' The Prime Minister would have to show
them that the government still hoped for conciliation and would
not resort to coercion. He would also have to be aware that Ulster
would not accept delegates to the United Kingdom parliament,
though the Southern Unionists should not for the moment be told
this. Midleton should be told that the separation of Customs from
Excise was technically more difficult than he imagined. Finally, it
was important to praise the Southern Unionists for all their work
and sacrifice.[174] Adams had another line for the Nationalists: 'The
whole of this interview should be directed towards getting the Bishop
[of Raphoe] in a more tractable frame of mind on the Customs
question and making him feel that the big question is to get the Irish
Parliament first and to get it by consent.' Adams thought of this as
an argument of expediency. He continued: 'It may well be, and
there is a strong case in support of the view, that Ireland should be
given control over Customs and Excise Duties, at least for revenue
purposes, and there is also the case for the still wider powers of
Dominion status.'

These were the conclusions of the Primrose report which Adams
had signed in 1911; they differed from 'fiscal autonomy' only in
restricting, by implication, Ireland's right to impose a non-revenue,
protective tariff. Nevertheless Adams's advice for the moment was to
get the Nationalists to accept temporary reservation of Customs,
with Excise if necessary, simply for the sake of agreement with
Ulster, with the reminder that they could press for wider powers in
an Irish parliament after the war.[175] The tactical schemes for dealing
with Nationalists and Southern Unionists were based on a four-part
policy prepared by Adams: a joint commission on Customs drawn

from the Irish and United Kingdom parliaments to be set up one year after the end of the war, the Irish parliament meanwhile to have no powers over Customs and Excise; an Ulster Committee in the Irish parliament; alternate parliamentary sessions in Dublin and Belfast; and industrial departments to be located in Belfast.[176] These propositions were the result of delicate bargaining with Barrie and Carson, but they amounted to rather less than the Midleton proposals, and Adams had been unable to obtain for the Nationalists an assurance that Ulster would accept Home Rule.

The conferences began with a meeting between Lloyd George, Curzon, Bonar Law and the Southern Unionist delegation. Midleton was not encouraging about the prospects for agreement; he thought that Redmond's nerve had gone and Ulster's intransigence hardened. The Southern Unionists found Lloyd George sympathetic to their complaints about Ulster, earnest in his denials of a compact with the province, and warmly opposed to partition. An interview the next day between Lloyd George, Duke and W. M. Murphy was less amicable, but the Prime Minister promised to find out what sort of Customs measure would pass in parliament.[177] The grand meeting between the Prime Minister and the whole delegation was fixed for 13 February, and the War Cabinet met that morning to prepare the government's position. Lloyd George opened by describing the political situation reached by the Convention, and Southborough explained the Customs question. Duke warned that if the Convention failed the government of Ireland would almost certainly have to be carried on by force. In the discussion Bonar Law and Milner suggested that the Customs question was more shadow than substance, and that it would be quite safe to concede Customs to get a settlement, provided the power to make commercial treaties was reserved. When Bonar Law remarked that Ulster felt that nothing would come of the Convention without a lead from the government, Lloyd George called on Adams to suggest the lines of a statement to the delegates. Speaking in the War Cabinet for the first time on record, Adams began by suggesting that the Convention should be told that an All-Ireland parliament was the only solution. Ulster would probably accept it if asked directly, and unless it was accepted the Nationalists and Southern Unionists would immediately leave the Convention. He suggested a Royal Commission for the Customs question, to sit after the war, Customs meanwhile to be reserved. In conclusion, he suggested that only a general statement should be made to the delegates, with the details of the government's proposals reserved for a letter to the whole Convention. This was seconded by Southborough, who hoped for positive suggestions from the Ulster delegates if they were not antagonised by a detailed statement. Lloyd George summed up, proposing a general statement which would call for imperial unity and insist on a settlement which provided for a single Irish parliament and the reservation of Customs and police to the Westminster parliament. This embodied the highest common factor in a difficult meeting which had been punctuated by rumblings from Walter Long threatening that 'the majority of those who thought with him in Parliament would never agree to the handing over of Customs to an Irish Parliament'. Nevertheless it was a policy to which all members of the War Cabinet would, for the moment, assent.[178]

When Lloyd George made his statement that afternoon the question of Customs dominated the discussion. The transcript of the meeting suggests a subdued hostility between the delegates disguised by a 'long and desultory discussion'. No new arguments were brought forward and all the old ones were repeated. The conference concluded with a blunt question from Midleton, who wished to know if the Convention would proceed without Ulster's assent.[179] For all the preparatory work this conference had won no concessions and Adams's advice to leave the substantial discussion to the Convention was vindicated. The next day the delegates met alone and went over the arguments. Lloyd George saw Ulstermen and Nationalists separately in an effort to bring them closer, but since the Ulstermen were unable to make any proposals without reference to their advisory committee, his meeting with the Nationalists was a futile, if good-humoured exercise.[180] Plunkett, who before the conference had warned the Prime Minister that 'if we break up, the record will show that a small minority...aborted the Convention and that the Government, by their pledges to that section, procured the abortion',[181] now recorded in his diary

If all the Government's business – especially the business of the big war – is conducted as is this Irish business God help England. The whole system has broken down at the heart of the empire and I am afraid that the next generation will have a ghastly time of it.[182]

The government was now faced with the choice of coercing Ulster or coercing the South, or perhaps coercing both. Cecil Harmsworth, writing to Plunkett at this point, saw only two possibilities: to accept fiscal autonomy and hope for further concessions from the Southern Unionists, or to reserve both Customs and Excise in the hope of

getting Ulster in.[183] Midleton's self-sacrificing attempt, meeting with
no response, had lost momentum, and the government's proposals
were now more important than ever. Adams drafted a letter to
Barrie, asking him to try to get authority from his advisory committee to accept an All-Ireland parliament, and suggesting for the
future a federal system such as the two men had discussed.[184] The
War Cabinet accepted his draft, but in the discussion Balfour
emphatically preferred partition to federalism, while Long expressed
support for the position recently taken by Carson, who had refused to
help the government further.[185] On 23 February Plunkett, Shaw and
Adams drafted a letter for Lloyd George to send to the Convention,
proposing a scheme based on the four-part policy prepared by
Adams for the conferences. The Prime Minister took the draft away
for the weekend and amended it with the help of Milner and Kerr;
but when Adams sharply informed Kerr that the revision would
wreck the Convention the original was restored, and Plunkett
returned to Ireland with the government's proposals in his pocket.[186]

The Unionists in the Convention took the deteriorating state of
Irish law and order as an excuse to stand still. Plunkett read the
Prime Minister's letter to the full Convention on 26 February.
Southborough thought that if the Nationalists and Southern Unionists came back together the Ulstermen might respond, but Midleton
was 'restive and obstinate' and would not budge.[187] Gwynn renewed
his efforts to woo the county-council chairmen away from fiscal
autonomy, but his plan was based on the hope that the government would alter its terms and came to grief when Lloyd George
refused:[188] in any case Midleton warned Adams that he could not
agree to it without losing Ulster altogether.[189] Gwynn also tried a
combination of Southern Unionists and Nationalists on the basis of
a fiscal autonomy to cease on the inauguration of a federal system
for the United Kingdom, but Lloyd George turned this down as
coercion of Ulster, and the Southern Unionists therefore declined to
embroil themselves with the scheme.[190] Lloyd George suggested to
Gwynn that if the Nationalists insisted on control of Customs he
would have to refuse them; but since he could thus demonstrate his
impartiality to Ulster, the chance of legislation might even be
improved.[191] Adams saw little hope in Gwynn's schemes, preferring
the resolution designed by Macdonnell which reflected the substance
of his own scheme as embodied in the Prime Minister's letter to
Plunkett. On 5 March the resolution was moved. Gwynn moved his
amendment, which met expected but not hostile criticism from

Midleton and blank refusal from Raphoe. The next day brought news of Redmond's death after a period of illness, and the Convention adjourned for a week. Plunkett and Midleton chafed at the delay;[192] but Adams was more concerned that Gwynn's amendment had been dropped and that Macdonnell's resolution was to be debated. After expressing his regrets at Redmond's death, he wrote to Plunkett:

The latest proceedings of the Convention seem to me to offer real hope. Personally I am convinced that it is very important to get from the Convention itself a scheme which can be carried through the House of Commons. We know perfectly well that you cannot get agreement and that factor must affect itself the chances and the character of the measure which can go through the House of Commons. I am satisfied that the Gwynn proposal would have failed when it came to the critical time. The case against it which could be made by Ulster and the Unionists in the House would have been too strong and in fact too reasonable to give the scheme a good chance...[Macdonnell's scheme] is simple and free from the objection of giving with one hand and taking back with the other and it is on the whole compatible with a federal settlement, which is certainly making still more headway, at least in the House of Commons.[193]

This testimonial for Macdonnell's scheme is no less sincere for being Adams's praise of his own handiwork.

When the Convention resumed its discussions the Macdonnell resolutions were put to a vote and accepted by a small majority. The Bishop of Raphoe and his supporters voted with Ulster in the minority. The conclusion of the Convention was decided by that division: when the report was put together and submitted to the Convention on 5 April the verdict was the same. A majority of 44 to 29 accepted it; various minorities attached reports or notes of their own. After ten months the Irish question was handed back to the government. The small majority did not constitute the substantial agreement which had always been the condition of the government's accepting the constitutional proposals of the Convention; some other way had to be found of satisfying all parties to the Irish dispute. In the words of its only modern historian, the Convention was 'one of the most striking failures in Irish history'.[194] The immediate causes of failure were Ulster's determination not to concede ground, and the dispute over Customs; in the long term the absence of Sinn Fein and the consequent insulation of the Convention from the realities of Irish politics would probably have undermined the success even of a scheme which met with 'substantial agreement'. Yet even in March 1918 the chances of an agreed constitutional settlement were not utterly destroyed, and the optimism of those such as Adams who had worked wholeheartedly to promote the Convention had not been proved groundless.

IV

Adams's influence declined markedly after the end of the Convention. The most important reason for this decline was the War Cabinet's decision to extend conscription to Ireland, which had hitherto been exempt. The temptation to conscript the Irish had always been strong, but the fear of consequent disorder, disruption of food supplies, and condemnation by foreign opinion, especially in America, had been stronger. The German spring offensive, which began on 21 March 1918, altered the balance of expediency. On 25 March the War Cabinet decided that it could not extend the scope of the Military Service Acts in England without extending their purview to Ireland. The decision had little to do with abstract justice: it was simply feared that further 'comb-outs' and extensions of the age limits would lead to strikes, disorder, and resistance to recruiting, all of which would be aggravated if Ireland remained untouched.[195] The question to be settled, therefore, was whether the gain in men and political support was worth the risk of precipitating catastrophe in Ireland. Adams was among the first to say that it was not, writing to Lloyd George on 26 March:

The immediate question comes down to this. Is the advantage to be gained from getting, say, 200,000 men a few weeks earlier into training equal to the disadvantage and risk which an immediate application of conscription to Ireland involves. My answer is emphatically 'No'...Wait for the Convention Report; declare at once your policy on that Report; then state your military policy for Ireland in the light of military exigencies. Make the appeal to Ireland as a matter of right, not as a bargain in the act of settlement, and the backing for your policy will be strong.[196]

The same position was strongly defended by various ministers in War Cabinet meetings from 25 March to 5 April, but without success. On 25 March it was settled that conscription must be applied: the question to be decided, as stated by Lloyd George, was whether to wait to impose conscription until Home Rule was granted on the lines of the Convention report, or to make the grant of Home Rule conditional on acceptance of conscription.[197] Duke and General Joseph Byrne, the head of the Royal Irish Constabulary,[198] both objected that to impose conscription would be impossible, and

General Mahon warned that the moment was inopportune.[199] They were supported in another meeting, perhaps surprisingly, by Carson and by James Campbell, the Lord Chief Justice of Ireland and a Protestant, who prophesied 'tremendous bloodshed.'[200] Nevertheless, after further consultations designed more to rally support than to add to the sum of wisdom at its disposal, the War Cabinet decided on 5 April to introduce conscription and Home Rule simultaneously. Bonar Law's objection, that without substantial agreement in the Convention this would mean coercing Ulster, was met by Lloyd George with the proposal that in that event the government would legislate on the basis of his letter to Plunkett of 25 February. Only Barnes, who disapproved of conscription, and Milner, who disapproved of delay, registered dissent.[201] When the proposals were presented to other members of the government on 6 April the contradictions underlying the decision were laid bare. Barnes, Addison and Churchill objected that Liberals and Labour were committed to conscription without a corresponding Unionist commitment to Home Rule; Bonar Law and Cecil expressed suspicion of Home Rule in a form known only by the outlines stated in the letter to Plunkett. The fragile compromise was made public as the government's policy the following day.[202]

Gill, who had been making enquiries on Adams's behalf, had predicted on 28 March that conscription, announced just a week before the Convention was due to report, would look like deliberate wrecking; Dillon, now leader of the Nationalists, would lead his party into the arms of Sinn Fein. Adams, who had already explained Gill's views to the Prime Minister and listened as they were considered in the War Cabinet on 26 March, sent in this further report on 29 March, supported by a minute:

I respectfully but most earnestly submit that this question of conscription for Ireland is much more deep-seated in its consequences than is easy for us to seize at the present juncture. The opinion expressed by the Chief Secretary, General Byrne, Sir Edward Carson, the Lord Chief Justice and Mr Gill – a practically unanimous opinion from those who know Ireland best – points to the urgency of taking a different course from what is at present proposed.

He suggested leaving Ireland out of the Military Service bill, putting the majority report of the Convention into force, and opening a voluntary recruiting scheme analogous to the 'Derby Scheme' which had preceded the imposition of conscription in the rest of the United Kingdom in October 1915.[203] But by that time the decision had been made. The effect in Ireland was dismally immediate. As soon as the decision was announced, Stephen Gwynn wrote despairingly to Adams:

The effect will be, if I am right, that the Government will by carrying the clause demonstrate that the Irish party is powerless by constitutional means to prevent conscription and subsequently, by refraining from putting the powers into operation, will enable Sinn Fein to say, irrefutably, that they have by their determination to resist prevented the application of the law which the Irish Party could not stop at Westminster.

The net result on the prospects of an Irish settlement needs no comment.[204]

Both Gill and Gwynn saw their predictions come true, in succession. The Military Service (Amending) Act passed the commons by 16 April. On 10 April the War Cabinet had learned that Sinn Fein had moved into action, advocating a transport strike and the shooting of recruiting officers.[205] On 24 April Dillon wrote to O'Connor that 'L.G. has let loose *Hell* in Ireland', and the next day he and Devlin, with O'Brien and Healy, met De Valera and Arthur Griffith[206] of Sinn Fein to concert opposition. Already the Catholic hierarchy had declared against conscription.[207]

Meanwhile the government was also preparing to fight. On 16 April Duke gave a pessimistic report on the military resources needed to enforce conscription, but the War Cabinet followed Lloyd George in preferring the cautious optimism of French, who was responsible as Commander-in-Chief of Home Forces.[208] On 19 April Adams minuted that 'All the evidence to hand is showing how opposition is going to be thoroughly organised and of a formidable character'.[209] The next day French reported that the troops in Ireland were sufficient only 'if they are used without any kind of doubt, hesitation or interference'.[210] Lloyd George, nonetheless, remained confident that the government's decision was right, and he had an enthusiastic supporter in Kerr. While Adams spent a weekend in the country discussing 'the Awful Irish Situation' with Plunkett,[211] Kerr attended the Prime Minister's interview with C. P. Scott on 21 April. Scott was shocked by Lloyd George's views. The Prime Minister declared that the demand for Dominion status was tantamount to a call for secession, and that he was determined to resist it. He agreed with Scott that conscription would probably wreck the chances of a settlement, but insisted that it was a political necessity if the Tories were to accept Home Rule. He wanted a short, sharp enforcement of the law. Kerr interjected that 'the executions after the Dublin rising...

a fresh batch every morning for breakfast, had been intolerable'. Lloyd George agreed. Ireland's challenge to the authority of parliament had angered him, and he was determined to force through a measure of Home Rule based on his letter to Plunkett, but made strictly parallel with conscription. Kerr remarked, 'I am certain that is the only policy. Make the two measures strictly parallel and force them through.' Scott noticed that Lloyd George valued his secretary's opinion; indeed, only his belief in Kerr's honesty, formed on a visit the previous year, persuaded him that the Prime Minister meant what he said and did not merely see conscription as a convenient excuse to smash Home Rule.[212]

Beset by the practical difficulties of imposing conscription, the government had also to settle the Irish constitution and find new rulers for Ireland, since the administration of Duke and Wimborne was losing plausibility. The 'dual policy' of Home Rule and conscription forced the constitutional problem on the War Cabinet's attention. When Lloyd George told the meeting of ministers on 6 April that the government would legislate on the basis of his letter to Plunkett, there was no more detailed scheme in existence, and Liberal ministers who pressed for Home Rule to be enacted quickly were asking the impossible. On 10 April Walter Long was put in charge of a committee to draft the new Bill;[213] on 16 April the War Cabinet instructed him to choose a small drafting committee to draft a bill based as far as possible on the Convention's report, subject to such financial changes as would promote acceptance, and to take account of American and United Kingdom public opinion.[214] Long's full committee, selected by Lloyd George, consisted of Curzon, Barnes, Smuts, Austen Chamberlain, Sir George Cave,[215] the Home Secretary, Sir Gordon Hewart,[216] the Solicitor-General, Addison, and H. A. L. Fisher. The three latter were Liberals, Barnes a Labour representative, Smuts an outsider, and the rest Unionists with a staunch anti-Home Ruler in the chair. Adams was secretary. Chamberlain had just entered the War Cabinet, making the condition that any Irish settlement would be compatible with a federal constitution for the whole United Kingdom.[217] Long was also a new convert to federalism; both men had been influenced by F. S. Oliver's pamphleteering.[218] At the first meeting on 15 April Long and Cave unsuccessfully urged that a federal bill should be prepared.[219] At the second meeting, after Long had received his instructions from the War Cabinet, Chamberlain lent his support to a measure compatible with federalism: a bill which would make Ireland the first country in the United Kingdom to achieve federal status. Addison, Barnes and Fisher feared this would delay the introduction of a bill, and pressed instead for the Convention's report to be rendered into the form of a bill by Adams and the parliamentary draftsman.[220] Though sympathetic to federalism, Adams himself warned Lloyd George on 23 April that 'As regards federalism, it is better not to make much play with this in the Home Rule Bill for the Irish are all agog with the *Federal Fraud*.'[221] When Long reported his committee's progress to the War Cabinet that day, he suggested a federal bill for Ireland with a preamble declaring an intention to set up a committee to examine federalism for the whole United Kingdom. Lloyd George grasped 'impetuously'[222] at the idea as a way to Ulster's heart after Chamberlain's 'determined effort to get the central scheme altered to this direction',[223] but he was overborne by Balfour, Curzon, Smuts, Barnes and Addison. The War Cabinet passed responsibility back to Long's committee by requesting a bill on Convention lines.[224]

Meanwhile Lloyd George was looking for a new Irish administration. His lack of confidence in the existing Irish government dated back at least to October 1917, when Duke had been unable to control agitations surrounding the death of Thomas Ashe, a Sinn Feiner being held in Mountjoy prison. Drilling and seditious meetings had continued, and Lloyd George began to complain of the 'muddle' of Irish administration. No action was taken, though Plunkett rather speculatively suggested either Adams or Harmsworth as replacements for Duke.[225] In February 1918 Adams had reported that 'I think the strain is telling on Mr Duke and there is a marked feeling that he is losing his grip'. He recommended that Wimborne and Duke should be replaced.[226] Duke evidently shared the view that he could not handle Ireland unaided, and French was sent to Dublin in late February to have conspicuous meetings with the Irish government.[227] In the first days of March Long was offered, but declined, the opportunity to go to Ireland with full powers of government: he also declined a seat on the War Cabinet.[228] On 22 March Duke, who a week before had received from Lloyd George notice of his intention to find a new Chief Secretary, concurred with the plan to renew the whole Irish government;[229] but it was not until late April, when the crisis of the German offensive had quietened, that the position of Viceroy was offered to Midleton, who refused it after negotiation,[230] to Selborne, who refused it summarily,[231] and to French, who accepted it. Edward Shortt, a Liberal with Asquithian leanings,[232]

became Chief Secretary, and Long was appointed as overseer of
Irish questions with direct access to the War Cabinet.

Neither Long nor French had confidence in the 'dual policy',[233]
and after pressure on Lloyd George from Long and Hankey, as well
as Adams, the War Cabinet consented on 10 May to a postponement
of Home Rule, for which there was in any case no definite scheme
yet in existence, and an appeal for volunteers before the enforcement
of conscription. Meanwhile French was to issue a proclamation
against 'Sinn Fein intrigues with the enemy' and follow this up with
arrests.[234] Although Lloyd George, in response to a direct challenge
from Bonar Law, averred that there was no intention to drop conscription and Home Rule altogether, Harmsworth could write to
Plunkett only three days later:

I have persuaded myself that Conscription will not be applied to Ireland
without the consent of Ireland. I have not much to go on but I hear that
the determination of important people here has relaxed somewhat during
the last week or so.[235]

Whatever the final intentions of the government, the decision to
postpone conscription was a watershed in policy. The suggestion
of conscription had thrown Ireland into turmoil; its postponement annoyed Unionists, besides shattering the Nationalist party
and strengthening Sinn Fein as Gwynn had sadly prophesied;
the appointment of a famous soldier as Lord Lieutenant to carry
out an aggressive policy against Sinn Fein, but with a deferred
promise of Home Rule to flourish at Ulster, practically ensured
that the government could count on the enmity of every Irish
party. Long's committee was relieved of the pressure to produce a
bill in a hurry, but that was a mixed blessing. Harmsworth, who was
being tutored in the development of Irish affairs by Adams, remarked:

The latest opinion in high quarters seems to be that it would not be very
difficult to introduce an all-round federal scheme in an Irish H.R. Bill that
would almost inevitably displease everybody. Tomorrow there will be a
different opinion which, if I hear it in time, I will endeavour to describe...
before another scheme takes its place.[236]

The committee's deliberations, and therefore Adams's subsequent
work on Irish matters, assumed an air of futility as it became obvious
that for most members the purpose was not to settle the Irish question
but to design a bill, of whatever content, which would pass the house
of commons.

Long shared the War Cabinet's desire to confine drafting to a small sub-committee,[237] which consisted initially of himself, Chamberlain, Cave and Fisher. His reservations were confirmed whenever the full committee met, for despite the predominance of Unionist sentiment, not even the Unionists were in perfect agreement on principles. At the meeting on 9 May, which supported Long's advice to the War Cabinet to restore respect for the law before attempting a constitutional settlement, Chamberlain still wished to see a modification of a scheme by Oliver, Curzon wanted an Irish parliament incorporating an Ulster Committee, and Barnes wanted to achieve that end by a return to the Convention report.[238] Between then and the next meeting on 4 June Long visited Ireland. He reported on his return that conscription would be impossible and that no bill on which the committee was likely to agree would be acceptable to any part of the Irish population.[239] The committee therefore began to prepare a bill which would appeal to the house of commons. Long and Chamberlain were already convinced that a federal bill would serve this end; information reaching the government from Guest and from Astor suggested that Unionists and Coalition Liberal back-benchers in ever larger numbers were coming to favour the principle.[240] Adams had been canvassing the committee since April in support of federalism, much to the dismay of Addison who had 'that lurking feeling that Salisbury, Selborne, Cave and others who are pushing these impossibilities, would not be sorry at all if they involved a postponement of the Home Rule Bill'.[241] Adams himself had no such intention, nor was he a henchman of Salisbury or Selborne. Oliver, Selborne's coadjutor in federal schemes, complained that Adams was 'much too apt to slur over a difficulty and to leave a ragged edge on the plea that to do the thing tidily would be "contrary to the spirit of the British Constitution" but the real reason would be that he is afraid of tackling the difficulty'.[242] Adams's purpose was rather to break the deadlock within the committee with a bold move away from the unworkable 'dual policy'.[243] Long and Adams together drafted papers for the War Cabinet arguing that the dual policy was no longer viable and that some sort of federal scheme offered the only hope of success.[244] Adams also produced a rough draft of a federal bill.[245]

This line of attack was not profitable. The War Cabinet discussed Ireland on 19 June, anticipating questions in the house of lords the next day. It was decided to announce, not that the dual policy had been dropped, but that it was in abeyance; and in response to urgings from Addison – who appears to have been succumbing to

Adams's persuasion – and from Chamberlain, the Prime Minister undertook to consider federalism, while reserving judgement until he had met an all-party deputation on 24 June.[246] Lloyd George's attitude to federalism was ambiguous. He told Long that he was going to tell the deputation that he was a life-long federalist. Long believed him and encouraged Adams to get him to 'really give a lead' in that direction.[247] Adams prepared papers on the subject but they do not seem to have been submitted.[248] Lloyd George told the deputation that it was impossible to proceed with a federal scheme. By the end of June Adams had circulated to the committee the draft of a bill for federal devolution for the whole United Kingdom, with supporting memoranda. His bill paid special attention to finance, specifying that the central government should reserve enough taxation to pay its way without contributions from the subordinate parliaments.[249] In private, however, he was losing hope. After talking to him on 20 June, Plunkett recorded: 'We see no light as to the way, though we have eliminated many courses of action.'[250]

Adams persisted in his support of federalism for some three months. Long's poor health interrupted the work of the committee and for almost the whole of July nothing was said or done about a settlement. The War Cabinet met on 29 July to discuss a response to a parliamentary question by Dillon. Adams prepared a detailed minute for the Prime Minister. His first concern was to get a rational decision about conscription. The Irish government had been allowed considerable latitude in running a volunteer scheme and in setting the date for conscription. It was at that time the intention to introduce it in October. Adams rejected the idea of admitting that it had to be given up, a course 'open to such grave and obvious objection that I do not even consider it'. Between imposing it in the autumn and meeting resistance as fierce as ever, and leaving it in abeyance while affirming the right to enforce it, he preferred the latter; a course of action which would inevitably raise the question of the political settlement. He was pessimistic about the chances of a purely Irish settlement; he rejected exclusion and was scarcely more enthusiastic about the Convention report, which, he argued, would never satisfy Ulster. As a *pis aller* he contemplated temporary exclusion as proposed in 1917, but he recognised that this was still quite unacceptable to the Nationalists. The unacceptability of other schemes brought him to consider an all-round federal solution which would mollify Ulster by not appearing to legislate separately for Ireland and thus would offer 'at least the prospect of relief'. To calm tension in parliament, he strongly urged the appointment of a parliamentary committee to sit through the forthcoming recess and investigate the question of all-round federalism. He had Chamberlain's support in this recommendation, which he hoped would convince the public that the government was not merely drifting and would have a good effect abroad, especially in America.[251] Most of this was in vain. Lloyd George, who wanted to defer a decision on Home Rule until after the recess, suggested Adams's idea of a recess committee to the War Cabinet. Curzon led the meeting in rejecting it as irrelevant and unhelpful. It was decided to announce in parliament that the government's policy had not changed since April, and that conscription would eventually be imposed. It was agreed that nothing could be done for the moment about Home Rule.[252]

August saw something of a new departure. On 6 August Long's committee met and agreed that two possibilities now remained: the 1917 bill with financial alterations, or a Convention report bill with both Customs and Excise reserved. Neither was put forward with great enthusiasm, and it was decided to state in the report that a federal solution, though not included in the committee's remit, was strongly to be recommended. During the discussions, in which it was gloomily concluded that the committee's own bill would never pass the commons, Shortt was asked what sort of bill he would have if it were possible to start again. He answered that he would give Ireland Customs and Excise, but give Ulster county option, claiming that this would be better than an All-Ireland parliament with an Ulster veto. Smuts supported him.[253] Stimulated by this, and following a suggestion from Arthur Murray,[254] brother of the former Liberal Chief Whip, Adams and the parliamentary draftsman decided that the attempt to write a bill acceptable to both sides in parliament should be abandoned. Instead a bill should be framed which would win the support of the Nationalists on the Second Reading, to be amended in Committee to meet Ulster's objections – a reversal, in effect, of the procedure planned in 1917.[255] Consent was to be achieved by meeting the government's opponents serially.[256] Adams took the idea to Shortt. A few days later Shortt and Adams approached Plunkett to seek help in bringing together Carson and Craig with Dillon and Devlin to discuss alternative bills which Long's committee might be brought to accept. Plunkett was highly discouraging, predicting that Dillon would not take responsibility for a bill and Devlin would not act independently.[257] No meeting took place, and the initiative quietly expired.

Adams's work on Ireland was now almost at an end. Long was ill and pessimistic, believing that if federalism was impossible his committee might as well break up. Adams shared his view, confiding to Plunkett that it had 'missed the tide...the government must have an Irish policy and...temporary exclusion in some shape is necessary'.[258] He returned from a holiday in September with a new bill much like the 1917 proposal but more favourable to the early inclusion of Ulster: this recommendation he passed on to Lloyd George in October, when the Irish government was pressing to introduce conscription on 1 November. He still believed that conscription would be a grave mistake.[259] On 14 November he forwarded to Lloyd George a strong letter from Plunkett on the necessity of a settlement;[260] on 23 November he told his old friend that 'the government had no Irish policy but drift',[261] which was an accurate interpretation of the agreement on Home Rule embodied in the correspondence between Lloyd George and Bonar Law concerning the coalition's electoral programme. Adams was justified in an acute and personal sense of disappointment as the Irish question lapsed into chaos at the end of 1918. His contributions to postponing disaster in Ireland had been considerable, first in informing the Prime Minister of the implications of alternative policies in early 1917, then in helping to establish the Convention, and finally in helping to manage the government's relations with the Convention so that breakdown was avoided until the very end of discussions. For a long time the government's policy, as expressed in discussion and in the Prime Minister's letter to Plunkett, was a policy designed by Adams. His work, which depended on the principle that a permanent settlement could only be achieved in a united Ireland in which both Nationalist and Unionist politicians could co-operate and lead their followers in co-operation, was no more successful than any other British policy towards Ireland in these troubled years. It was defeated firstly by conscription, which he strongly opposed and whose first effect was to destroy the political credibility of the Nationalist party, and secondly by the residual strength of exclusionary policies, which appealed powerfully to Lloyd George as a 'compromise' which could be enforced rather than achieved by the rare commodity of consent.

6

Imperial questions

I was very pleased to read L.G.'s interview about 'The Imperial
Council'. Speaking through that megaphone our friend P.K. has a
great chance of making himself heard throughout the Empire.

Milner to Sir Hugh Thornton, 3 February 1917, Milner Papers 19.

I

It has been possible, in examining domestic supply problems, foreign
affairs, and the Irish question, to indicate the part played by the
Garden Suburb in helping Lloyd George to run the government, to
illustrate the defects in war-machinery which its work disclosed, and
to assess its independent contribution to great events. Kerr's work on
imperial policy speaks to the fourth question with which this book is
concerned: the ideological colour of the Prime Minister's Secretariat
and its importance in transmitting imperialist values to Lloyd
George. Kerr's imperial and Indian responsibilities make the Garden
Suburb an obvious place to look for signs of clandestine Milnerite
influence on policy-making. Such signs, however, are rare and ambiguous. Although the years 1916 to 1918 have been identified as the
high point of Round Table influence,[1] that movement, the core of
'Milnerism' after 1909, had like the Liberal party shown evidence of
deterioration before its collision with the rampant omnibus of war.
The Round Table was inaugurated in 1909 by former associates of
Milner in South Africa.[2] It preserved a specious institutional continuity through its quarterly journal, which Kerr edited until
December 1916. The movement's original commitment to closer
imperial union through federation was nourished by anonymous
articles in the quarterly, and by the indefatigable Lionel Curtis,
whose series of memoranda culminated in 1916 in the publication of
The Commonwealth of Nations. Even before the war founder-
members were drifting away, either because they disliked Curtis's
formulations of imperial federation or because competing modes of

imperialism, such as Tariff Reform, regained their attractiveness. The war, besides directing energies elsewhere, further eroded the intellectual foundations of the movement. In 1915 and 1916 articles in *The Round Table* lamely insisted that the absence of machinery for consultation ought to have inhibited the willing participation of the Dominions:[3] but it had not done so. In 1916 the group repudiated Curtis's second book, *The Problems of the Commonwealth*, and Milner himself declared against formal constitutional arrangements as a means to achieve closer union.[4] A division gradually became apparent between the prophetic wing of the movement, led by Curtis and including Robert Brand, Lionel Hichens and Kerr, and a more conservative group associated with Milner and including Leopold Amery and F. S. Oliver.[5] Some of the prophets talked of a Fourth Party[6] and eventually joined the Liberals; among the conservatives were those who welcomed the end of the coalition in 1922. In March 1917 the Imperial War Conference resolved to postpone discussion of imperial constitutional reform until after the war, in terms which excluded the possibility of an imperial parliament or an imperial executive.[7] The prophets were disappointed; the conservatives rather welcomed what they saw as progress towards the substance of imperial union without institutional trappings.[8] This diversity of view within the Round Table prevented its having a collegiate influence, although Milner and Amery, respectively in the War Cabinet and in its Secretariat, were well placed to further their individual views.

A similar diversity prevailed over India. In 1912, on his return from a visit there, Kerr urged the group to consider the very gradual extension of self-government and the immediate incorporation of India in the planned imperial parliament. A cautious statement of his views was printed in *The Round Table*. He was accorded a mixed reception, generally hostile to self-government.[9] In 1915 he and William Marris,[10] an Indian civil servant who had worked with the 'Kindergarten' in South Africa and subsequently joined the Round Table, prepared separate drafts for the chapter on India in the planned second volume of *The Commonwealth of Nations*. Both supported movement towards self-government, Marris more strongly. Then Kerr, Curtis and Reginald Coupland[11] constituted themselves an 'Indian Moot' and co-opted five Indian civil servants to help in their investigation. One of these, Sir William Duke,[12] was responsible for the detailed scheme of 'specific devolution', later known as 'dyarchy', which provided for the gradual transfer of powers in the provinces from bureaucratic councils to councils responsible to an Indian electorate. The Indian Moot preferred this scheme to any extension of the reforms instituted by Morley[13] as Secretary of State and Minto[14] as Viceroy, under which Indians elected on a limited class and communal franchise sat on the existing bureaucratic councils. Although dyarchy was suggested to Duke by the Indian Moot,[15] and later publicised by Curtis during an extended tour of India between 1916 and 1918, the appearance of a form of it in the Montagu–Chelmsford Report and in the Indian Government Act of 1919 does not amount to a convincing example of Round Table influence. On the one hand, the Round Table repudiated dyarchy in 1917 as implying too rapid a progress towards self-government;[16] on the other hand dyarchy added little to the well-understood technique of devolution in colonies destined for self-government, which had been known since the Durham Report in 1832 had recommended it for Canada and which was widely canvassed in the Indian civil service and in other interested circles.[17]

Kerr therefore brought to Lloyd George's service views on India and the imperial constitution which had been elaborated in Round Table discussion, but not a set of principles which could be called 'Round Table policies'. He had himself welcomed the change of government and Milner's appointment to the War Cabinet as a chance to get a sound imperial policy, writing to Milner on 11 December 1916 that Lloyd George should be persuaded:

to say that he recognises that for the purposes of the War he is the Prime Minister not of the British Isles so much as of the Empire, and that as such he wants the assistance of the outer Empire not only on the battle field but in the Council Chamber...Mr Lloyd George with his faculty for democratic oratory has an unrivalled opportunity in a few sentences of transforming the whole Imperial position, provided at his first public utterances he talks not only to the people of these islands but the people overseas.

Kerr suggested what probably was in Milner's mind already: an Imperial War Conference to co-ordinate the use of imperial military and economic resources for war.[18] In War Cabinets on 19 and 20 December it was decided to summon the Prime Ministers of the Dominions to a conference, which met in March 1917.[19] Dominion leaders sat with the War Cabinet to co-ordinate the war effort in special meetings called Imperial War Cabinets, and on alternate days the same leaders sat under the chairmanship of the Colonial Secretary, Walter Long, to discuss matters of more general scope which could be, and all of which were, postponed until after the war.

The latter meetings constituted the Imperial War Conference of 1917, a lineal descendant of pre-war Colonial and Imperial Conferences.[20]

II

The gathering of Dominion Prime Ministers brought Kerr his first opportunity to consider imperial questions on Lloyd George's behalf. The Imperial War Conference was in some ways a Round Table dream come true. Admittedly the representation of India, a Round Table ambition, was owed not to the Round Table but to the insistence of Austen Chamberlain, the Secretary of State for India.[21] However another innovation, the distinction made between the conference organised by the Colonial Office and the cabinet organised by the War Cabinet Secretariat, can be attributed principally to Milner's insistence in the War Cabinet, supported by Amery, who was convinced that the Colonial Office was not fitted to conduct relations between the British government and the self-governing Dominions.[22] Amery's attempts to institute direct communications between Prime Ministers, corresponding to his preference for administrative over constitutional methods of achieving closer union, were thwarted in January 1917 by Hankey, who described them as 'a gigantic scheme of propaganda against the Colonial Office';[23] but he was closely consulted by Milner when the Imperial Conference was first discussed, and bore the brunt of organisation within the War Cabinet Secretariat and assisted in planning the agenda of the Imperial War Cabinet.[24] Long, who thought he had 'neither tact nor manners',[25] fully recognised the power of his attack on the Colonial Office.

Kerr, who knew of Amery's work on the Imperial War Cabinet Agenda,[26] saw the opportunity to extend the government's original scheme of associating the Dominion Prime Ministers in the prosecution of the war. In late February he wrote to Long, Balfour and Lloyd George:

It has occurred to me that we ought to make a point of asking Sir Robert Borden to attend the meetings of the War Cabinet whenever the question of our relations with America are under discussion, and this independent altogether of the special meetings of the Imperial War Cabinet.

As he is over here I think that both the Canadian people and the Canadian Government would resent it if he were not asked to be present whenever a matter which affects so vitally their own national interests is under discussion.[27]

In an attempt to get himself invited to War Cabinet meetings, from which Lloyd George had deliberately and persistently excluded him,[28] Long affected assent to this proposal. He wrote to Balfour on 27 February:

P. Kerr writes suggesting that Borden should come to Cabinet when you are discussing affairs connected with U.S.A. Of course this does not rest with me, but I venture to say just this. Borden is very sore about U.S.A. and thinks Canada shd. have a decided preference. Further since we have New Zealand and Newfoundland here...I think it would be a mistake to ask one of them alone...I think it is very desirable all should be asked to our Cabinet without delay.[29]

Long clearly hoped that he might be invited to a War Cabinet in which many Dominion statesmen participated, but he had no help from Balfour, who wrote a non-committal, if essentially favourable, reply to Kerr[30] and consulted Lloyd George, whom he found to be in favour of the proposal. He told Long that the Foreign Office would welcome Borden's participation on the rare occasions on which American matters were discussed.[31] When Long wrote back that 'the only sound principle seems to me to be to invite all or none', Balfour merely referred him to the Prime Minister.[32] It was probably in innocence that Kerr advised Lloyd George on 27 February:

I think it is very important that you should talk with Mr. Walter Long before the first meeting of the Imperial War Cabinet on Friday. There are a number of points personal and otherwise about which he ought to inform you before the discussion.[33]

Two questions raised and settled at the Imperial War Conference had been of particular interest to Kerr in his Round Table work: the 'closer union' of the Empire, and the Indian emigration question. Smuts, who represented South Africa because the Prime Minister, Louis Botha,[34] needed to remain at home for political reasons, and Sir Robert Borden, the Canadian Prime Minister, were both determined to resist any pretensions the British government might have towards closer union. Smuts, who had a wide circle of Radical and other intellectual friends in England, as particularly suspicious of the new government in which his old enemy Milner was so prominent. Shortly after his arrival he was invited to dinner by Milner, and found himself discussing closer imperial co-operation with Milner, Amery, Kerr, Hankey, Sir Joseph Ward, leader of the minority in the New Zealand coalition government,[35] and sundry others. 'Smuts most reluctant to discuss it at all, and, I thought, very suspicious of Milner', Hankey recorded.[36] Milner's diary records frequent meetings with various combinations of Dominion leaders, at which Kerr and Amery were often present. There is no reason to doubt that some form of closer union was discussed at these meetings, nor that they could be said to constitute an attempt by Milner and his friends to secure the assent of the Dominion leaders to a more formal and effective machinery for the regulation of imperial matters. On the other hand it is most unlikely that any serious attempt was made to persuade the overseas leaders to accept imperial federation. Kerr's part in these talks, which included two long conversations with Borden,[37] cannot be seen to have had any effect on the outcome of the conference, whose constitutional decisions, in particular the resolution of 28 March noted above, were determined by the insistence of Smuts and Borden that constitutional alterations should only be undertaken after the war and should respect the autonomy of the Dominions. As Kerr reported to Curtis, Borden in private had emphasised 'in the strongest possible terms' that it would be inadvisable to suggest imperial federation immediately after the war.[38]

Kerr was more satisfied with the consequences of the conference for India. Besides bringing India more fully into the confidence of the Empire and thereby improving the chances for a constitutional settlement, the conference had settled, at least to his satisfaction, the awkward question of Indian emigration to other parts of the Empire. Sinha[39] had come to England as one of the Indian assessors to the conference, determined to secure the right of Indians to live and work freely in all other parts of the Empire. The representatives of the white Dominions were uncomfortably aware of the extent of racial prejudice in their own countries, and were unwilling to come to terms with the Indian demands. Most parts of the self-governing Empire had imposed linguistic, educational or financial qualifications on immigrants which were waived as a matter of routine for whites and rigorously applied, if necessary in an arbitrary fashion, against the Indians and Japanese.[40] Frustrated by their exclusion from the areas of white settlement, Indians represented by the Aga Khan had called for the cession of German East Africa to India as a colony. The solution appealed to Chamberlain when he had to resolve the question to the satisfaction both of India and the white representatives; but it did not meet the essence of the demand, which was for Indians to have the same opportunities as whites throughout the Empire.

The question of Indian emigration had been raised in the Round

Table when Curtis began to talk of a Commonwealth citizenship and of including India in the Commonwealth. The members of the group had no illusions about the acceptability of Indian immigrants in the other Dominions, and were principally concerned to provide a justification for restrictions which was not offensive to educated Indians. The substitution of a 'civilisation bar' for a 'colour bar' met the difficulty, as Kerr pointed out to Chamberlain when he took the matter up with him in February 1917 during consideration of the agenda for the Imperial War Conference.

I do not believe you are likely to get a more favourable opportunity to negotiate a settlement of the Indian emigration problem between India and the Dominions...We have always urged that the basis of agreement should be, that the permanent settlement of the proletariat of either colour in a country predominantly occupied by the other should be prohibited...free contact between the peoples of different colour must be for the present confined to the more or less well educated and civilised classes, and that intermingling of the proletariats must be prevented because it invariably produces evil results on both sides.[41]

So sceptical was he of Indian assertions of the need for room to expand that he denounced the idea of giving German East Africa to India, and in a second letter warned of the consequences if Indians were allowed to mix with Africans who would, on reaching political maturity, resent their presence.[42] At most, he suggested, Indians should be restricted to the exclusive occupation of a tract set aside for their use. These views were not his alone. Curtis, who had the previous year addressed to the Viceroy a vigorous memorandum about the evils of allowing Asiatics to settle in the same countries as whites,[43] wrote to Kerr on 25 March that every effort should be made to control Indian migration in a manner which would ensure that Indian populations did not mix with populations of other races. Kerr sent the letter on to Chamberlain. The Secretary of State, better aware than Curtis that the settlement of Indian affairs had to be achieved by consent, greeted it with weary tolerance. 'He always writes with a delightful dogmatism and perhaps sometimes has not seen as far into a problem as he thinks.'[44] He pointed out that Sinha could not take responsibility for such a settlement of the immigration question. Chamberlain's immediate purpose was to reach a satisfactory agreement at the conference which Sinha could take back to India, and the position put forward by Curtis, however logical, appeared to favour the white Dominions without offering any concession to Indian sentiment.

In the event the immigration question was settled, like most issues which came before the Imperial War Conference, by the private discussions of the Dominion leaders and not by British ministers, their advisers, nor the private pressure groups who importunately advised them. Borden convened a meeting attended by Smuts, Sinha and Sir James Meston[45] at which all agreed to accept a proposal put forward by Chamberlain that migration within the Empire should be governed by the principle of 'reciprocity'.[46] While entry to any Dominion for study or temporary residence was to be open, the regulation of labour and permanent settlement was to be left in the hands of Dominion governments, subject to the Government of India's right to impose any restriction on the citizens of a Dominion which that Dominion's government imposed on Indians. When introduced as a resolution in the conference, accompanied by general support for the East African plan and a plea from Chamberlain that Indian *amour-propre* should be treated with more delicacy than had been customary, the agreement appeared substantial. In reality, since the inhabitants of the white Dominions had always shown a singular disinclination to emigrate to India, it cost their governments nothing in popular support and both sides recognised it as a victory for Canada and South Africa. Sinha declined the responsibility of moving it formally in the conference, and Chamberlain recognised that it was for Borden and Smuts 'certainly the most that they will agree to'.[47] The East African scheme was quietly forgotten at the Peace Conference when the League of Nations Mandate was invented.

Kerr, though unshaken in his beliefs, recognised reluctantly that the Imperial War Conference had been a setback for the aspirations for imperial unity which he shared with many of his Round Table colleagues. He made no attempt to press his views in government circles, which would in any case have been futile since the Dominions had the last word in constitutional questions. Instead he confined himself to writing an article for *The Round Table*, which like every contribution to the quarterly appeared anonymously, and a supplementary memorandum for private circulation among Round Table members. The published article, which was drafted in late May 1917 by Kerr in discussion with other members of the Round Table's editorial 'Moot',[48] gave an optimistic outline of the opportunities for closer imperial co-operation available within the framework established by the conference.[49] The memorandum laid down, with a firmness that Kerr clearly felt he could not display in print, the doctrine that imperial federation, with imperial ministers responsible to an imperial parliament, was a necessity.[50]

III

The question of the future constitutional development of India was brought to the War Cabinet by Chamberlain in May 1917. The question of proceeding beyond the Morley–Minto reforms had been discussed in the Viceroy's council under Lord Hardinge.[51] On succeeding as Viceroy in April 1916, Lord Chelmsford[52] had set out to prepare a declaration of British policy in India which would both secure political stability and give the British administration a sense of purpose. Chelmsford's council, which had considered a variety of evidence including Duke's memorandum, sent its final proposals to London in November 1916 for consideration by the India Office.

Political realities in India were meanwhile changing fast. In December the Indian Congress party and the All-India Muslim League agreed at Lucknow to work together for Indian Home Rule. The 'Lucknow Pact' closed, for a short time at least, the fundamental division in Indian nationalist politics upon which the British had tacitly relied to preserve the *Raj*. Startled by the rapid growth of the movement, especially after Lucknow, the Government of India sought to discern a silent majority ('an influential though timid unorganised and comparatively inarticulate body of opinion which is opposed to and afraid of any sudden and violent changes in the constitution and looks to Government for support against the extremist propaganda', in Chelmsford's words[53]) to which an appeal could be made. On 18 May 1917 Chelmsford asked Chamberlain's permission to make a public statement of policy, including an elaborate, if oblique, definition of the goal of British administration in India and a promise to extend the Morley–Minto reforms by increasing both the non-official membership and the powers of the local and provincial councils. Chamberlain disliked both the statement of a goal, on the grounds that it was too formal and that it would not win consent, and the proposal to extend the Morley–Minto reforms. An India Office committee, sitting under Duke, to examine the Indian government's proposals, had already won Chamberlain's support for a commission to enquire into Indian constitutional reform. Chamberlain therefore brought his dispute with the government of India to the War Cabinet, to whom papers were circulated on 22 May 1917.[54]

The Indian constitution was thus brought, indirectly, into Kerr's purview. He had had an opportunity to discuss Indian politics with two knowledgeable Indians when Sinha and the Maharajah of Bikanir,[55] in London for the Imperial War Conference, had met the half dozen active members of the Round Table group in England in April 1917. The company 'came to no conclusion, of course', as Kerr reported to Curtis on 23 April, but Sinha and Bikanir convinced the Englishmen that some political concessions would have to be made to stifle dangerous agitation.[56] Kerr also had the benefit of Curtis's voluminous letters from India and of discussions with Chamberlain, whose approval of a commission and dislike of the Morley–Minto reforms he shared. He addressed to Lloyd George in early June a compact statement of the condition of India.

The root of the difficulty lies in the fact that British policy in India has never been clearly defined. The British Government has never declared that the goal of its policy is Indian self-government. Agitation therefore, for Indian Home Rule inevitably has something of the character of sedition. So long as the policy of the British Government in India remains a negative policy which it is today, it is extraordinarily difficult for it to allow a raging, tearing, Home Rule propaganda of the type conducted by Mrs Besant in 'New India'. Unquestionably I think the Besant agitation for the immediate introduction of a quite impossible form of Home Rule must be productive of serious political results, if it is allowed to continue unchecked. The spirit which underlies it is really not dissimilar to that which has lain at the bottom of Sinn Fein. . .When we consider what ought to be done, the situation seems to me to fall into two parts. The first is a formal and official declaration that the goal of British policy is Indian self-government. I would make that statement without any qualification or reserve. The second question is the steps to be taken towards this goal at once. The more one looks into it, the more obvious does it become that you cannot progress along the Morley lines, that is to say the gradual substitution of Indians elected on a very restricted franchise for the bureaucratic executive councils. To do that would simply be to condemn India to a far worse form of the disease from which France has suffered ever since its people thought they could democratise the Napoleonic bureaucratic system by substituting the Chamber of Deputies for an Emperor. India contains 315,000,000 people. It can only be governed from one centre if it is governed as a democratic empire. If democracy is to have the slightest chance in India, it must be converted into a federation of nations; in other words the Government of India will have to become a truly Imperial Government in the sense that it is mainly concerned with Defence, Communications between the provinces, Foreign Policy, Tariffs, and other common affairs. For all other purposes as in America, Canada, and Australia the responsible government will have to be the provincial governments.[57]

In urging Lloyd George to send a commission to India Kerr echoed what had been said again and again by the India Office and by Chamberlain; in recommending federal devolution in India he was repeating a conventional wisdom. The proposal to announce self-government for India 'without any qualification or reserve' was perhaps only a manifestation of his own enthusiasm. His minute made a substantial suggestion about the Indian constitution, in the sense that it went further into detail than Chamberlain's mere desire for a commission, but it clung to the garments of generalisation in which Round Table thought was habitually clothed.

War Cabinet discussion of Indian reform was delayed by more pressing business – notably Ireland and the submarine question – and by Curzon's insistence on reading all the papers before discussion.[58] On 27 June Curzon circulated a paper adumbrating the conservative view of the Indian question. He complained about the pace of reform:

> Thirty-three years elapsed between the first Indian Council Act of 1861 and the Indian Councils Act which, as Under-Secretary for India, I carried through the House of Commons...in 1892. Sixteen years passed between this Act and the next great forward step in the legislation of Lord Morley and Lord Minto in 1909. Eight years only have elapsed, and we are invited to make a further considerable move. It will be observed that the progression is strictly geometrical...

He wanted it recognised that the government was making concessions out of expediency and not out of conviction. In this paper Curzon offered no fundamental objection to Chamberlain's proposals, except that he wanted Chamberlain to go out to India in place of a commission of enquiry: his purpose seems to have been to claim the right to be consulted about Indian questions.[59] In the War Cabinet he was supported by Balfour, who warned of the dangers of haste, and with his help developed a conservative position on India, whose essence was a refusal to countenance any act of policy which would indicate the possible establishment of India as an autonomous political unit, or as a federation of autonomous states. In Lloyd George's absence the War Cabinet came to no conclusions,[60] and Curzon embodied his arguments in a paper on 'Indian Self-Government'.[61]

At about this time Kerr abruptly became more conservative in his opinion of Indian reform. Perhaps he was persuaded by argument: it was after a discussion with Balfour that he reversed himself on the subject of 'self-government'.

> With reference to our talk about Indian reforms ought not the government's

statement of its policy to be based upon the idea of 'constitutional government', not 'self-government'. 'Constitutional government' is the idea which
has underlain all our political history, it emphasises the need for the reign
of law, it provides for the authority of the Crown, it is a reproof to revolution yet it obviously implies the gradual increase of popular control as the
people are fit to exercise it, without specifying either time or precise
method.[62]

It was a far cry from this to Indian self-government 'without any
qualification or reserve'. From being an advocate of liberal and even
progressive reforms, Kerr now seemed to take up a position which
appeared, both for the short and the long term, to be at least as
conservative as the position adopted by Curzon. On 5 July he
attended a War Cabinet meeting which continued the discussion of
29 June;[63] at the meeting Chamberlain revealed more clearly that
he regretted having to make any declaration about British policy in
India, but felt that the decision was forced on him, and Balfour
suggested a formula of the most exquisite vagueness in which the
government would promise to increase the share of natives in Indian
administration 'as rapidly and to as great an extent as circumstances
will permit', without in any way specifying the form of that administration. His formula stated that Indian conditions were profoundly
different from conditions in the white Dominions and demanded
different terminology. He concluded:

> The Government therefore think that it would be inconsistent with the
> interests of India to attempt now to mark out the precise course which
> Indian reform must take in the remote future, and the precise shape which
> its constitution will ultimately assume; but they are resolved to do all in
> their power to develop the policy of increasing the influence of educated
> Indian opinion in the conduct both of central and local affairs.

Curzon repeated his suggestion that Chamberlain should go out to
India to examine the situation, to be opposed, probably by Balfour,
on the grounds that the appointment of a Secretary of State to such
a mission would raise false hopes of major change. In the discussion
three attitudes, all conservative, can be discerned. Chamberlain
wished to see some progress, but not on the Morley–Minto lines, to
be made so that revolution should not take hold. Curzon apparently
welcomed the flexibility offered by the Government of India's proposal to extend the Morley–Minto system to different degrees in
different provinces.[64] Balfour wanted any change to be postponed
into the distant future, and apparently had no views about the form
of change.[65]

To these views Kerr added a fourth. On 7 July he sent Lloyd George a 'criticism of Lord Curzon's proposal to send the S of S or anybody else to extend the Morley–Minto reforms – a *fatal* policy'.[66] Instead of the 'strong Commission. . .to look into the whole question of government reconstruction and political reform'[67] which he had looked for earlier, he now suggested that a Cabinet committee should sit in London, sending only one member to India. Instead of the formal and official statement of policy which he had suggested before, he proposed that Chamberlain should make a speech which should include the warning 'that to talk about self-government for so huge a continent as India as a practical policy at present, is meaningless and premature'. The burden of his argument was carried by the ideas, familiar in his writings since 1915, that the present system of councils, however extended, could not govern India, and that devolution of certain powers to small local authorities was the only way to incorporate Indians safely and progressively in the machinery of government. But after putting all the negative arguments for devolution, he baulked at involving the Indian population in the devolved authorities. The low level of education in India determined that 'for a long time to come the real responsibility for the larger aspects of Indian Government must rest with the British Government'. These were the views of Balfour, but with the difference that Kerr asserted, at least in private, that he knew the form which Indian self-government would take when, in the extremely distant future, it finally materialised.

Kerr's change of opinion in July, a reversion to the views expressed in his article of 1912,[68] might be explained in many ways. His conversation with Balfour in early July perhaps shook his confidence in the grand magnanimous gesture, and the discussions of the Moot were apparently doing the same. On 22 July he wrote to warn Curtis that the Moot thought dyarchy too progressive. In the same letter he confessed his personal anxiety that Bolshevism, Sinn Fein and the Indian Home Rule movement all laid 'all emphasis on national self-realisation and little on national duty', and urged Curtis to publicise national duty in his writings in India.[69] The pessimism which affected Kerr in June and July, leading him to advise Lloyd George to concentrate less on war-aims speeches directed against the Germans and more on 'the growing forces of pacifism and unrest' at home, is noted below:[70] the only explanation given by him for this sinking of mood was an incidental reference to the success of the German eastern offensive.[71] The threat posed to Britain's imperial mission, both by German military success and by propaganda for a democratic peace, which he had welcomed until he realised its implications for British interests, was much on his mind. Such a comprehensive anxiety might account for his susceptibility to persuasion by reasoned argument to a view which he had so recently rejected.

Kerr's move to conservatism about India coincided with the manifestation in Lloyd George of a slight interest in India, but in the turmoil his voice was scarcely heard. After the report of the Mesopotamia Commission had disclosed incompetence in the Indian administration,[72] Chamberlain resigned. Lloyd George replaced him, to the consternation of some Conservatives, with Edwin Montagu,[73] a Liberal who, by accepting, signalled his separation from the Asquithian camp. Montagu had been Under-Secretary of State for India from 1910 to 1914, and had become popular in India through a speech in 1912 which had been interpreted to promise an early advance to self-government.[74] In 1917 he had been outspoken in his criticism of Chamberlain,[75] and he was made to promise not to touch 'the great fabric of the Government of India without careful investigation' before taking office.[76] His name was associated with federal reform in India, and on 30 July 1917 he circulated a series of proposals which would result, at some future time, in an India organised as a group of self-governing provinces linked by a central authority.[77] By pertinacious lobbying Montagu secured his colleagues' assent to an announcement in the commons on 20 August 1917 which proposed an instalment of self-government for India;[78] in October, having thwarted a plan to send Chamberlain instead, he left for India to collect the evidence for the report on the Indian constitution which became known as the Montagu–Chelmsford report.[79] With Montagu's appointment to the India Office the conservative predominance in the making of Indian policy was destroyed. He differed from Chamberlain not in the policy he would recommend, for in July 1917 neither was committed to a specific measure of reform except in that both rejected an extension of the Morley–Minto reforms, but in the fact that he welcomed reform instead of fearing it.

Kerr's anxiety about hasty change in India found little outlet. His hand can be detected in a small obstacle of which Montagu complained in August:

The P.M. is really the most extraordinary of mortals. I saw him at breakfast, explained the whole position to him, and got a promise that he would back me up. Before I had been speaking three minutes, he chipped in with an objection to quarrelling about words and a statement that 'self-government' was really what Lord Curzon in his second Memorandum described it as being. Fortunately Lord Curzon was more helpful than the P.M., and did not take this view; but I could not get the word 'self-government' out of him. For some reason that I am absolutely unable to understand, people prefer 'responsible government' to 'self-government'. I do not know the difference.[80]

Curzon in his memorandum of 2 July had insisted that 'self-government' for India could only mean a very different and more restricted form of government than that found in the white Dominions.[81] Montagu knew that in asking for 'self-government' he was asking for more than Curzon had envisaged, and that Indian opinion would share his view of what 'self-government' would mean even if it did not share his view of the time it would take to implement it. That was presumably what he had explained to Lloyd George, only to be met in the War Cabinet with the views expressed by Kerr in his memorandum of 7 July. Montagu's low estimate of the importance of a word was probably right. He later used the terms of the declaration of 20 August 'ruthlessly' to 'demand that the new constitution should acknowledge the principle of executive responsibility';[82] he would certainly have exploited the word 'self-government' to a similar end, and it is difficult to see how Kerr's preferred alternative of 'constitutional government', though implying nothing more, perhaps, than orderly procedures and civil liberties, would have been less open to such use in the excited condition of India after the war.

Montagu made his announcement, and in due course departed for India with a small party, including Sir William Duke, to gather evidence for the Montagu–Chelmsford report. The effect of his mission was to take India out of British cabinet politics, much as the Irish convention had taken another troubled dependant out of parliamentary politics. Out of sight, it was out of the Prime Minister's mind and therefore outside the range of his private secretary's duties. Kerr continued to receive information about India from Curtis and from Duke, but there is no record of his having given written advice to Lloyd George about it, even after Montagu had returned and given his report. In an embarrassing episode in February 1918, Kerr gave an interview to a representative of the Indian Home Rule movement, Joseph Baptista, who hoped to discover the secret mind of the British government and had therefore requested an interview with the Prime Minister. In a discursive interview Baptista gained the impression that 'the Cabinet had decided to give India the fullest possible measure of Home Rule without delay', and Kerr warned the India Office that his interlocutor was trying 'to make political capital out of which [sic] was a purely private and friendly conversation' by proposing to publish an account of the interview in the Indian press.[83] The incident illustrates the intellectual gulf between Kerr and an educated Indian nationalist, which prevented the former making it clear that his interpretation of the declaration of 20 August implied a very slow progress, not the rapid establishment of representative institutions which Indian politicians had inferred as the significance of 'responsible government'.

IV

It cannot be said that through Kerr the 'New Imperialists'[84] or the Round Table gained useful access to the highest circles of policy-making about the Empire. In 1918, as in 1917, he corresponded with Amery about the Imperial War Conference and about the vexed question of communications between the governments of the Dominions and the United Kingdom government, but to little effect: the tide had begun to run against closer imperial union in 1917. Professor Kendle has noted the Round Table dinner of 4 May 1917, when to the dismay of some of their colleagues the majority of the London group, including Kerr, accepted without protest the arguments put by Smuts against closer union.[85] In the same way, this account has suggested that Kerr chose to bide his time with Lloyd George over the imperial question. He had no influence because he did not try to use his position as secretary to the Prime Minister to gain influence. His attitude to Indian questions was more positive, but there were profound ambiguities in his approach. In June 1918 Montagu described him in a letter to Chelmsford as having 'much influence with the Prime Minister, being strongly a supporter of our alternatives':[86] but that could only have meant that Kerr rejected the Morley–Minto reforms. Otherwise, while he might use the same words as Montagu or the Nationalist movement used, his assumption about the timing of Indian constitutional advance was based on a far lower estimate of Indian capacity for self-government. In any case India was not a subject which fascinated the Prime Minister. Neither on Indian nor on imperial questions did Kerr make any great use of his position to advance the policies dear to him or to the Round Table.

7

The political culture of
10 Downing Street

...upon Narcissus was imposed the further duty of rapidly
assimilating the popular idea or tendencies of the day, and
presenting them to his chief, as it were, in concentrated pellets.

H. W. Massingham, 'All in a Garden Fair', *The Nation*, 24 Feb. 1917.

...His main position seems to be that the war is primarily 'the war
for public right': and that our main object is to make Germany
accept and keep treaties...But there are some considerations which
I wish (if you agree) you would argue with him when you next have
a chance. (i) Supposing we really got Germany on her knees (and
she will be there, before she agrees to the reconstitution of *Serbia*),
ought we not to keep her there a little longer, if we can, even at
some sacrifice, in order to readjust the map in the *real* interests of
national freedom? As we hope for no more war, we may never have
another chance...

Reginald Coupland to A. E. Zimmern, concerning Kerr,
18 November 1916, Round Table Papers 817.

I

As contemporaries had anticipated, members of the Garden Suburb
did much to interpret Lloyd George to the world and the world to
Lloyd George: 'cultivating the Prime Minister's mind',[1] in Massingham's hostile phrase, and cultivating public opinion at the same
time. They helped to create a body of thought which influenced the
Prime Minister's public statements and, to a lesser extent, his acts of
policy. They had no monopoly in the cultivation of Lloyd George's
mind, nor were they unaffected by his own active intelligence, but
they were frequently in his company and therefore able to put their
positions to him more often than others who competed for his
attention. Their interpretation of events, their own private and
published writings, and their recommendations for the public presentation of the government's case all contributed to the intellectual
foundations of Lloyd George's political position. Where it can be

documented, the discussion of public events within 10 Downing
Street is a unique working demonstration of a 'Coalition Liberal
Mind': not the collective mentality of a political faction such as
Dr Bentley has described,[2] but the ratiocination of a small group of
well-informed individuals whose arguments can be followed in a
connected form and related closely to the world outside.

Downing Street was not a seminar: this intellectual development
took place not for its own sake but as a product, and an essential
part, of three of the regular duties of the Secretariat. First, Lloyd
George very often called for advice not on what to do, but on what
to say. Thus Kerr and Joseph Davies prepared a substantial dossier
for a commons speech on the Indian Cotton Duties in March 1917.[3]
Before consulting his secretaries, Lloyd George had acquiesced in
the decision to allow the Government of India to impose import
duties on manufactured cotton goods to protect native industry.
When the measure had to be carried in parliament against the
Lancashire members and doctrinaire free-traders, he turned to
Kerr and Davies to help him justify the decision after it had been
made. Another example, noted above, was his request to Adams
for encouraging material about the Irish economy when he wished
to deflect Irish demands for constitutional reform.[4] Such trans-
actions were of little significance when, as even in the Cotton Duties
answer, a largely factual answer was returned to a factual question:
they acquired importance when the response was opinion, argument,
or even polemic. Thus in April 1917 Adams, who had been giving
prosaic information and advice about food and agriculture policy,
broke out in enthusiasm when asked for speech materials:

...what we are doing today is no temporary work. We must provide for a
continued production from the land far greater than we have hitherto
secured. During war-time we must strain our resources to make ourselves,
as far as possible, independent of overseas supplies of the essential articles
of food. This problem cannot be solved simply by production; it must be
done also by altering our consumption. We have let our wheat acreage fall
too low, but we have still in these islands a large acreage of oats and a
considerable acreage of barley. We must use these supplies to a much
larger extent for the necessary food of the people, and we must adjust our
consumption to these new supplies of wholesome food.[5]

Such transmutations of mundane policy into confessions of faith
generally form part of the histories of policy questions to which they
are related, but there is one series of quasi-doctrinal statements which
stands alone, calling for separate attention. Kerr's memoranda
on the progress of the war were almost all concerned with public

statements. One can trace in them a development of thought which came to embrace foreign affairs and domestic politics, and thus to connect politics to policy. They are examined in detail later in this chapter.

A second duty which encouraged the secretaries to pronounce on the meaning of events was their contact with the press. By talking to editors and correspondents, and in Kerr's case by writing anonymously in *The Round Table*, they could add to the campaign of publicity which Lloyd George conducted throughout the war in speeches and through other agents. A third relevant duty, which far outmatched the others in scope and perhaps in consequences, was the preparation of editions of the *War Cabinet Report* for 1917 and 1918. These documents were ostensibly accounts of stewardship, setting out the administrative work of the new government and concentrating on the new departments and on constitutional innovations such as the War Cabinet itself. Inevitably their political function far outweighed their educational value, and Adams and Kerr as editors set their faces firmly against doubt and pessimism. The raw material was furnished by departments which were not anxious to shadow their own achievements, and the result was a tendentious and selective history of the war's achievements. The reports therefore had consequences both for immediate politics and for the early historiography of the war, representing an informed view of how the coalition government hoped it would be remembered.

In these three areas it is possible to document to some degree the Garden Suburb's involvement in forming the world view adopted by Lloyd George during his first premiership. There remains the nice question of who influenced whom in the dialogue between secretary and Prime Minister. In one sense it is impossible to answer without access to the inner mental processes of the participants. Lloyd George wrote his own speeches, usually transforming out of recognition the advice given him. Even when a secretarial submission seems to result in a speech or a policy there may still be doubts. A case in point arises when one finds Lloyd George, who sat regularly in the War Cabinet with Milner, expressing apparently 'Milnerite' views which were being pressed on him by Kerr. Who then is the grey eminence, Kerr daily or Milner four times a week? Another difficulty is that one cannot tell how much the secretaries wrote what the Prime Minister wanted to see; both Kerr and Adams tried, with only modest success, to adopt an authentically demagogic tone in their speech notes, and perhaps the substance of their memoranda as well as the form should be considered as evidence of Lloyd George's influence over them. Probably the most that can be drawn from the Garden Suburb's records is a description of the ideas and attitudes which flourished in 10 Downing Street with Lloyd George's assent and perhaps with his encouragement; but even that is not an insignificant matter.

It is nevertheless possible to trace continuities between the secretaries' earlier thinking and their advice to Lloyd George. These continuities are important because they establish the degree of intellectual independence which the secretaries can claim, and because they represent, much better than crude inferences from Kerr's association with Milner or Adams's Irish experience, the substance of the influences brought to bear on the government through the Secretariat. To set beside the continuities are the records of the secretaries' responses to passing events. All can be compared, albeit only indirectly, with changing policy and attitudes in government. While it is exceedingly difficult to attribute specific responsibility for a particular governmental decision to a member of the Garden Suburb, there are reasons for attaching great importance to the atmosphere created around the Prime Minister by his Secretariat. Lloyd George's aversion to the written word was notorious, and his reliance on conversation to gain information and ideas was correspondingly great. This seemed to lead to intellectual promiscuity. Adams lamented that Lloyd George 'can't be got at by the right people',[6] and after days of work on a speech Kerr would report that 'To-morrow L.G. is going to make a speech about Ireland. I don't quite know what he is going to say. Nobody does...So that we are all on tenterhooks.'[7] But Lloyd George, to the bewilderment of slower minds, was more concerned with ends than means and more constant in great matters than in small. The continuing presence of his secretaries gave them an advantage over other influences upon him which a minute consideration of the details of policy would tend to conceal. If this seems an argument *a priori*, one might consider the observations of C. P. Scott, who, after his meeting with Lloyd George in April 1918 to discuss Home Rule and conscription, described Kerr, 'on whom he evidently relies increasingly', as 'quite a good Liberal (though an opinionated and rather cranky one) and very much in George's confidence'.[8] Scott was reflecting on an interview in which Lloyd George had voiced opinions about Ireland which Kerr had expressed in *The Round Table* before he came to Downing Street, and again in his earliest memorandum on the subject in January 1917.[9] Lloyd George had resisted Irish conscription for the first fifteen months of his premiership and while there were undoubtedly good reasons for imposing it when he did, there had been good reasons before which had been overridden. In the light of Scott's remarks it is difficult to ignore the convergence of views between the Prime Minister and his secretary, however that convergence had come about.

Such convergence also presses for attention when the language used by Lloyd George to describe and reflect on events in public is similar to that used by his secretaries, especially by Kerr, whose constant attendance on the Prime Minister is noted so regularly in the diary of another constant attendant, Sir George Riddell. The Garden Suburb's interpretation of events retains its interest because it was disseminated as part of the government's official propaganda, either by Lloyd George or by themselves. The secretaries shared the view that truth was the best propaganda: the formation of their beliefs about what was true can be traced in their papers. In their introductions to the *War Cabinet Reports* they told the world what they had been telling the Prime Minister. There is no obvious discrepancy between the private and public analyses: a single, fairly coherent body of thought furnished the material for both. Shaped by the vicissitudes of war and developed with the advantages of a central position and full access to information which Downing Street conferred, this thinking was distinct from the tradition which has been described as 'social-imperialism', and from pre-war Liberalism, while drawing elements from both. In the hands of Kerr and Adams it made a fairly stable intellectual basis for the Prime Minister's own thinking.

Both Kerr and Adams, as editors of political reviews, have left published records of their opinions and preoccupations in the years before they came to the Garden Suburb. In their editorials and other miscellaneous writing both had committed themselves to political and social ideas of some generality, and although it would be an exaggeration to call them like-minded, they moved in the relatively small circle of English academic writers on public affairs, and where their interests touched their opinions showed common features which owed much to the common language of that circle. Adams's journal, *The Political Quarterly*, had a wider scope, and in the seven editorials which appeared during its short life (from 1914 to 1916) he expressed himself on Ireland (twice), the war in Europe, international control of war, the reorganisation of the government for

war (twice) and the resolutions of the Paris Economic Conference of
1916. Outside the journal he was not prolific, his weightiest publication being two chapters in the *Oxford Survey of the British Empire*
on trade and public administration. Only these chapters and the
editorials on Ireland discussed above[10] are unaffected by the war,
and it is therefore difficult to detect any change which might have
come about because of the conflict. Writing on trade in the *Survey*
he was steadfastly factual, basing his article on the recently inaugurated Census of Production, which he explained carefully for the
non-specialist reader. As befited the publication, which appeared in
1914 after British trade had begun to expand, he remarked on the
growing proportion of British exports destined for the Empire. The
only passages which were even slightly controversial were on the
export of coal – a well-worn theme of Tariff Reform economists,
which he noted as 'a subject of serious concern, affecting as it does
not only directly the general system of industrial production which
has been built up in the United Kingdom, but also the general cost
of living, and thereby again the comparative costs of industrial
production'[11] – and on agriculture:

> The production of agriculture has not kept pace with industrial production,
> and there are respects in which agriculture is the most unorganised and
> backward of British industries. Moreover, there are features in British
> agriculture which are disquieting. The shrinkage of the area of tillage, and
> the decline in the labouring population are symptoms of an unsatisfactory
> state of affairs, while in many parts the low wages of labour, the under-
> capitalized conditions of a great deal of the farming, and the slowness to
> adapt the methods of combination and co-operation which have revolu-
> tionized European agriculture in the past generation, and are being adopted
> in the old East and the new West, are all matters of no little concern for
> the economic welfare of the United Kingdom to-day.[12]

He also took the opportunity, in his chapter on public administration,
to praise his *alma mater*, the Department of Agriculture and Technical Instruction, as 'the pioneer department in the United Kingdom
as regards the development of state action in relation to agriculture'.[13]

Adams's writing in 1914 was preoccupied with Ireland until the
European war forced him to think of larger matters. He was ready
in the September issue of the *Political Quarterly* with a spirited
apologia for the British part in the war, attributing 'direct responsibility' to Austria and Germany and emphasising Britain's 'clear
obligation' to France.[14] In his view the war was being fought to
uphold the rights of small nations and the sanctity of treaties, and to

defend freedom against militarism. This led him directly to an editorial on 'International Control' in February 1915, in which he urged the universal adoption of the principle that international disputes should go, if not to arbitration, then at least to investigation by an international commission before war was declared.[15] By May 1915 he had turned to domestic problems. In 'The Cabinet and the Nation' he suggested a moratorium in party politics. His language is strikingly reminiscent of the anti-party sentiments of the 'social-imperialists':

> It is felt on every side that the man who puts private interests before public duty, or party interests before country, or self-indulgence before efficiency, is a traitor.[16]

More impressive still:

> If the different parties have learned to work together in times of war, some of this spirit of co-operation may be carried over to face the grave domestic problems of the near future. It will surely be a matter for regret if, after the war, we should fall back again into acute party controversy.[17]

Ironically these sentiments, published in the month which saw the downfall of the last Liberal government, were quite closely accompanied by a rejection of coalition as a political device 'improbable, doubtful in its results, and unnecessary'.[18] It is clear that even under the strain of war Adams was not a coalitionist or a protectionist. In March 1916, writing on 'National Organization and National Will', he emphasised the need for sensible policies which balanced military conscription with industrial needs, and while praising Germany's industrial organisation for war, sounded an old-fashioned Liberal warning:

> ...we are fighting for the rights of nations, small and great, for the faith of international law and the punishment of the transgressor, and for the security of the Empire and of our Allies from a domination which, whatever its military, economic and social efficiency, is incompatible with our ideas of freedom, national and individual.[19]

This rejection of efficiency as a touchstone of virtue was carried further in his notes on the Paris Resolutions. He approved of the abrogation of most-favoured-nation clauses in treaties with Germany, and of the measures taken to secure strategic industries, but with reservations:

> But there is also place for a word of warning. We have entered this war to defend international rights, to advance international peace and goodwill, to safeguard the independence of small states, and to bring about an era of

greater freedom. Our economic policy must be in line with our political aims. Economic defence is a necessary part of national safety. But nothing will do so much to continue a state of war and insecurity, and to defeat the larger political aims of freedom, as an exclusive economic policy. The spirit of economic reprisals must not carry on into the period of peace.[20]

The most striking characteristic of Adams's writing is its preference for what he called 'progressive' ideas: these included international arbitration and the extension of state intervention in industry and society. He was best informed, and most interested, in the machinery of public administration, and saw its extension as benign. Even in his wartime writings his enthusiasm for international competition was restrained, and he looked to international affairs largely to create conditions in which trade could prosper.

A different set of presuppositions brought Kerr to similar conclusions, both in foreign and domestic questions. As a writer for *The Round Table* he was restricted both by the imperial focus of its parent group and by the editorial policy of the 'Moot', an editorial committee which considered and often changed articles submitted to it in draft. But Kerr was responsible for ten articles in the journal before the war, five of them about European politics in which other members of the group were less interested. His knowledge of Europe was gained in some haste, but by March 1912 he had drawn from his observations of Anglo-German rivalry the conclusion that without some supranational authority to resolve disputes the competition between powerful states could only lead to war. The British system, based on liberty, was superior to the German system, based on authority, but it would have to be defended by superior military strength. He was therefore fully prepared for the outbreak of war, and met it with a coherent, if idiosyncratic analysis. From the outbreak of war to December 1916 he wrote for every issue of the journal an article which would typically combine a homily on the origins of the conflict, an exegesis of British war aims, and some reflection on the prevention of future wars.

Kerr blamed the war on Prussian militarism and state-worship and on the irresponsibility of the Austrian ruling group.[21] At first he explained British intervention as an act of *realpolitik*:

England joined the war, and with her the Dominions oversea, because the existence of the Empire was at stake and because her own honour was involved. The triumph of Germany would have meant the triumph of the Prussian spirit and the destruction of all effective resistance to it in Western Europe. A greater Germany, fronting possibly at the channel, with more territory and larger resources, with no enemy save Russia in the distant East, organized once more as a huge fighting machine, and confirmed in her belief in the method of winning her way by blood and iron, would have threatened the essential liberties of the peoples of the British Empire, and the safety of the communication between its parts. A German victory over France and Russia would have carried with it the certainty of another and a more terrible attack on the British Empire later on.[22]

The justification of expediency was soon abandoned and eventually, in 1916, repudiated.

It is sometimes said that we entered this war through enlightened self-interest. Such a view will not bear the test of an examination of the facts, save in the sense that it always pays to do right. Because honesty is the best policy, it is absurd to regard every honest man as a calculating schemer.[23]

Kerr was convinced that the war between 'two irreconcileable principles, autocracy and democracy'[24] must be fought until the 'utter and decisive defeat of Germany',[25] since 'nothing could be more disastrous than that by signing a premature peace the slightest ground should be afforded to the rulers of Germany for proving to the German people that they have gained by their policy of armaments and aggression'.[26] Although these recommendations resembled official pronouncements of British war aims both in content and level of generalisation, it is unlikely that Kerr was consciously writing official propaganda. If the remarkable homogeneity of his writing on war aims suggests artifice, its indigestibility and enormous length belies the interpretation: in sixty-six pages on 'The Schism of Europe' or thirty-two on 'The Harvest of War'[27] he was presenting the war as he saw it, a moral problem to which the correct solution was fighting to the end.

His unchanging vision of the moral justification of the war served as a foil to his developing ideas of post-war international organisation. In June 1915, pending 'an organic union of the world', he looked to 'a change of heart in Europe, coupled with a readiness on the part of the most pacific powers to defend the right by force'.[28] In September he pronounced that 'the cure for war is not to weaken the principle of the state, but to carry it to its logical conclusion by the creation of a world state', failing which an association of the most liberal powers, on the model of the British Commonwealth, might take charge of European affairs.[29] By December 1915 he had settled on a comprehensive theory of peace-keeping and an appropriate administrative mechanism:

The real cure for war is to overthrow the idol of selfish nationalism and put in its place the service of humanity.

...Any serious attempt to put the welfare of humanity first involves the establishment of a permanent conference of the world powers.[30]

These are perhaps the first stirrings of support for the League of Nations, but they must be interpreted in the light of Kerr's subsequent retreat from the idea of a permanent conference to a system of treaties to defend 'public right', an ethical concept borrowed from Gladstone *via* Asquith to express the canons of an international community which lacked the organised coercive powers necessary for 'international law'. In September 1916 he proposed that the peace of Europe should be secured by a guarantee of public right achieved

...by embodying in treaties, such as that which neutralised Belgium, or which might reaffirm the national liberties secured under the Monroe Doctrine, practical safeguards for the liberties and rights of the civilised world. When the Great Powers have erected these practical safeguards for public right and, in addition, have made them effective by undertaking, severally and jointly, not only to enforce them, but also to be sufficiently prepared to be able to do so with certain success, there will be good hope of lasting peace.[31]

In European questions Kerr was not a typical 'expert' such as those who were brought into the Political Intelligence Department of the Foreign Office. He lacked the profound knowledge of Europe which, for example, Seton-Watson, Namier, or Headlam-Morley brought to their work:[32] he had scarcely travelled on the Continent, knew no German, and had 'got up' his information about central Europe superficially for a discussion which reappeared with little variation in every article he wrote on the subject during the war. Only with the information available to him in Downing Street did he develop his knowledge, and even then he retained a primarily moral interest in Europe.

Outside the Round Table group, Kerr was probably best known in 1916 not for his European writing but for an essay on 'Political Relations between Advanced and Backward Peoples', contributed to a collection of essays on international relations, and an essay on 'Labour and Industry' in a collection on class misunderstanding.[33] His position on backward peoples was unequivocal: 'The truth is that the government of backward races by advanced races is...the result of "natural laws".' The natural laws in question were the consequences of the average innate superiority in character, intelligence and culture of the white races over all others. Kerr argued that immediately a superior race came into contact with an inferior one it was necessary for the government of the superior race to intervene to protect the inferior from corruption caused by commercial exploitation. He did not condemn commercial activity overseas: he merely thought that those nations which profited from it had a duty to protect the native races from its consequences. He also insisted that contact between the lower classes of white and coloured races was undesirable, and drew upon his experience in the Transvaal to show that Asian immigration into areas of white settlement caused economic and political trouble, and should therefore be prevented. He thought white government of coloured races should be assumed early and maintained for a long time: 'A nation which has had to assume the responsibility for maintaining good government among a backward people, cannot relinquish that responsibility until the latter have given some clear evidence of their capacity to do so in its place.'[34] This straightforward version of the White Man's Burden was supported with slabs of quotation and paraphrase from Lyall's history of the conquest of India and from missionaries' reports of the degradation of the native races in New Hebrides.

On labour he was less confident. He began well: 'Modern industrial unrest dates from the industrial revolution.' But after explaining that the division of labour widened the psychological gulf between employer and employee, and that the failure of the community to intervene exacerbated the situation, he was forced to disclose that he had no solution except 'a change of heart'. There were some interesting side roads on the way to this conclusion. He made a stirring, if unspecific, call for an improvement in the 'higher direction of industry' and took the surprising position that the 'real evil is not the rate of interest, i.e. profit, but the concentration of excessive quantities of capital in a few hands. And that evil can only be dealt with by the state itself through income taxes, death duties, and means of limiting or redistributing capital holdings.'[35] He recognised and approved of labour's demand for a minimum wage and a shorter working week, and spoke favourably of 'industrial democracy' while admitting that he did not know what form it should take.[36] For all its vagueness, this essay and another version of the same thoughts printed in *The Round Table* are both clear examples of social thought in the Milnerite tradition of state intervention. Kerr rejected emphatically the Labour party's prescription of nationalisation, but he was no friend of unrestrained private capitalism: 'We shall never get the right idea of work until we see that at bottom it is public service which everyone ought to perform, rich and poor alike.'[37]

On the strength of this essay Kerr was first considered as overseer of labour matters in the Garden Suburb:[38] but although he had large views, he was uninformed about detail and his responsibility for imperial affairs was far more appropriate.

Kerr's ideas do not fit readily into any category. Many of his themes were reflections of Milner's views, whether on home or foreign affairs; but he added to the corpus of Milnerite thinking some idiosyncratic applications of moral analysis which set him apart from any 'social-imperialist' movement. Like many Round Table members he was opposed to Tariff Reform and dismissive of the profit motive in domestic or foreign affairs. There is more than a little truth in Beatrice Webb's description of him as a 'refined aristocratic dreamer'.[39]

II

Kerr's earlier writing and experience influenced the style with which he approached his work for Lloyd George, but his activities were governed by the Prime Minister's immediate needs, which could not always be turned to his somewhat millenarian purposes. His first known effort on Lloyd George's behalf, notes for a speech in response to President Wilson's Peace Note in December 1916, has unfortunately not been found.[40] His first surviving work was to prepare foreign policy notes for Lloyd George's speech at Caernarvon on 3 February 1917. Wilson's initiative still dominated his thought. In his earlier writing he had represented Britain as the guardian of international morality; now he realised that Wilson would usurp the position unless the British government protested its agreement with all that the President said. He searched Wilson's speeches for hints that American neutrality would soon be over, and rather prematurely found what he wanted in the speech to the senate on 22 January, the so-called 'Peace without victory' speech. Kerr thought that although Wilson had been determined to keep his country out of the war 'at almost any price', the President now realised that the United States could not tolerate 'a murderous hold-up of the world by sea'. Wilson had hoped to avoid intervention by bringing about a peace that winter by means of his peace note, but he was now seeking to warn Germany that the United States would intervene if the submarine campaign continued, and to unite his country behind him.[41] Kerr's guess exaggerated the President's willingness to go to war:[42] but his wishful thinking is less important than his assumption that peace was an avoidable calamity. The War for Public Right must go on; the Allies had outflanked Germany by their joint reply to Wilson's peace note,[43] and could retain public sympathy both at home and in the United States by proclaiming their agreement with Wilson's point of view and by insisting that the war was continuing because of German militarism.[44] Lloyd George's speech should emphasise that the new government had subordinated everything to winning the war. He should deal with the co-ordination of Allied and Dominion activity, and with the efforts being made at home. Then: '*At the end of recital of war measures*, I think you must say something about *peace*.' The Prime Minister should emphasise that the Allies' tremendous efforts were directed at crushing not the German people but the military machine.

Kerr temporarily moderated his antipathy to an early end to the war under the influence of Smuts, whose arrival in London for the Imperial War Conference coincided almost exactly with the revolution in Russia. The coincidence seems at first to have overwhelmed Kerr's assimilative powers and his first attempts to introduce Smuts's ideas to Lloyd George embodied ambiguities in the interpretation of the February Revolution which were only to be resolved in his bitter disappointments at the Bolshevik *coup*. Smuts himself was more interested in *realpolitik*, and cared more for the outcome of war than for its ideological significance. He believed that a crushing defeat of the Central Powers was neither feasible nor necessary. German attempts to dominate Central Europe through a Germanised *Mitteleuropa* could be thwarted by an appropriate settlement with Austria. That done, British interests lay in the destruction of the German and Turkish colonial systems, which had largely been achieved by 1917, and otherwise in a return to the *status quo ante* in Europe. Smuts hoped to rely on nationalist and democratic movements in Europe as allies against Germany and Austria, and to keep 'world opinion' on the Allied side by taking care about such questions as 'the severer forms of reprisals, our coercion of small neutral nations, and even an added emphasis to our traditional generous policy in purely domestic affairs.'[45] His first formal statement of the case came in a speech to the Imperial War Cabinet on 23 March.[46] It pleased Milner, who had come to similar conclusions himself and had already tried to float them in public,[47] but the Dominion leaders were unconvinced.[48] To a casual observer, and even to the usually perceptive Hankey, Smuts's recommendations might appear to have been 'on the lines adopted by Massingham in the *National Review*',[49] but his preoccupation was not so much radical as imperialist: he sought to protect colonial gains from being bargained away to achieve an unrealistic European settlement.

Kerr's first opportunity to hear these views probably came at a dinner which Milner gave for the newly-arrived South African on 14 March.[50] Before the Dominion leaders had arrived in England Kerr had considered their likely views and concluded that they would be prepared to discuss negotiations on any basis, even the return of the colonies, except that France, Belgium, Serbia and Roumania would have to be restored. Because 'no commonsense man would gamble on...the Allies getting their terms in 1917', he expected the Dominion leaders to want to discuss the 1918 campaign.[51] By 20 March he had reconsidered, advising Balfour that:

I think you will find that General Smuts and possibly some of the other overseas representatives will want to initiate a discussion at once on the possibilities of a diplomatic policy directly calculated to separate the German and Austrian peoples from their governments. As you probably know better than I do, there is a good deal of criticism of the Allied reply to President Wilson on the ground that it tended to restore the unity between the German and Austro-Hungarian governments and their subjects, by being open to the interpretation that the allies would be satisfied with the break-up of Austria and its partition among other states, and with nothing less.

The Russian Revolution makes the question of the general direction of allied diplomacy both one of greater urgency and importance and easier to consider, if it is thought desirable.[52]

Kerr's choice, surprising in a professional imperialist, was to emphasise in Smuts's argument not the imperial purpose but the European instrument. Remarking that the Russian autocracy had inhibited the western Allies from emphasising the democratic aspect of the war, he proposed a new slogan for Entente diplomacy in a letter to Lloyd George on 20 March.

By making democratisation of Europe a primary object, we would give to our Allied diplomacy a new meaning and a new power, for, while beating upon the machine from without with no less vigour than before, we should be directly weakening its hold upon its subjects within its own territories.[53]

Working upon this inspiration from Smuts, Kerr became steadily more obsessed with the idea of democracy as a theme of Allied foreign policy, until in late May the collapse of the Russian war effort shattered his faith in the solvent properties of democracy in enemy territory and its tonic effect on the Allies.

Kerr attended the first meeting of the Imperial War Cabinet, on 20 March, at which Lloyd George proposed the democratisation of Europe as the second of five British war aims.[54] Although the Dominion leaders might, as Kerr suggested, have been thinking about 'whether the general direction given to Allied diplomacy by the Allied reply to President Wilson is now sound in view of the Russian revolution',[55] their conversation was about the spoils of war. Rather than the democratisation of Europe, the Dominions were looking for a *quid pro quo* if they were to answer the British government's call for men and material. Smuts's speech on 23 March, and Milner's support of it, led to the establishment on 12 April of committees on the territorial and non-territorial desiderata of peace. Curzon's territorial committee reported on 28 April, calling for the destruction of the Turkish empire and the establishment of a set of priorities in the disposal of the German colonies which favoured Dominion interests.[56] European war aims were treated perfunctorily. The negotiation of any European settlement was to be left to the Foreign Office and the War Cabinet, which meant in the event that it was left to Lloyd George.[57] Kerr helped his master not with secret diplomacy but with speech notes.

His preference for the public and principled over the private and practical approach to the Central Powers was explicit. He welcomed the declaration of war by the United States because:

The War has taken on openly the character of a war for democracy versus autocracy, as well as for the liberation of Belgium, France, Serbia, etc.[58]

But he shunned any attempt to use this development diplomatically. A refusal to negotiate with autocratic governments would commit the Allies against negotiations with *de facto* governments; and the offer of easier terms to democratic governments, besides being an unwarrantable interference in the domestic affairs of Germany and Austria, would be to bargain about the Allied demands for right and justice which were not negotiable.

The practical problem therefore is how to take advantage of the recent events to induce the army and the popular majority to insist on the acceptance of our terms. If autocracy resists it will end in revolution, if it acquiesces democracy will have become an accomplished fact.

The solution to the 'practical problem' was the speech to the American Luncheon Club on 12 April for which these notes were a brief.[59] Lloyd George should emphasise that the Allies sought not conquest but a settlement which represented the wishes of the population concerned. He should forswear economic penalties against Germany so long as 'militarist economic penetration' was abandoned, and should state British determination to break up the Turkish empire. The promise of self-determination exposes one of the ambiguities in the position which Smuts had adopted at the Imperial War Conference: self-determination for the peoples of the Austrian empire might conflict with the proposal not to break up the Monarchy, for the subject peoples were not necessarily prepared to remain even in a federal relationship with the Habsburgs. If the rulers of the Dual Monarchy were to make peace and form a bulwark against *Mitteleuropa*, they might not be pleased by Allied attempts to make their subjects disloyal. Smuts had not made clear to what end democracy was to be a means; Kerr reconfounded the confusion by arguing as though democracy was an end in itself.

He took the point further after the reconstruction of the Russian government in May. On the face of it the dismissal of Miliukov, the Foreign Minister and leader of the moderate Cadet party, at the bidding of the Soviet representing soldiers who no longer wished to fight the Germans on behalf of the Entente, represented a setback for the Allies. Kerr, who associated the move with a strengthening Russian desire for a 'democratic peace', juxtaposed it with evidence of a peace coalition in Germany and concluded that it offered the Allies further opportunity to make diplomatic capital out of the democratisation of Europe. In late May he wrote to Lloyd George:

So far as the main political situation is concerned the important things are:

(a) The appearance of a definitely democratic party in Germany much wider in extension than the Social Democrats.
(b) The growth of the doctrine of a democratic peace in Russia and elsewhere. . .I have little doubt that Germany will become more and more pre-occupied with the internal struggle between the adherence [sic] of the old order, who will be out for annexations and war to the knife, and a party which will represent a large majority of German opinion which will be in favour of a no annexationist peace.

As to the second [point] it is evident that the notion of democratic peace is spreading not only in Russia but elsewhere, that is to say the notion that the only way of preventing these Imperialist Wars is to allow every nation to settle its boundaries for itself, and not to have them carved about over their heads by diplomatists in secret conclave. There are of course immense difficulties in the way of applying this principle but fundamentally it is sound. I think, therefore, that it is inevitable that if Russia is to gain a stable government, possessed of authority both over the army and the people, it will have to make a re-statement of its War Aims in these terms, and ask the Allies to do the same as a condition of adhering to the Treaty of London.

I don't think the first move ought to come from us but we ought to be prepared to meet it when it does come.[60]

This memorandum, admitting that the principle of no annexations was 'fundamentally. . .sound', represents the furthest point of Kerr's journey towards acceptance of the consequences of the Russian revolution. So long as he retained his optimism about Russia he was prepared to follow democracy wherever it led, in contrast to Balfour and Smuts who regarded the notion of democracy with scepticism. Balfour, as long ago as October 1916, had talked of 're-arranging the map of Europe in closer agreement with what we rather vaguely call "the principle of nationality" ',[61] but only as an instrument for achieving the war aims already stated by the Allies and for reducing the economic and military resources of the Central Powers. It was not an end in itself, any more than democracy was an end to Smuts in his speech to the Imperial War Cabinet. Kerr went further than either of them in believing that democratic institutions would of themselves produce a territorial settlement which would prevent wars; democracy was to be the guiding principle, not merely the excuse.

It is a measure of Kerr's intellectual relationship with Lloyd George that he was later than his master to realise the implications of developments in Russian politics. On 1 May Lloyd George had hinted to the War Cabinet that the war might have to be brought to an end by exchanges of territory.[62] On 9 May he suggested bargaining the return of captured German colonies for the evacuation of Belgium.[63] Only in very late May did Kerr warn Lloyd George that a detailed restatement of war aims on the lines demanded by the Russians would do no good.

My own impression is that what the new Russian democracy is exercised about is not 'no annexations' but peace. What they want is that the war should end so that they may get on with their own internal revolution.[64]

He concluded that the Allies should postpone their statement until the autumn, when the submarine campaign would have failed, so that 'the autocracies will be faced with the alternative of capitulating to our demands or facing revolution at home'. His respect for the power of public opinion soon led him from qualified optimism about the collapse of the Central Powers to a deep pessimism about the stamina of the British people.

Kerr now began once again to emphasise the moral arguments for continuing the war, urging the Prime Minister on 1 June not to allow the Serbians, through British neglect, to be tempted to make a separate peace with Austria; the Allied guarantee to Serbia was an essential excuse for continuing the war until Britain had secured her position against Germany in Europe and overseas.[65] He wanted Lloyd George to insist in his Dundee speech on 30 June that British war aims were not imperialistic, as pacifist critics alleged, but that Britain had entered the war to prevent Germany's dominating Europe by armed force and would dispose of the captured colonies in accordance with the wishes of the inhabitants. Controversial aspects of the European settlement, such as the fate of Alsace-Lorraine, Roumania, Poland, and Yugoslavia, should be avoided in favour of the more limited and moral desiderata of the restoration of Belgium and Serbia.[66] He insisted that it was 'essential to avoid a detailed reply' to Chancellor Michaelis's ambiguous response to the Reichstag's equally ambiguous Peace Resolution of 19 July. In his speech at the Queen's Hall on 22 July, Lloyd George should emphasise the fundamental issues of the war, such as the defence of public right, and stay clear of the 'very delicate' question of peace.[67] Kerr's privately expressed opinion in July was that

Having broken away from autocracy the world is now rushing headlong towards the abyss of anarchy under the guidance of such phrases as 'self-determination', 'nationalism', 'Home Rule' and so forth.[68]

The apprehension that Britain was also rushing towards the abyss came ever closer to the surface. Kerr feared that the British people, demoralised by high food prices and profiteering,[69] would fall prey to pacifist agitators – a risk which his colleague Harmsworth was investigating in his liaison with the Commission on Industrial Unrest.[70] As the opportunities for a restatement of positive war aims diminished, Kerr pressed Lloyd George to deal with domestic morale in his speeches. As Michaelis and Czernin, the Austrian Foreign Minister, tried in July to raise an argument about war aims, he warned Lloyd George:

I do not think it will do much good to be drawn further into the controversy with Michaelis and Czernin. Nothing that you say will affect German opinion as long as the offensive in the East is successful. And the French are bound to talk back. I think your main aim might be to reason with the growing forces of pacifism and unrest in this country and among the Allies...The main point is can we get that stable peace for which every-

body longs, so long as the Prussian military machine remains in control
from Belgium to Palestine...[71]

In the same notes he began to hark back to the themes of his *Round
Table* articles.

On the question of negotiation I think you might well ask: how can we
consider negociations until we know whether Serbia and Belgium and
other small nations are going to be restored?...Finally, the peace for
which we fight is not mainly a question of territorial adjustment. It is a
peace which will be the beginning of a new world – a world in which all
nations will live happily side by side, because military autocracies will have
been universally overthrown.

The note of reserve soon changed to watchful defiance directed at
the Germans – 'There has been no real change of heart in Germany
as yet'[72] – but more particularly at subversive forces at home. In
October he had come to consider most of the government's domestic troubles, whether from the right or the left, as manifestations
of German intrigue: 'Kuhlmann's "psychological atmosphere",
Boloism, Pacificism [sic], Jingoism, Industrial trouble.'[73] The study
of foreign affairs had brought him inexorably to the problem of
dealing with trouble-makers at home.

On 29 November 1917, the *Daily Telegraph* published a letter,
rejected as unconstructive by *The Times*, in which the Marquess of
Lansdowne called for the restatement of British war aims to remove
the impression that Britain wanted to destroy the German régime, to
strip Germany of territory, to penalise her economy after the war, to
exclude her from the League of Nations, or to impose upon her an
interpretation of the 'freedom of the seas' which would be detri-
mental to her interests.[74] Lansdowne had first suggested a negotiated
peace in November 1916, when he was still a member of the government, and his opinions were known, and to some extent shared, in
the new government. The War Cabinet had discussed a negotiated
peace during the Imperial War Conference and on other occasions
thereafter. Nevertheless a savage attack was launched, in parliament
and through the press, on Lansdowne and any who appeared to
support him. The motive was apparently to prevent the consolidation
of a peace movement at the parliamentary level which might
threaten the stability of the government. Many participants in the
public debate had ulterior motives and the question of defining war
aims was rapidly obscured: in particular, it was in the interests of
many disputants to have it believed that there were two clearly

separated sides to the argument, led respectively by Lansdowne and Lloyd George.

The Prime Minister in particular needed to make a distinction between Lansdowne's views and his own. He was in France when the letter was published, attending the first meeting of the Supreme War Council and a series of Inter-Allied Conferences. During difficult sessions he was presented with the extra problem of persuading his Allies that the letter had not been inspired or approved by the government: the French feared that the British would sell them out for an early peace, and from the other side Colonel House was pressing the British government to accept Lansdowne's interpretation of the freedom of the seas.[75] Lloyd George returned to England full of complaints. Fortunately *The Times* had already printed a statement authorised by Cecil that the letter had not been seen or approved by any member of the Cabinet and that it contradicted the policy of the government; the stage was therefore already set for conflict.[76] Lloyd George turned to his entourage who warned him of political danger.

In August, when Henderson had left the government because he wanted the Labour party to send delegates to an international socialist conference in Stockholm where German socialists would be present, Kerr had recommended a brusque and impatient tone with Labour's pretensions to develop an alternative foreign policy.

If Labour is dissatisfied with the war aims of the government its course is not to go to Stockholm but to induce the government to adopt war aims which it can accept, or resign from the government.[77]

The Lansdowne letter found him more sensitive to domestic political problems and more anxious that Lloyd George should triumph in open debate over the proponents of an early negotiated peace. He also took the opportunity to urge on the Prime Minister some of the ideas of international organisation which he had first floated in *The Round Table* in 1916.

On 4 December Kerr sent the Prime Minister a note, probably written by someone else, which warned that Asquith's supporters were pressing him to come out in public for Lansdowne. On the other hand the writer was confident that after Bonar Law's firm handling of his party's meeting on 1 December the Unionists were soundly behind the government and the war.[78] Astor, who commented on the parliamentary situation the next day, was less confident.

A surprisingly large number of Unionists don't judge the letter by the 'effect' it did and was bound to produce. They seem to concentrate on the passages in it with which they agree.

A few are asking (just as many persons were asking a year ago) – can we win the war? If we continue through 1918 can we be fairly certain of victory?

I find the most effective reply to them is (1) that in our economic offensive we have a weapon hitherto not fully used and that it should assist us materially if developed...(2) that if we ended now and made a bad peace without victory we should lose the respect of America and probably lose some portion of the Empire (e.g. S. Africa).

If you could rekindle the high moral tone and spirit of self-sacrifice which existed in the early years...you would counteract the present war-weariness. We want to get away from the sordid questions of profits and high wages.[79]

Kerr, who apparently did believe that there were two sides to the argument, tried to furnish the material which would persuade an audience that Lansdowne was in favour of a 'bad peace without victory' and that Lloyd George was against it – neither proposition being wholly true.

To this end, Kerr combined his own moral sensibility with his master's demagogy in a lurid text for a speech at Grays Inn on 14 December. Defining two heresies in Lansdowne's statement, that Britain could properly negotiate with an autcratic Germany and that an autocratic Germany could properly be admitted to a post-war League of Nations, he explained why the nation should not be seduced from orthodoxy.

This is in truth a war against war. But that can only be attained through victory for our cause. That is the issue before us to-day. On the one side compromise with the Prussian League of subject nations, a great military camp armed and drilled and controlled by a clique whose passion is domination, a constant menace to liberty, a source of perpetual intrigue, with whom peace is impossible. That is what a Lansdowne peace must mean. It means hell for every man, woman and child for years and years.[80]

Kerr went on to explain that the war was being fought to establish a League of Nations on a firm footing, which would be open to all free nations and would guarantee public right for evermore. In a more reflective note, intended to form the basis for a major speech, he took up old themes and developed a new one. Because 'the industrial masses' had been allowed to lose sight of the moral issues of the war, they were at risk from pacifists, the treacherous, and the faint-hearted. They must be persuaded that a premature peace would make it impossible to establish an international order which would uphold right. He suggested an imaginative scheme for Lloyd George to put forward as a first step. The Supreme War Council should be set up as a permanent international organisation, extended first to all neutrals, then to the Central Powers after they had restored international right and made reparation for the war. The Allies should declare that they would go on fighting until the Central Powers accepted those conditions, and immediately invite the accession to the Supreme War Council of every nation which had broken off diplomatic relations with Germany.

I believe that if you made it clear that you were going to work for proposals of this kind (while emphasising that the only road to making a success of them lay through victory) it would have an immense effect. It would dispel the idea that the war had degenerated into two groups of powers each trying to punish the other...It would tend to bring more neutrals into the war, and so exercise economic pressure on Germany. It would appeal to the best elements in Russia and Italy, and it would give the German people a real reason for standing out against their government.[81]

A little of this note of Kerr's survived in Lloyd George's speech. The passage quoted on p. 159 is recognisable, though hardly more than that, in the Prime Minister's analysis of the choice before the Allies:

Let there be no doubt as to the alternatives with which we are confronted. One of them is to make easy terms with the triumphant outlaw, as men are driven to in order to buy immunity in lands where there is no authority to enforce law. That is one course. It means abasing ourselves in terror before lawlessness. It means, ultimately, a world intimidated by successful bandits. The other is to go through with our divine task of vindicating justice, so as to establish a righteous and everlasting peace for ourselves and for our children.

It is striking, however, that Lloyd George, instead of embarking on a vigorous personal attack on Lansdowne, dismissed him with no more than heavy irony. Lansdowne had announced his agreement with President Wilson, to which the Prime Minister responded:

I understand that all our anxieties as to this epistle were groundless... It is satisfactory to know that Lord Lansdowne was misunderstood both by his friends and by his critics...[82]

Kerr's second note contributed to a stream of advice and argument which flowed to the Prime Minister during the weeks before his major war-aims speech, delivered at the Caxton Hall on 5 January 1918. The major new idea, to extend the Supreme War Council, had been conceived independently by Hankey, but even with two secretaries to support it the project came to nothing. The government's desire to meet the threat of the Lansdowne letter grew into a determination to reaffirm that there could be no peace without victory. As German and Russian negotiators used tendentious public statements to advance their diplomacy at Brest-Litovsk, the British government laboured over a public pronouncement which would define British aspirations loosely enough to satisfy most points of view within the government and to fulfil the manifold functions of a war-aims speech.

The Caxton Hall speech had its roots not only in the private ruminations of the government but also in the situation outside. Peace feelers from Austria prompted discussion of the terms which Britain might seek in a separate peace. While colonial aims which did not touch Austria were scarcely revised, much attention was paid to the flagrantly anti-Austrian ambitions of Britain's Allies. A difference became evident between Smuts, who seemed prepared to neglect Allied war aims entirely, and Balfour and Cecil who felt obliged to maintain at least some of them.[83] The possibility of a meeting with an Austrian was first raised in late November, shortly before the Supreme War Council meeting which Lloyd George was attending when Lansdowne published his letter.[84] The Prime Minister obtained his Allies' consent to the meeting and secured from Nitti, the Italian Minister for Finance, a fabulous story of Italian reasonableness about the *irredenta* which encouraged him to think that Italian ambitions would not stand in the way of a settlement with Austria.[85] An atmosphere of hope encouraged kindness towards the Austrians. Both Smuts and Drummond resurrected the idea of a reconstruction of the Dual Monarchy as a four- or five-part federation, to include both Poland and Serbia.[86] Smuts proposed that Austrian squeamishness about deserting the German alliance should be overcome by making a genuine offer of peace to the Germans which would offer a free hand in Russia's Baltic provinces in return for the cession to Britain of all German colonies except Togo and the Cameroons and a revision of the frontier between Germany and France in Lorraine. Balfour protested not only about Smuts's indifference to France and Serbia, but also at the reversion to the proposal to take the colonies which the Dominions wanted and leave those which the British government wanted. Thus a wide-ranging debate on British war aims and their public presentation grew out of a discussion of terms with Austria for a separate peace. Kerr made an early contribution, urging Smuts to change his argument for retaining the German colonial empire.

...there is one point I think you ought to alter. It is absolutely fatal to suggest that the German colonies must be retained because they are essential to British communications. The U.S.A. won't look at that for a moment...Personally I am against handing back the colonies, but I am of this opinion because I am sure it is contrary to the best interests both of the inhabitants and the world that they should be given back to a nation inspired by Prussian ideals...I believe this argument will prevail, where the purely British argument will not.[87]

Kerr's insistence on this point, recalling his essay on Backward Peoples also testifies that he had already gone further than Smuts in realising that peace terms could not remain a matter for secret discussion between Britain and Austria. The month of December 1917 saw that belief spreading among Britain's leaders.

Cecil had been among the first to see the point, stimulated by his disquiet at the savage treatment accorded to Lansdowne's letter.

I think its publication was exceedingly inopportune, some of his proposals I altogether disagree with, and I believe the tone of the letter was far too apologetic. But the substance of it, apart from the exceedingly unfortunate passage about the freedom of the seas, does not seem to me very objectionable.
In effect, he argues that we ought to re-state our war aims: that undoubtedly some of those which we put forward in the Wilson note have become obsolete, and that we should remove the impression that we desire the political annihilation of any of our enemies.[88]

Smuts came to support the idea of making a public statement after Mensdorff had told him that the absence of an up-to-date statement of the Allies' definition of victory made it impossible for the Central Powers to consider their position about negotiations.[89] From the same mission Kerr brought back his report that a moderate statement of Allied intentions towards Turkey would help the Ententophil minority of the Committee for Union and Progress to rally opinion against the pro-German majority.[90] The decision to make a statement in public was clinched by the publicity given to the armistice and peace negotiations between the Russians and the Central Powers at Brest-Litovsk. The victors accepted Trotsky's demand that negotiations should be completely public. On 22 December Joffe, who led the Russian delegation, presented his conditions of peace, which encompassed full national self-determination, no annexations, no indemnities, and a settlement of colonial questions on the same lines as European questions. Czernin and Kuhlmann, the Austrian and German Foreign Ministers, overcame the General Staff and accepted the Bolshevik terms in principle, well aware that they would seriously embarrass the Entente.[91] The subsequent breakdown of the Brest-Litovsk talks did nothing to mitigate the discomfort felt in London. Cecil in particular was confirmed in his view that British *morale* would crumble unless an adequate statement of British war aims was made public.

Cecil's plan was to consult France and Italy about their essential interests and add these to a statement of Britain's 'irreducible aims'. The latter he defined thus, in a letter to Balfour on 28 December 1917:

...the status quo in Europe (Personally I do not regard an independent Poland, or Jugoslavia, or even Bohemia as a British interest), Autonomous Armenia, Mesopotamia, Palestine, Independent Arabia. Retention of German Colonies in Pacific, S.W. Africa, Internationalisation of East Africa. Restoration of Cameroun and Togoland. In addition we are bound to support the reasonable demands of our Allies when stated, including Alsace-Lorraine and some rearrangement of Treaties.[92]

Cecil made it quite clear that he would not welcome negotiations if the Germans tried to exploit the similarity between these terms and Czernin's statement of Austrian aims. He thought that the ability of a future League of Nations to keep the peace depended on a military or economic defeat of Germany.[93] It followed that the communication of such war aims to the Central Powers in secret would be worse than useless, and that the statement should be made in public if at all. His conviction that something had to be done won him the effective leadership of the Foreign Office on the point, for his cousin Balfour professed himself indifferent to the definition of war aims,

...a problem in which I take no very great interest because, as it seems to me, there is not the slightest difficulty in defining what ends we want to achieve by the war. The real difficulty is to find out how far we shall be able to attain them, and how far our Allies are prepared to fight till they are attained.[94]

Lloyd George disagreed with the Foreign Secretary. Cecil and Smuts were asked to suggest the substance of a reply to Czernin's statement, and there was even talk of putting Smuts in Balfour's place.[95] The question of war aims was discussed frequently and at length in the War Cabinet, and it was Balfour's own fault if advice on the forthcoming public statement was drawn from everywhere except the 'constitutional' source.

Both Kerr and Hankey were involved in the preparation of the counter-blast to Czernin. Kerr was asked to prepare a draft answer on 29 December. He cast his advice in the form of an exegesis of the text 'restoration, reparation, and adequate guarantees' which Lloyd George had used in December 1916 as an anodyne paraphrase of earlier statements of British war aims. Kerr accused the negotiators on both sides at Brest-Litovsk of an attempt to 'becloud the moral issue by suggesting a peace on the basis of crying quits all round'. Restoration did not mean 'no annexations': the Entente would restore nothing and the Central Powers would restore everything that they, as aggressors, had conquered. The Allies would also expect reparation, not 'in the sense of contributions by the vanquished to the victor in the war', but as 'the outward and visible sign of restitution for wrong inflicted and of penitence therefor'. They would therefore repudiate 'no indemnities'. As to 'adequate guarantees', he was decidedly less savage in his suggestions for territorial rearrangement than his otherwise apocalyptic language would suggest. He called for:

a re-drawing of the boundary between Germany and France in Alsace-Lorraine, the retrocession of the Trentino and the separation from the Turkish Empire of the peoples whom the Turks have so mercilessly misgoverned. . .a settlement of the racial problems of South Eastern Europe on the basis that the various nationalities therein contained should be as far as possible grouped in autonomous units with securities for religious and language rights of minorities. . .As to the relations which exist between these national entities they have no fixed ideas, provided they are not brought under the political and military domination of Berlin.

These desiderata were very modest, slightly less accommodating to Austria than Cecil's in their insistence on securing the position of the subject nationalities, and altogether very like the proposals lately put forward by Smuts. Kerr's moral preoccupation found its outlet in his insistence that the autocratic political system of Central Europe be replaced in 'the democratisation of Central Europe'. On colonial questions he repeated his view that the settlement should secure 'what is best for the peoples concerned and humanity at large'. For post-war organisation he suggested that the Allies should 'convert the Treaty of London into a permanent international agreement,'[96] to which 'a liberalised Austria Hungary' should be invited to accede. Kerr argued that by rearranging the map, reconstructing the political systems of certain states and setting up an international organisation interested in preserving the peace 'on liberal principles', it would be possible to secure a lasting peace. Accordingly he suggested a statement on much the same lines as his memorandum of advice.[97]

Only one passage in Kerr's draft found its way in a recognisable form to the Caxton Hall speech. On the settlement of Africa and the Pacific he proposed:

It is of the greatest importance that they should be placed under an uniform and benevolent administration whose sole purpose is the education and advancement of their inhabitants, and not their exploitation for the benefit of any European capitalists or governments.

It was an important point which he had raised before. In the final draft it was rendered:

The governing consideration. . .in all these cases must be that the inhabitants should be placed under the control of administrations acceptable to themselves, one of whose main purposes will be to prevent their exploitation for the benefit of European capitalists or governments.[98]

Although no other direct parallel is obvious, Kerr's contribution to the finished product cannot be dismissed. *The Nation* tartly, but correctly, observed of the speech that it was 'of the "school of Lloyd George" rather than an unadulterated and acknowledged product of the Master's free-flowing brush'.[99] In the final process of composition, Kerr amalgamated papers by Smuts and Cecil to furnish a text for the War Cabinet;[100] but there is some meaning to claims such as that of Hankey, who was not simply boasting to his diary when he observed: 'In a sense it originated in my Memo written last Saturday; none of the actual text of this, but many of the ideas remained in the final statement.'[101] The final text epitomised a conventional wisdom, extending beyond the government to Asquith and Grey[102] and to the statement on war aims of the Labour Party Conference.[103] Kerr, like Hankey, had during 1917 contributed to this conventional wisdom, and in those parts of the text which cannot be attributed confidently to Smuts or Cecil appear points on which he had on other occasions contributed ideas, often drawn from his earlier writing.

We had to join in the struggle or stand aside and see Europe go under and brute force triumph over public right and international justice.
. . .the adoption of a really democratic constitution by Germany would be the most convincing evidence that in her the old spirit of military domination had died in this war.
Unless international right is recognised by insistence on payment for injury done in defiance of its canons it can never be a reality.[104]

It was in passages such as these, with their emphasis on the moral significance of the war, that differences between Lloyd George and

Lansdowne were made most prominent. The attitude towards territorial claims shown by the government was quite compatible with
the Lansdowne view; a professional diplomat trained to think in
terms of territory commented on the similarity.[105] The spirit which
had animated Kerr's condemnation of Lansdowne shows through in
these references to international justice and public right.

The speech was delivered to an audience of trade unionists at the
Caxton Hall on the morning of 5 January 1918. It was greeted by
radical journals as the first tangible consequence of the Lansdowne
letter,[106] and by jingoes as 'defeatism'.[107] The final text and the
discussion which preceded it within the government and between
government and leaders of opinion all suggest that its collective
authors were quite as much interested in justifying the prolongation
of the war as they were in seducing Germany and Austria to the
negotiating table.[108] In this connection it is significant that Kerr, who
constantly emphasised moral arguments for continuing the war in his
recommendations for public statements, used them in private argument during the preparation of the speech.

In the early months of 1918 Kerr seems to have grown closer to
the Prime Minister; his opinions on Ireland, for example, were increasingly shared by Lloyd George. But the importance of public
statements receded as brute military and economic force brought
Germany to the point of defeat in Europe. Speech-writing, with its
opportunities for Kerr to express his opinions, regained its significance as preparations were made for a general election. In August
Kerr accompanied Lloyd George to Criccieth where, with Addison,
Sir Henry Norman and the Deputy Whip, Dudley Ward,[109] the
Prime Minister planned his campaign to renew the coalition. A wartime election was expected, the first stage to be a speech at Manchester in September in which Lloyd George would rally support for
a new coalition government to finish the war on the proper terms
and supervise reconstruction.[110] It was important, as Guest observed,
that the tone of the campaign should be 'sufficiently spiritual' to
avoid the charge that Lloyd George was making a personal bid for
power.[111] Kerr's speech notes emphasised the need to fight the war to
victory to secure 'a change of heart in Germany' and a proper
foundation for the League of Nations.[112] On domestic matters he
emphasised the nation's health, which had been much discussed at
Criccieth, but concerned himself even more with the perils of
Bolshevism, the dangerous implications of the Metropolitan Police
strike of late August, and the 'shibboleth of class'. His notes for the

election campaign itself gave equal weight to the international question and to the ghosts of domestic strife called up by the war. On the League of Nations he noted that people were not interested in detail, only in knowing that Lloyd George, with the help of America, France, and Italy, was going to 'make another war impossible'.[113] He suggested explaining why it was necessary to try the Kaiser, to abolish conscript armies, and to treat colonial possessions with justice and responsibility.[114] At home he suggested references to new conditions of life, national unity, and a reconciliation between capital and labour not imposed by the state. It was, once again, the doctrine of a change of heart,[115] in Europe and in industry.

These items, with the notorious addition of a harsh policy against the defeated enemy, were present in Lloyd George's election speeches and reflected the Criccieth discussions in which Kerr had taken part. Far more than in his war-aims speeches, Lloyd George used in his election speeches the large issues of principles which Kerr recommended to his attention. While others were no less disposed to think of the election as an attempt to prevent the Labour party from taking full advantage of wartime conditions, Kerr was quite explicit in relating the election campaign to the lessons of the war. Writing to Lloyd George from a post-Armistice holiday, he urged him to:

expose without fear or favour what the Labour machine really consists of, i.e. the men who were against the war, who have from the first day hindered the output of munitions, who have always been for fraternisation with the enemy and a compromise peace, and who are now really Bolsheviks and doing all they can to condemn this country to class hatred and social strife, inevitably ending in Bolshevist ruin.[116]

This analysis of future peril had arisen quite as directly from Kerr's work on foreign affairs as had his positive recommendations for a League of Nations and a proper colonial settlement. It can be traced to his disillusionment with the achievements of Russian democracy in 1917, and it embodies themes which first appeared in his comments on Henderson's resignation and on the Lansdowne letter. The election campaign, rather than any consideration of the diplomatic future, must be regarded as the culmination of his two wartime years of work for Lloyd George and the development of thought which preceded them. After July 1917 he never flagged in his insistence that the Empire was threatened from within as well as from without. So long as the war continued his moral preoccupations were played down in his master's speeches, which were acts of policy and therefore drew on wider sources of advice. In the frankly political speeches of the election campaign the extent to which his analysis of domestic and foreign events reflected a conventional wisdom within Lloyd George's circle can clearly be seen.

III

Kerr's analyses of the progress of the war were part of a discussion which was internal to Downing Street and sometimes, when the Prime Minister did not respond, internal to himself. It is illuminating because it puts into words and arguments the interpretation of events current in Lloyd George's entourage. It is complemented by the contribution of the Secretariat to a wider discussion carried on in the press and among public men. Lloyd George used William Sutherland, one of his ordinary private secretaries, to manipulate the press from day to day. Sutherland's egregious reputation for rumbustious intriguing only served to confirm Lloyd George's own doubtful character in the minds of those who did not or could not compete in the same race for popularity. Although but few instances of his methods are documented, the occasion in May 1917 when he altered a communiqué signed by Addison and the leaders of the Amalgamated Society of Engineers to give the impression that Lloyd George had settled the engineers' strike single-handed is so completely documented that it is impossible to dismiss the allegations of Conservative politicians that Sutherland regularly, and crudely, manipulated the public account of events to enhance Lloyd George's personal popularity.[117] The Garden Suburb had more elevated methods. Although Sutherland was universally condemned, the maintenance of some sort of relationship with the press was recognised as part of political and public life. Even the rather strait-laced Hankey recorded without obvious embarrassment in his diary that he 'was commissioned to turn Sutherland on to get the press right in this matter, which I did with good results'.[118] In wartime, when the secure position of the government could be thought of as a military asset in itself, cultivation of the press could have a non-partisan respectability; and it was in an ostensibly non-partisan spirit that the Garden Suburb met the press.

There were ambiguities in the position taken by the Secretariat towards public relations. In a laboured and ambivalent defence of Lloyd George's attitude to the press in 1918, a Liberal M.P. remarked that 'it is said...he has encouraged, if not inspired, such raking and harrowing of the ground he intended to plough as has

given the effect of special and unfair advantage in the use of government secrets to private organizations. . .'[119] Leaving aside the issue
of commercial competition between newspapers, it cannot be denied
that in briefing the press and in his own writing Kerr sometimes
raked and harrowed the ground which Lloyd George might plough,
giving information and guidance on subjects which were still under
discussion in government. As early as March 1917 he was passing
hints to an American journalist about the likely attitude of Britain
at the peace conference; this information was published in the
United States, but only after being passed back to the White
House.[120] In his article on 'The Irish Crisis' he went further, arguing
strongly in an otherwise largely historical article for the position
which Lloyd George, in May and June of 1918, was defending in a
divided government.[121] It is far from clear that these interventions
had much effect in altering the political situation: *The Round Table*
was an esoteric publication, and the American public did not keep
Lloyd George in power. Kerr, who claimed to dislike 'doctoring'
the news,[122] was perhaps writing partly for his own benefit, elaborating the truth in an attempt to understand it.

The case of the War Cabinet Reports is more clear-cut. The
Report for 1917 originated in the calculations of Christopher
Addison, who feared in October 1917 that pro-Coalition Liberals
were losing support in the country. Believing that there was no
argument like success, he suggested to Lloyd George and Guest that
a record of the government's achievements would redress the situation: the form of the record was then discussed by Lloyd George,
Addison, Milner and Kerr. The report was to be a counter-attack
against Asquith and the right wing of the Conservative party,
whom Addison suspected of destructive intrigues. It was therefore to
concentrate on questions on which Asquith's administration had had
a poor reputation, such as food supply and the use of shipping.[123]
Addison wanted the report available by the end of October, but the
project was conceived on such a scale that it did not appear until the
new year. Adams, Kerr and Cecil Harmsworth took charge. Every
department was asked to submit an account of its principal achievements during the year, and the editors synthesised the contributions.
Even the table of contents says much about the issues deemed important by Addison and the secretaries: after discussion of military,
naval, foreign and imperial events, separate chapters were devoted
to national service, industrial relations, transport, import restrictions,
the control of industry, food production and control, welfare, and

reconstruction. The departmental material in these chapters was supplemented by twenty pages of introductory matter by Adams and Kerr; but their editorial control is evident also in the decision to give 29 pages to food and 26 to the control of industry, making those the most substantial chapters.

The introduction opened with a bold statement on the 'Significance of 1917', which was that the character of the war had been altered by submarine warfare and the Russian revolution, together with the entry of the United States and other neutrals such as Greece, Brazil, and China, from

...a battle for the liberty of small nations and the defence of public right in Europe into a world-wide struggle for the triumph of a free civilisation and democratic government. Though the cause of popular government received a set-back towards the end of the year owing to the disorganisation and anarchy which prevailed in the Russian Republic, this new character of the war was clearly brought out in the speeches of the Allied statesmen in the first days of the new year.[124]

The editors stressed inter-Allied co-operation and the development of imperial relations, and explained the superiority of the new administrative institutions. Then they recounted their view of the most important problems of 1917. First came manpower and munitions, then the submarine campaign. The measures taken were reviewed: naval counter-measures, the Ministry of Shipping, increased shipbuilding, restriction of imports, increased home production of food, timber and ores, and the control of consumption. Then a somewhat brief account of military achievements was followed by reflections on the long-term effects of war. These remarks are of critical interest. They were approved by the War Cabinet for publication, and they must therefore represent to some degree the self-image of the coalition; they are also clearly related to the previous writings of the editors.

The consequences of the war were presented under four heads. The first, National Organisation, is perhaps the most striking:

In the first place, the organic life of the community has been greatly strengthened...not only have enormous numbers of men, and latterly of women also, been mobilised for military and naval purposes, but the vast majority of the people are now working directly or indirectly on the public service.[125]

The paragraph continued in a sustained encomium of state intervention, concluding:

Taking the year as a whole the Administration has been brought into far
closer contact with every aspect of the life of the people, the provinces and
the metropolis have been linked more closely together, and the whole
community has received an education in the problems of practical democracy such as it has never done before.[126]

This remarkable synthesis of the views of Adams, in his chapter on
Public Administration for the *Oxford Survey of the British Empire*,
and of Kerr and Milner in their shared views on the role of the state
could scarcely be matched. Next the editors turn their attention to
'the industrial problem': state control of profits and labour conditions, the suspension of trade-union regulations as testimony of the
workers' willingness to work for the common good, and the institution of Whitley Councils are all praised. Then, presumably at
Adams's insistence, 'agriculture has been restored to its proper
position in the national economy'.[127] Other matters of significance
for the future are noted: Montagu's India Declaration, the appointment of the Irish Convention and the Joint Committee on the
Second Chamber, the Education Bill, the Ministry of Pensions, the
Ministry of Reconstruction. Then, in a final paragraph, Kerr and
Adams ride their hobby-horses in turn:

Looked at as a whole 1917 has been a remarkable year. During it the war
has assumed more and more the character of a struggle on the part of all
the free nations for the final destruction of militarism and the establishment
of an international order which will give real securities for liberty and
public right throughout the world. The nations of which the British
Commonwealth is composed have been drawn together in their joint effort
for the common cause. And within the United Kingdom there has been a
growth in the sense of public service and of the power to improve and
adapt economic and social and administrative methods which will make it
far easier to build up a healthier and more equitably organised society in
future. This record, indeed, shows that the British peoples have good
reason for confidence that the spirit in which they have set themselves to
deal with the problems of the past three years will enable them to master
successfully the still greater problems which lie ahead.[128]

It is noteworthy that almost all the subjects touched upon in the
introduction had been investigated during the year by the Garden
Suburb: a reflection both on the document's authorship and on the
central position occupied by the Secretariat. In administration and
in ideology the secretaries had come to occupy a central position in
the coalition.

By comparison the Report for 1918 was a pedestrian document.
Since it was published in 1919, after the war and the election had

been won, the cutting edge of political partisanship was absent: the introduction was modelled closely on the introduction of the previous report, except that it reported the achievement of what had been foreshadowed. Notes for the future were avoided.[129] It is in the 1917 Report that one can see the apotheosis, at book-length, of the political culture of 10 Downing Street in the latter years of the war.

8

Two malcontents

Adams, Kerr, Harmsworth and Joseph Davies, who have all figured prominently in earlier chapters, maintained for two years the conviction that the work of the Garden Suburb was worth doing. This opinion was not shared by Waldorf Astor and David Davies, who were disgruntled because their expectations for the Prime Minister's Secretariat were not fulfilled. Both men imagined that a post in Downing Street would give them entry into the highest circles of government, where the authority of the Prime Minister, whom they expected to supply with ideas, would crush obstacles to the march of righteousness. Davies hoped thus to spur the military authorities to greater efforts in new directions, and Astor to nationalise the liquor trade. It proved beyond the power of the whole War Cabinet, let alone David Davies, to deflect the military authorities from their course, and the liquor trade remained safely in private hands. The two secretaries decided almost simultaneously in June 1917 that the Garden Suburb was worth nothing if it was not a lever to accomplish tangible change, and made moves to resign. Davies, less tactful and more energetic, was immediately successful; Astor lingered unhappily in Downing Street for a further year. The contrast between what they wanted and what they found is illuminating. While others found satisfaction and purpose in improving the quality of decisions by keeping Lloyd George informed, and in shaping to some degree the body of ideas from which he derived his thinking on current and future policy, Astor and Davies demanded attention to their views on specific decisions. Service in the Secretariat was for them a substitute for office, and they behaved like junior ministers who were entitled, indeed almost obliged, to resign if their deliberate advice were ignored.

Though self-righteous, this attitude to the Garden Suburb was not altogether unreasonable. Both were comparatively young men who had inherited wealth and its concomitant power, and who perhaps expected too easy a passage in political life. But in 1916 others, without advantage of age or longer parliamentary service, were receiving promotion. Both Astor and Davies were entitled to think that they had been longer on the winning side than many who were carrying off the spoils of victory. Furthermore, both had ideas about war or reconstruction policy which, in their own minds, enhanced their value to the new government. In the event they were denied promotion by deficits in their characters, attainments, or political careers about which they could not be expected to agree with those who blackballed them. It was implicit that invitations to join the Garden Suburb were a substitute for the Parliamentary Secretaryships which Lloyd George was unable to offer; men of political ambition would expect the appointments to give comparable scope for action. For the others the job had a different significance. Adams and Kerr were outside the political career, and Joseph Davies had not yet entered parliament; Harmsworth had preferred the Garden Suburb to the position of Chief Whip. They could accept different constraints, and it was their interpretation of the purpose of the Garden Suburb which contributed most to its constructive work. Astor and Davies, ironically, shared with the Secretariat's detractors a distorted view of the influence conferred by service in Downing Street, and came to grief while trying to exercise this imaginary power.

II

Astor's principal interest during his service in Downing Street was the Drink Question. Since its establishment in June 1915 he had been an enthusiastic member of the Central Control Board (Liquor Traffic), which had powers under the Defence of the Realm Acts to regulate the strength and price of liquor, to limit drinking hours and close superfluous public houses, and to take the whole licensed trade under control in areas where it was thought necessary.[1] The original justification for the Board and its powers had been to curb excessive drinking among munition workers and servicemen, and its limitations of hours, strength and price were applied only in munitions and troop transport areas. By late 1916 it had extended the restrictions to the greater part of the country and seen a substantial reduction in reported drunkenness, absenteeism, and inefficiency. As shipping difficulties and the bad harvest of 1916 came to threaten food supplies, more importance was attached to reducing consumption in order to conserve raw materials. To achieve reductions equitably with the minimum of unrest the Board decided that the licensed trade would have to be nationalised, a scheme which had been suggested in 1915 but abandoned in favour of control through the Board. When first suggested, nationalisation, called State Purchase, had stirred up an extravagant row. While some temperance organisations had welcomed it, a vociferous section of the movement condemned state participation in a sinful trade; the brewery interests were persuaded to accept it by generous terms, while a strong movement on the Conservative back bench, the traditional defender of Trade interests, thwarted it partly on principle and partly to embarrass the Conservative front bench by provoking a conflict with the government. After causing the maximum of trouble, the proposal was abandoned in the last stormy weeks of the Liberal government and Lloyd George, who had instigated it, passed on to other interests. Agitation for and against State Purchase had regained strength in 1916, and the stage was set for a repetition, in somewhat different political circumstances, of a controversy which senior politicians could remember only with discomfort.[2] Astor, a temperance reformer by conviction, a total abstainer himself, and an advocate of prohibition by local option, was anxious to play an effective supporting part.

On 20 December 1916 the War Cabinet decided to restrict the supply of brewers' materials as part of the food programme;[3] the Liquor Control Board urged that State Purchase was the only safe way of doing so.[4] On 12 January the War Cabinet sidestepped the proposal on the grounds that 'more urgent measures' for restriction had to be settled first, and ordered that brewing should be limited to 50 per cent of the 1915 figure.[5] The Board responded that without the degree of state control which only Purchase could achieve, such a reduction would cause 'hardly less irritation than a policy of total prohibition'; the chairman, Lord D'Abernon,[6] submitted a scheme for reducing demand by doubling the beer tax which he offered as an effective preliminary to Purchase.[7] On 23 January the Food Controller's detailed proposals for reductions in supply were accepted and the tax proposals taken under consideration, but the question of Purchase was once again postponed.[8] The Control Board was by now impatient with the War Cabinet's procrastination and Astor tried, without recorded success, to arrange an interview with Lloyd George for three of his fellow members.[9] The War Cabinet was eventually forced to act by parliamentary pressure, and on 14 February Sir George Cave, the Home Secretary,[10] was appointed chairman of a committee to investigate the financial impact on the trade of further restrictions of output. He was authorised to announce in the commons that the government was 'keeping the question of nationalisation of liquor before them'.[11] Meanwhile the beer output for 1917 was fixed at 10 million standard barrels, rather more than the 50 per cent of 1915 production previously suggested.[12] Another administrative and political controversy was set in motion, which was to last until Purchase was finally shelved in June 1917.

Astor, who represented Lloyd George on the Cave committee, now began to intervene directly with the Prime Minister. He followed the Control Board's December policy statement in arguing that:

A reduction of beer to 10,000,000 standard barrels would in fact mean practical prohibition for certain sections of the community. The Government may find that they have aroused almost as much ill-feeling and discontent as if they had introduced total prohibition without any of the advantages of the latter policy.

After making that point, however, he broke away from the Board's recommendations, and instead of rejecting prohibition as a political impossibility seemed rather to welcome it as a bold and practical act of statesmanship. Some of the advantages he claimed for it were practical ones described in figures: 200,000 men and women employed in the trade could go into factories; 300,000 tons of malt could be fed to pigs; more than 300,000 tons of fuel could be used in other industries; rolling stock and shipping could be saved in large quantities. He also suggested redistilling all the spirits in bonded warehouses for use as munitions alcohol, thus saving 27,000 tons of shipping every month. Other advantages of prohibition were more spiritual:

Drink is a recognised factor in increasing sexual desire and in leading persons into trouble. Were alcohol prohibited, morality would increase...

He concluded by remarking that if total prohibition were imposed other luxuries would more easily be restricted, and neutrals would be convinced that England was indeed a righteous and determined nation.

Only two real arguments can be brought against complete prohibition, namely finance and public opposition. The experience of the Board of Control (Liquor) is that the people will make any response or sacrifice, provided that the appeal is made to them on the highest grounds. The loss of revenue is, at a time like this and with present issues, comparatively insignificant.[13]

Astor was brought round to State Purchase by the work of the Cave committee, which reported on 21 March that the brewers were prepared to accept a reduction of output of beer with a corresponding reduction of the sale of spirits. The committee, which had had some difficulty with the brewers because of uncertainties about Purchase, urged that a decision about it should be made quickly to clear the air, and an investigation of financial details begun immediately.[14] Pressure from Conservatives in the government, responding to powerful brewing interests which positively wanted to be bought out by the state, brought about a War Cabinet decision in favour of the principle on 27 March, and Milner was delegated to prepare a draft bill.[15] Astor, who did much of the detailed work on Milner's behalf, seized his opportunity. He had already canvassed some constituents and received favourable replies,[16] and tendentiously drafted a letter for Lloyd George to send to Joseph Rowntree, a veteran campaigner for public control of the liquor trade:

You know I am a strong advocate of State Purchase. We missed a great opportunity in May 1915 of putting it through, but I do not despair even now of accomplishing something on these lines.[17]

Astor soon turned his confidential memorandum to Lloyd George, arguing for total prohibition, into a circulated Cabinet paper using substantially the same arguments to justify State Purchase.[18] In a separate paper he attacked a Ministry of Munitions committee which had dismissed the possibility of recovering munitions alcohol from potable spirits,[19] and in a final gesture he circulated a report of a conversation with Herbert Hoover, the American Food Controller, who warned that American opinion would not stand for the manufacture of beer and whisky from American grain.[20]

The draft bill was presented to the War Cabinet by Milner on 4 May.[21] He was keen to get on, arguing in a supporting memorandum that 'the trouble over this question cannot be avoided and delay in taking it seems certain to render the trouble worse'.[22] The reluctance of other members of the War Cabinet was overcome by 7 May, but the next day Lloyd George, on his return from a conference abroad, expressed doubts about the parliamentary difficulties of a Purchase scheme, and Milner was asked, while these were investigated, to work out a scheme of temporary control.[23]

Although a firm decision had not been taken, a meeting was

arranged for 11 May between representative brewers on the one side and Lloyd George, Milner and Henderson, with Astor in attendance, on the other. Lloyd George's presentation of the government's position injected the germ of confusion into an already complicated situation. The brewers came away with the impression that the government was not determined on Purchase, but was still considering a temporary assumption of control without full compensation, and a campaign of agitation was begun against the government's proposals.[24] It took two further meetings, on 17 and 25 May, for Milner to persuade the brewers that Lloyd George had meant to say that, precisely because the cost of compensation for temporary control was high, and because the temperance movement would oppose it, it was necessary to choose instead the expedient of Purchase.[25] Meanwhile Lloyd George tried to convince temperance groups that State Purchase was a social reform.[26] On the strength of Milner's report of the terms he had negotiated with the brewers, the War Cabinet on 31 May decided to take immediate control of the Trade after the Second Reading of a two-clause bill providing in principle for the appropriation of funds, and appointed three committees to work out the financial terms of Purchase.[27] At that point there seemed nothing to prevent State Purchase becoming law.

At this late stage the policy was suddenly diverted. Reports from farming and munitions areas in early June began to suggest that any shortage of beer would cause unrest and gravely threaten production. On 19 June, in three separate memoranda, Milner, the Control Board, and the Ministry of Munitions asked the War Cabinet for a decision requiring the brewers to dilute their beer.[28] In Lloyd George's absence the War Cabinet accepted the advice of the Board that immediate control was the only way to enforce dilution. It was decided to take over the trade immediately, and Milner was asked to present his bill at the next meeting, on 21 June.[29] The meeting took place in Bonar Law's room in the house of commons. Lloyd George took the chair and suggested an alternative means of increasing the available supply of beer: to allow the brewers to increase their standard barrelage by one third during the summer months, and to require a slight measure of dilution. He then persuaded his astonished colleagues that full control was not a necessary condition of dilution, nor of a constructive liquor policy. The scheme of control preparatory to Purchase, which had been occupying so much of Astor's and Milner's time, would therefore not be proceeded with. The minutes record his argument that:

While this increase would be opposed by the Temperance party, the Parliamentary position was unfavourable to the introduction of a Bill embodying the policy of control and purchase and members of the War Cabinet were also preoccupied with urgent questions of war policy.[30]

Many years later Astor recalled with bitter regret that 'Milner was taken completely by surprise and put up no fight.'[31] Although the policy of State Purchase was not formally abandoned, the War Cabinet's decision condemned it to death. Dilution and the release of more raw materials for brewing demonstrably solved the immediate problem, and when the three committees on financial terms reported in May 1918[32] the sense of emergency, which had almost carried Purchase to success in 1917, had largely dissipated. State Purchase of the liquor trade had missed the tide.

Those who knew of Astor's work recognised it as a personal defeat for him. Milner, who grasped the significance of the hesitation, wrote in sympathy on 22 June:

I must send you one word of sincere regret for the breakdown of our Liquor Policy. Of course we shall have infinite trouble about Liquor yet, but the fatal swerve of Thursday evening has, I fear, made it impossible to take the one straight road wh. would have got us out of these difficulties, besides opening up a prospect of an almost immeasurable social reform.

I feel it is particularly hard on you after all the splendid work you have done to keep us in the straight path. I wish you had a better backer in the Cabinet. I have given all the strength I could spare to the business but it was not sufficient. . .I am afraid I think that the Prime Minister never really meant to face the music, and Bonar was glad of any chance of 'running out'.[33]

Though Astor felt betrayed by Lloyd George, there is much to suggest that he had gravely misunderstood the liquor problem and had therefore given advice which deserved to be rejected. His support of prohibition in February 1917 suggests no more than a lack of political sense; his outspoken attack on the committee on the re-distillation of potable spirits was less excusable, since he had not troubled to discover that whisky distillation would in any case have to continue in order to preserve the yeast supply.[34] On the central question of State Purchase neither he nor Milner seems to have understood what would win the brewers' consent. To many brewers State Purchase was preferable to a scheme of control for the duration of the war. What they feared most was an extension of restrictions which would ruin their businesses and leave them at the end of the war in full possession of badly damaged assets. Apparently because of Lloyd George's ambiguous remarks on 11 May, many did not trust the

government to buy them out at the end of the war if it took immediate
control without Purchase. They therefore insisted on generous
terms of compensation for wartime loss of business, and a new
system of regulation, more responsive to their wishes, to replace the
Central Control Board. Although the terms, which Milner accepted
in the belief that they were necessary conditions for the brewers'
consent to Purchase, were so costly to the government that D'Abernon
could describe them as a 'frame-up',[35] they did not meet the brewers'
essential demand for certainty.[36] Consequently the policy which
Milner presented to the War Cabinet on 21 June was unattractive to
both sides, and it was easy for leading brewers who lobbied Lloyd
George, such as Sir George Younger and John Gretton,[37] to argue
that the government should meet the immediate problem in an
entirely different way by allowing an increase of production and
postponing control and Purchase *sine die*. Not apparently realising
this, Astor in his later reflections preferred a simple conspiracy
theory: 'L.G. I think had some private talks with George Younger
and Gretton – Dirty work was done behind our backs.'[38] Astor's
relations with the Prime Minister never fully recovered from this
blow, though he forbore from resignation on Milner's advice.[39] The
rest of his service in the Garden Suburb was fruitless and unhappy.

III

The same episode was the occasion for David Davies's resignation,
not because he was personally committed to State Purchase but
because he deplored the apparent swerve from rectitude and chose
to express his displeasure in strong terms. Davies was the most para-
doxical character to find himself in the Garden Suburb. Those who
knew him saw him as a passionate idealist, somewhat egotistical but
essentially a good man. Others, amongst whom were numbered many
of the people who met him in the course of government business,
thought him a schemer and an ambitious troublemaker. The two
sides of his character would easily be reconciled if it were assumed
that he was a political innocent, but that would be to contradict
evidence of his shrewdness in assessing political conditions at home
and abroad. His tactlessness was obvious to all, but it is not a
sufficient explanation of his misfortunes or his dismissal from the
Garden Suburb.

Although his ambitions had played a large part in the establishment of the Secretariat, the new organisation gave him little satis-

faction from the first. Thomas Jones remarked on his mood on 2 January 1917, the day after Lloyd George had approved a scheme of organisation for the new body:

I spoke to D.D. He was not very enthusiastic, but now that his fate for a time is settled he'll be more willing. It has been rather a job handling him since L.G. went to No. 10 and the 'breakfasts' dropped. He fancies himself as something of a strategist and pours in letters and memos to the chief. I have begged him to write nothing for a month...[40]

Davies had formal responsibility for liaison with military departments on matters of supply and, technically speaking, on matters of strategy, as well as responsibility for pensions with all relevant departments. He tried at first to interpret these duties widely. On 15 January he reported to Lloyd George that Northcliffe and Rothermere wanted Sir Henry Wilson to replace Robertson as C.I.G.S.[41] At much the same time he had some conversation with Wilson himself on 17 January, as a result of which he was diverted into the Russian expedition described above.[42] He returned from Russia to find that his circumstances were unlikely to improve. Jones found him chafing at the futility of his employment.

I can *feel* he is rarely free from thoughts of the Nursing Home and generally unsettled – wondering e.g. if he could go out with the 'Mission' if the U.S.A. comes in or go out as military attaché to Venizelos etc.[43]

While completing his awkward report on Russian conditions, Davies looked round for ways to help the war effort, but found only trouble. Any affectionate memories of the campaign to unseat Asquith did not soothe Addison's irritation at an attempt to probe the mysteries of the Ministry of Munitions in late March:

Another of the worries has been the mess made by the Prime Minister's secretaries who seem to have as much notion of the way to get information from departments as novices. The latest performance is that of Colonel David Davies in connection with tanks, the sum of whose efforts has been to get Stern and Edgar Jones up against one another, and to give an entire misreading of the facts to the P.M. and not help things one little bit.[44]

On 10 April Davies asked to be allowed to resign if he could not be given a staff appointment in his old rank of Lieutenant Colonel;[45] but the American declaration of war had given him something to think about, and he called on the American military attaché to discuss military co-operation. He then submitted a five-page memorandum to Lord Derby at the War Office, covering the British contribution to the training of the American army and to American munitions production. Derby was not amused, and complained to Lloyd George on 28 April:

I am sorry I must trouble you in a matter which has given me a certain amount of concern. I have received the enclosed from Major David Davies...There is not a single point in the memorandum which has not been considered by myself...I could therefore pass over the letter with a bare acknowledgement were it not for [Davies's final sentence]. Now this shows to my mind that somebody is discussing my business with Colonel Lassiter [the military attaché] and that is an arrangement that I cannot possibly accept...If it is your wish that this document should be taken as a statement from you, I naturally accept it as being the views of the Prime Minister. But if, as I cannot help thinking, reading between the lines, that they are the views of Major David Davies and that he has been in communication with Colonel Lassiter, either he should be put in my place or else he should be requested not to interfere with matters of which he has no knowledge and, as far as I know, no qualification to speak, as that can only end in confusion.

I confess I feel strongly on this matter...[46]

Davies, who had thus destroyed his working relationship with two of the most important departments with which he was engaged, was losing patience both with his job and with the behaviour of Lloyd George and his government. On 17 April his boredom and revulsion had exploded. The occasion was the commons debate on the government's action in prohibiting the foreign circulation of Massingham's journal, *The Nation*, because of hard things said about Haig which had been reprinted in the German press. Massingham himself believed that the Garden Suburb was responsible for the ban, and wrote a powerful lampoon of its presumed discussions.[47] Radical allies of the journal united to attack the government for a blatantly illiberal and self-serving restriction of the freedom of the press. Lloyd George defended himself by throwing the blame on Lord Derby, and defended the decision by playing on the jingoism of the commons.[48] Davies met him after the speech and, when asked his opinion of the performance, replied, 'A very fine speech on a very bad case.' Lloyd George told him to 'go to hell', and Davies went instead to complain to Thomas Jones.[49] It emerged from his conversation with Jones that far more than the *Nation* episode, bad as that was, was at issue between Davies and Lloyd George.

Poor D.D. has been restless for days, because he feels he has no definite job and is not pulling his weight...What angers [him] so much is that the P.M. yields constantly to the War Office and defends their stupidities in public instead of letting them know what he thinks of them...D.D. came to my room this morning about twenty to nine dressed and about to go off to

No. 10 with an ultimatum to the P.M. saying he was going to join his regiment in Egypt etc. I told D.D. it was very unfair to fling a letter like that at the P.M. at such a moment...[50]

For the moment Davies accepted this soothing advice, and indeed the close harmony of his views on the Salonika question, described above,[51] with the Prime Minister's inclinations masked the serious decline in their relations. As negotiations with the French government became more and more frustrating, he returned to the government's inadequacies, making explicit criticisms on 27 May of the appointment of Northcliffe as Head of the British Mission in the United States, of Devonport's incompetence as Food Controller, and of the poor state of Lloyd George's relations with the Labour movement. He concluded with a pathetic description of his role in Downing Street:

I know you think I am a harmless sort of lunatic – always grousing and criticising. Well, I shouldn't be much use to you if I didn't – and there are heaps of people to do the other thing – aren't there?...If I cannot truly serve you inside perhaps I may have better opportunities outside.[52]

His opportunity came soon after the unsuccessful mission to Paris which did not persuade the French government to sack General Sarrail.[53] Hearing of the War Cabinet's decision to extend brewing, he sounded a last blast of the trumpet on an offensive chord:

I have seen various people of all colours this week and the impression left on my mind is that the Government stock, and yours in particular, is tumbling...It's no good, my dear Chief, you can't go on fooling the people indefinitely. They take you at your word – if you play them false they will send you to Coventry with Winston. They thought you *were* a man of his word...Making the fullest allowances for all the tremendous difficulties which have beset your path...have you run the straight course?[54]

Though he complained also of Salonika, the brewing decision was reckoned by his acquaintances to have precipitated the letter. By thus 'writing a letter to say he was no better than Asquith'[55] Davies brought his quarrel with Lloyd George to a climax. The next day Lloyd George asked him to resign on the grounds that an attack was being mounted on the government because the Prime Minister was sheltering a healthy young officer.[56] Davies thereupon tendered his resignation, reflecting that '...I have felt for some time that our views on various questions were becoming more and more divergent...'. He warned Lloyd George to stay on the straight path and not to exhaust himself, concluding that although his own time in

Downing Street had been of some service the Prime Minister was unwilling to devolve sufficient responsibility on others. He ended his letter with a moral homily warning against wasting 'the great opportunity of your life by sacrificing these precious gifts [Lloyd George's ideals] on the altar of expediency'.[57]

Davies's dismissal has been attributed to Lloyd George's brutality and to Davies's own more generous defects of character.[58] Neither is an adequate explanation. On Davies's side the decision was not impulsive. He had long been frustrated by the lack of results for his labours, and by the lack of support against the War Office and others. He was not free to speak in the commons. He was disillusioned by the policies of a government on whose honesty and determination he had rested his hopes: Salonika, the *Nation* episode, and the failure of State Purchase had all offended his moral sensibility. On the other hand, Lloyd George had endured for Davies's sake not merely candid criticism, but also the complaints of offended departments. It would be a mistake to infer from the final, intemperate correspondence that levity on either side contributed much to the break. Lloyd George was not altogether unwilling to listen to criticism, but his Secretariat served a different purpose. Davies was not qualified temperamentally to fill a place in the Garden Suburb; nor was the Garden Suburb an appointment to fill his needs.

IV

After the *débâcle* of 21 June Astor spent an unhappy year trying to find other ways to urge his favourite policy on the government. His sustained enthusiasm for State Purchase annoyed D'Abernon, who had turned against the policy in May when he saw how the government would implement it, and by August merely wanted it forgotten. D'Abernon wrote to his wife in June that 'I always said it would not get through the H of C and have kept absolutely clear of it', and in August in exasperation:

Drink returns excellent but a good deal of fighting and intrigue going on. The worst element Waldorf Astor, who is a sentimental, priggish million-aire, dog-stupid with an exaggerated sense of his own importance.[59]

Astor's attempts to move the government were complicated by his relations with Garvin. In early 1917 Astor had tried in vain to prevent Garvin's embarrassing Lloyd George by pressing, in *The Observer*, for the reinstatement of Admiral Lord Fisher and the

inclusion of Churchill in the government.[60] Later, when he wanted
to exercise his opportunities as a newspaper proprietor to put pressure
on the government, he found Garvin recalcitrant again. Returning
from a holiday in Scotland bent on resigning to act independently if
Lloyd George took no action on drink, he was met with a counter-
threat of resignation from Garvin:

> I can only say that by a course so out of proportion in a war like this you
> would wreck your career and your paper on that line. As for me I could
> not possibly follow it...rather than that I would give up the paper made
> almost with my heart's blood.

This was accompanied by a tart reminder that Lloyd George had
taken Astor on to his staff 'under exceptional circumstances and
with great goodwill'.[61] Garvin was probably sincere in his belief that
Astor's resignation was not in the public interest, but he had, in
September when his threat was made, other reasons for displeasure.
The coldness between editor and proprietor arose in part from their
substantial differences over policy, since Garvin was unfaltering in
his support of Lloyd George, and in part from a quarrel over finance
and editorial responsibility. During the autumn the two men
wrangled over salaries and the distribution of liability for excess
profits duty; Astor consulted counsel and complained that he
sensed an 'auction' in Garvin's hints that he could get better terms
elsewhere.[62] Astor found no ready co-operation for his plans.

Lloyd George failed conspicuously to take any initiative about
drink. On 28 September the War Cabinet decided to extend the
increase in brewing sanctioned in June for a further three months.[63]
Astor did not immediately resign, but clearly continued to express
dissatisfaction, for Nancy Astor wrote to Milner asking him to
persuade her husband not to try to leave Lloyd George. At Christmas
he told a constituent that he had almost given up any hope of a
constructive liquor policy.[64] However, the New Year brought an
unexpected opportunity, as it became obvious that shipping shortages
would be very severe. On 1 January Lloyd George suggested to the
War Cabinet that the import of brewers' materials should be restricted in favour of cotton for explosives.[65] Astor saw a chance, and
wrote to Garvin:

> I believe our little friend is again getting interested in beer and barley
> and shipping...*The Observer* policy in the immediate future should be:
> 1. Fair and equal distribution of all alcoholic drinks – i.e. rationing.
> 2. No profiteering...

3. No expensive, wasteful luxury beers. . .
4. Give the people either as a whole or by localities the power of deciding
   themselves whether they will. . .go dry during the war.[66]

This was a bold programme, with the last point in particular taking
up the idea of prohibition by Local Option which had been favoured
in extreme temperance circles before the war. Garvin was in no
mood to be sympathetic, drafting a number of replies which all
mentioned the narrow legalism of Astor's position on the newspaper's
finances. Even the most forthcoming draft was discouraging about
Drink:

> The P.M.'s view I know is that amidst the overwhelming war work and
> anxiety he has not immediate time or fair chance to go into the big
> question, and that until he has time and a fair chance the less said about it
> the better. But your notes, I am glad to think need not conflict with that
> view. We can manage the thing both effectively and considerately.[67]

This was lukewarm at best, and when Astor came up with another
scheme in the middle of the month, a plan to ration each consumer
by tickets for beer interchangeable with bread tickets, both Garvin
and Lloyd George ignored it.[68] Even then he was not discouraged.
On 1 February 1918 he sent the Prime Minister an essay on political
expediency.

> I am sure that looking at it from the lowest motive it would pay you
> politically to get the Drink Question out of the way some time before the
> next election. . .you are now getting the maximum of opposition and the
> minimum of political advantage through the present unsettled drink
> position.[69]

If Astor thought that in appealing to 'the lowest motive' he had
found the secret of successfully influencing Lloyd George, he was
wrong. Nothing happened. Though Astor's essentially moral commitment to the restriction of drinking was unflagging, the prospect
cannot have seemed hopeful.

Meanwhile a storm was blowing up in the commons over the
connection between the government and the newspaper press.
Despite his insignificant role in the editorial management of *The
Observer*, Astor felt that his own position was under attack. He had
been embarrassed when, at the beginning of February, Admiral Sir
Hedworth Meux, M.P.,[70] had criticised him in a speech for using
The Observer on Lloyd George's behalf to mount an attack on
Robertson in preparation for his dismissal from the post of C.I.G.S.
Meux had replied in brief and insulting terms to Astor's letter of
complaint asserting *inter alia* that 'The day you. . .accepted the post

of Parliamentary Secretary to the Prime Minister that same day *The Observer*, your personal property, *ipso facto* ceased to be an independent newspaper.'[71] To make matters worse Robertson, when sent copies of the correspondence, disclosed that he had felt a personal attack in *The Observer*'s attitude to him and had therefore refused an invitation to Astor's house at Cliveden.[72] Astor was considering his reply to Robertson when Austen Chamberlain rebuked the government in the commons for its press connections. During the debate on the Army Estimates in which Robertson's dismissal was a major issue, Chamberlain remarked:

My right hon. Friend and his Government have surrounded themselves quite unnecessarily with an atmosphere of suspicion and distrust because they have allowed themselves to become so intimately associated with these great newspaper proprietors.[73]

Astor was probably alone in numbering himself among the 'great newspaper proprietors': Northcliffe, Beaverbrook and Rothermere were the usual objects of suspicion. But he was deeply affected by the debate and tendered his resignation to Lloyd George on the grounds that his presence in the Garden Suburb was becoming a source of weakness to *The Observer* and to the government. At the same time he sent in an exhortatory memorandum on Drink, which appears to exclude the possibility that disagreement over policy was on this occasion the source of his desire to leave:

I regret leaving you before the Drink business is settled, as I stayed on purposely to finish it when I should have gone out previously if I had merely consulted my personal feeling.[74]

Astor's friends learned of this letter indirectly, and Goulding tried to persuade him that Chamberlain's disapproval was misplaced and that it was the government's duty to choose the best men, whatever their business connections. Since Goulding was not supposed to know of the resignation letter he could not discuss it directly, and he told Garvin that the best hope was that Lloyd George himself would persuade Astor to stay.[75] The Prime Minister was receiving insistent advice from his Chief Whip that he could repel Chamberlain's attack only by standing his ground,[76] and it was probably in response to this calculation that he did indeed persuade the reluctant secretary to carry on. The arrangement was not much to Astor's liking. Apart from his work for the Prime Minister, Astor had long been interested in the project to establish a Ministry of Health, which was making little progress against the obstruction of the Local Government

Board.[77] He supported conscription for Ireland. His position in Downing Street kept him silent in the commons. This situation became untenable when the War Cabinet, in late April, postponed indefinitely its discussion of the reports of the committees on the financial terms of State Purchase.[78] On 6 May Astor wrote his last letter of resignation, making it explicit that policy was the cause.

I wanted to resign some time ago and I still do not want to remain at my present job as the particular policies I was working at are in abeyance and so my utility is very limited...I appreciate however the number of persons who for various reasons are trying to weaken you, and I do not want to help them by any action of mine. If, therefore, you think it inadvisable that I should go at this moment in view of the difficulties ahead, I will continue to carry on for a time, if you see no objection to my acting more in the House, and doing so with a reasonable measure of independence.[79]

Now came a hiatus in Astor's work. He neither wrote memoranda for Lloyd George nor acted independently in the commons for the next two months. The most plausible explanation is that he was fully occupied with the affairs of *The Observer*. In March he had suggested a reconstitution of the newspaper's management which was apparently intended to increase Garvin's income and financial security, while strengthening Astor's grip on the paper's editorial control. One proposal was to set up an editorial 'cabinet' under Astor's chairmanship and including Philip Kerr. Garvin refused, as usual on personal grounds:

As soon as ever I am satisfied that there is no attempt to get me out of the editorship...my whole mind will be given to make working suggestions in the interest of your proposals.[80]

In the interest of good feeling, Astor, somewhat unwisely, offered to get Garvin a knighthood in the newly created Order of the British Empire.[81] Through the medium of Goulding, Garvin stipulated for an honour in one of the older and better known orders such as St Michael and St George, or the Bath.[82] The exchange of letters became more acrimonious. By 21 April Goulding was seriously suggesting that Garvin should join *The Sunday Times*.[83] There is no evidence of a resolution of the dispute, whereas letters survive to indicate that Astor was trying to play a larger part in the editorial direction of the paper.[84] Certainly by July, when an appointment as Parliamentary Secretary in the Ministry of Food became vacant as Clynes was promoted to fill the place of Rhondda, Garvin was keen to see his proprietor kept busy elsewhere. Though Lloyd George was anxious to give Astor the job, it was first necessary to overcome resistance from the same quarter which had blocked Astor's appointment to the Local Government Board in 1916. Walter Long and F. E. Smith thought that Astor was too progressive and had no claim on the Conservative party.[85] Goulding went directly to Bonar Law.

> A.B.L. was most friendly had a gt. talk and I think your man will get the Under Sect. to Clynes.
>
> There is gt. opposition in the Party. F.E. not enthusiastic, so many other men with claim. T. [Lord Edmund Talbot, the Conservative Chief Whip] had told my chief [apparently Bonar Law] that W. would be a most unpopular move – however I think it is all right. Your pal worked the thing today as I knew your wishes about your proprietor.
>
> Burn this.
>
> May the Proprietor absorb his mediocre abilities with Government officials.[86]

A little more effort was needed before the matter was clinched, so Goulding called on Beaverbrook.

> I had a long talk with Max – today at War Council he urged L.G. to appoint W. My chief has already given his consent, but W. Long and all the fossil crowd are out ag. the appointment – another par. will appear in the Express tomorrow – but Max said he would like to have a note under the support par. of today and tomorrow 'due to friendship and admiration for Jim G'.[87]

Thus Astor's friends, who had thought to put him out of the way in Downing Street, helped to make him a junior minister and removed him from the Garden Suburb.

9

Conclusion

...the Secretariat whose special function it was to protect a powerful
Chief from the interference of ordinary politicians, including
Ministers and the heads of public departments. The Chief was thus
saved from frivolous interruptions in his pursuit of far-reaching
designs, and gained in power...by a mysterious aloofness, like
Juggernaut hidden in a secret shrine into which no alien may gaze...

H. W. Massingham, 'All in a Garden Fair'.

I

In their first memorandum for Lloyd George, Adams and Kerr
envisaged that members of the Secretariat would act as intermediaries between the Prime Minister and the departments, write
reports on important matters concerning the departments assigned
to them, and interview people who wished to see the Prime Minister
on departmental business.[1] These specific and limited aims were only
partly fulfilled during the two years of the Garden Suburb's life.
The receipt of regular reports from departments was soon transferred
to Hankey's Secretariat on the grounds that the information was of
interest to many ministers besides Lloyd George.[2] Nevertheless a
regular contact was maintained between some of the secretaries and
their assigned departments, which resulted in the submission of
reports when that was merited: though Harmsworth's reluctance to
comment on the National Service question 'because there was
nothing very material to say'[3] was perhaps extreme in its self-denial.
The quality of contact with departments varied from secretary to
secretary. Adams, Joseph Davies and Harmsworth maintained close
and, for the most part, harmonious relations with their departments.
Kerr dealt infrequently with the Foreign, Colonial or India Offices,
reserving himself for the higher interpretation of the war. Davies
declared war on his assigned departments, commented freely on
matters outside his responsibility, and lost his job in consequence.

One aim of this book has been to show the importance of the regular liaison work performed, or occasionally neglected, by the Garden Suburb. British government in the last years of the war had reached such a state of complexity that even a Prime Minister with Lloyd George's energy and sensitivity could not manage it without an active liaison staff. But to say that the need existed is not to say that it was fulfilled. In 1918 the Machinery of Government Committee, after hearing evidence from Adams and Hankey, felt unable to decide whether the Garden Suburb was adequately organised for its liaison task. After the fuller review which has been possible in this book one can say more, but without reaching a conclusive verdict.

It is important, first, to specify why it was thought that the Prime Minister needed the degree of control over the machinery of government which such a staff might give him. The reason most likely to win public acceptance in 1916 was that without it the pace of war would slacken and that the warmaking machinery, given its head, would do the wrong thing, in the wrong place, at the wrong time. The political debate of the first two years of the war, stimulated by Lloyd George and his political allies of the moment, had thrown up a Platonic ideal of the wartime Prime Minister as an omniscient dictator. Since this had been accompanied by the demand, met in abundance, for more government exercised through bevies of sub-dictators, it was especially necessary to provide the means of omniscience. This was done in the form of the Garden Suburb and the War Cabinet Secretariat. In the event the War Cabinet Secretariat was little more than a clerical organisation. The Garden Suburb, consisting of five junior men without executive responsibility and with only clerks and typists to assist them, could do little to maintain the comprehensive and continuous oversight of government demanded by this presidential concept of war-leadership. One has only to reflect on the staffs maintained in modern times by real presidents to comprehend the difficulty: the Executive Office of the President of the United States has a staff in excess of four thousand, compared with hundreds in 10 Downing Street today and no more than fifty in 1918. What was created instead was the appearance of omniscience, which was enough to infuriate Radical critics of the new government[4] and presumably to please the pro-dictatorship lobby in due proportion. The real task, as seen from Lloyd George's point of view, was to strengthen the Prime Minister's position in an environment which, despite the unusual circumstances of war, was not presidential but subject to the risks of parliamentary politics. Lloyd George's first coalition was far from being impregnable. It could have been over-thrown at any time by a fortuitous combination drawn from Asquithians, extremist Conservatives, Labour members, and the Irish party. All of these groups made special demands of the government as a condition of holding their hand in the commons. A re-markable proportion of the Garden Suburb's time was devoted to politically sensitive administrative questions which touched on the special interests of volatile groups in parliament. The Irish settle-ment, the interests of farmers in the food-production campaign, the energetic prosecution of shipbuilding when it was causing trouble in the commons, National Service and industrial unrest, food supply which immediately affected the constituents of Labour members, all stood to win or lose perceptible degrees of support for the govern-ment. On the other hand much of Kerr's time was spent pursuing, albeit in a naive manner, the hearts and minds of a wider public which in his view maintained the government in power despite the fickleness of an unrepresentative parliament. Lloyd George was, to a peculiar degree, the lynchpin of the government which he led because both he and other politicians felt that he commanded popular support. This support was gained not just by his demagogic talents or his executive energy, but by his capacity to restrain any one group of his supporters from acts of government, whether of omission or commission, which would antagonise the supporters of another group. His ability to do this depended in part on the sort of informa-tion the Garden Suburb provided for him in the course of their reports on the continuing administrative work of the government. In using his Secretariat he was defending not merely his own position in the coalition, but also the coalition's position in parliament and beyond.

The success of the Garden Suburb, measured on this criterion, is rather greater than would appear if it were assumed that it aspired to some ideal of administrative efficiency. Its contribution to admin-istrative efficiency was real enough, although that was incidental to its overriding purpose, but that contribution was confined to weaker, politically vulnerable departments. It is an ironical reflection on the new government that these were predominantly new departments, created in response to the same demand for novelty and energy which had brought Lloyd George to power. The older departments, better accustomed to the conduct of public business and better able to defend themselves from the attention of the Prime Minister's secretaries, were dealt with at arm's length or not at all: Kerr com-

municated with the Foreign Office through the private secretary to
the Secretary of State, the service departments were left alone after
David Davies resigned, and the Home Office, the Office of Works,
and the Local Government Board seem never to have kindled the
Secretariat's interest. The Garden Suburb concerned itself with the
quality of administration in a few areas, and thereby fulfilled a
political function. Even in this effort it was not wholly successful.
The disgruntlement of Astor and David Davies was in large part a
result of their attempt to substitute for the mundane labour of
collecting administrative intelligence a number of functions which
did not so readily fulfil the needs of the hour. The Garden Suburb
was not the keeper of Lloyd George's conscience, even supposing he
had one; nor was it a means for ambitious young men to impose bold
new plans on their obstructive elders. It did not serve Lloyd George's
purpose to be told the gossip of the clubs by David Davies, nor to be
given tendentious information about parliamentary opinion by Astor
when Guest's more acute and detached intelligence was fully engaged
on the same task. It might have helped if they had given more and
better information on munitions supply or industrial unrest, as
Harmsworth tried to do when he stepped into Davies's shoes. As it
was, the Garden Suburb's effort to maintain a high level of communication between Lloyd George and the departments was unsuccessful in large part because some of the secretaries were patently
trying hard to achieve the same sort of political end by doing a
different job.

If members of the Garden Suburb were confused about their role,
it is hardly surprising that their contemporaries outside Downing
Street, as well as historians, should share their confusion. Lloyd
George's ineffable reputation for not being quite a gentleman has
suffused the Secretariat's memory. During his premiership the structure of his entourage was not understood, and the term 'Garden
Suburb' sometimes applied indiscriminately to his other secretaries
and political dependants. In the turmoil of 1922 the very word
'secretary' could arouse hostile editors and back-benchers to un-
differentiated rage, as Hankey found to his chagrin as he tried to
defend the position of the Cabinet Secretariat.[5] Eminent persons
such as Churchill and Henry Wilson criticised the work after the war
of Kerr and his successor Edward Grigg, and it has been but a short
step to conflate this criticism with what is known of Sutherland
'hawking baronetcies in the clubs'[6] into a most unsavoury description of Lloyd George's entourage, and to apply it anachronistically

and without qualification to the Garden Suburb. Later historians, without particular animus against the Secretariat, have described its members as 'denizens of the Garden Suburb'[7] as though it were a political reptile-house, or taken pains to explain, without justification, that it was altogether different from Churchill's Statistical Section.[8] This is unjust to Lloyd George and the Secretariat even when, as in some of the alternative versions, those surrounding Lloyd George are given new brooms and the critics portrayed as mouthpieces of a decaying political caste. The wrath of critics and the praise of sympathisers have been poured on the Garden Suburb because it has been assumed that its influence over the policy of Lloyd George's government was great, or at least disproportionate to the standing of its members, and that its influence was anti-liberal, or imperialist, or malevolent in some other way which is not explained.

A second aim of this book has been to examine those assumptions. It has been shown that the secretaries subscribed between them to a range of views on the present and future condition of government and society and that, in world-view as in the politics of party and faction, the group was fairly eclectic. Any influence it had on policy was exercised through Lloyd George: the notable successes, as, say, on Ireland and shipbuilding, came about because the Prime Minister's energy and authority were exerted in directions which the Secretariat had charted for him. Those occasions arose naturally from the work of administrative intelligence which was its first duty, and outside that sphere there is strikingly little evidence of clandestine policy-making in the Prime Minister's back garden. The two secretaries of whom most might be expected were of course Astor and Kerr; but they chose to work on their most 'Milnerite' schemes with fellow Milnerites or with Milner himself, and without Lloyd George's support they had no success. Instead there is evidence of a different sort of influence, not over policy but over attitudes and language which may constrain policy without determining it. The substance of that influence is on balance surprisingly liberal, humane and optimistic, in contrast to the cynicism attributed to Lloyd George and his circle by Liberal critics or the defensive pessimism emphasised by the historians of social-imperialism. The political culture of the Garden Suburb was the precursor of the Coalition Liberalism whose honour has been convincingly defended by K. O. Morgan.[9] Its tone was harsher, since it was deeply affected by the vicissitudes of war, in particular the difficulties posed by poor labour relations;

but it was not narrowly confined to the struggle against revolution or the adulation of Lloyd George as Prime Minister. It reflected confidence and sincerity in the pursuit of 'progressive' measures at home and abroad.

II

T. P. O'Connor once described the Garden Suburb as Lloyd George's 'kindergarten'. A kindergarten is, or should be, the very first step on the path to great achievements. What, then, became of the secretaries after they left Downing Street? In fact the Garden Suburb was not the nursery of outstanding political careers. Astor's eclipse had been predictable since 1916, when his ailing father accepted a peerage. The son succeeded in 1919, after he had moved from the Ministry of Food to become Parliamentary Under-Secretary at the Ministry of Health. His seat at Plymouth was passed on to his redoubtable wife, Nancy, and after he left office in 1921 he turned his attention to *The Observer*, temperance reform, charitable committees, and, notoriously, Appeasement. In the thirties he wrote extensively on agricultural topics; his only public appointments were as British delegate to the League of Nations Assembly in 1931, and as Lord Mayor of Plymouth from 1939 to 1944. He died in 1952. David Davies, who also had large business and philanthropic interests to occupy him, remained in parliament until 1929. He was active in the League of Nations Association, and took collective security as his subject when he too blossomed as a writer in the thirties. He died in 1944. Joseph Davies, like so many of the new M.P.s in the 1919 House, retired from public life after 1922; he died in 1954. Harmsworth was Under-Secretary of State for Foreign Affairs and acting Minister of Blockade from 1919 to 1922, thus occupying the two posts previously held by Robert Cecil. He also retired from politics in 1922. He wrote a book on fishing and an unrevealing volume entitled *Immortals at First Hand* (1933); he died in 1948. Of the four politicians in the Garden Suburb, Joseph Davies, Harmsworth and Astor took at the end of the war the further steps in their careers which they would in any case have expected if they had not been in the Prime Minister's Secretariat: David Davies's service, or rather the manner of its end, destroyed any hope and probably any ambition he had for political advancement.

Adams and Kerr were in a different situation. Adams returned to the Gladstone Chair of Political Theory and Institutions at Oxford, which he held concurrently with a Fellowship of All Souls. He served on the Royal Commission on the Universities of Oxford and Cambridge and a number of other public and private bodies, most of them concerned with rural development, including the Plunkett Foundation, of which he was a trustee. He was chairman of the National Council of Social Service from 1920 to 1949. In 1933 he was elected Warden of All Souls. He retired in 1945 and died in 1966. The Garden Suburb was an interruption to his academic career, which did not materially change course: he rejected, after some deliberation, the chance of a couponed seat in the commons.[10] Only for Kerr did the Garden Suburb mark a turning point, and it is arguable that his later service for Lloyd George was of more significance than his war service. He continued to serve Lloyd George as a personal adviser after the demise of the Garden Suburb, and was closely associated with his policy at the Paris Peace Conference and over the Graeco-Turkish dispute. In 1921 he retired from Lloyd George's service to become editor of the *Daily Chronicle*, which Lloyd George had acquired in 1918. He was by now a thoroughgoing apologist for Coalition Liberalism, although he left the *Chronicle* after less than a year for personal reasons. He tried to maintain a central position amidst the shifting political tides of the twenties, and served briefly in the National Government in 1931 as Under-Secretary at the India Office, despite his very close association with Lloyd George in the late twenties over the new policies of the Liberal party. He had been deeply affected by the mistakes of the Paris Peace Conference, to which he thought he had contributed, and for that reason he worked hard during the thirties to maintain Anglo-German relations. He was appointed Ambassador to Washington in 1939, and died in post in 1940. Kerr's biographer has observed that he was one of the few men to work closely with Lloyd George without quarrelling with his master. Neither Harmsworth nor Joseph Davies appears to have left any unequivocal statement of their opinions about Lloyd George after they left Downing Street:[11] but the other secretaries appear to have been sorely tried by the experience. Astor complained in 1918 that Lloyd George often acted 'in a way which showed that he had never been at public school';[12] David Davies by the autumn of 1918 was working in the Asquithian interest;[13] and even Adams, after thirty years, remembered his service in Downing Street as a period of frustration.[14]

III

In its passing the Garden Suburb was not greatly mourned, even by
its members. In his evidence to the Ministry of Reconstruction's
Machinery of Government Committee Adams suggested that a reorganised Prime Minister's department, including the Whips, should
be incorporated as a section of the Cabinet Secretariat, to comple-
ment the clerical and record-keeping work then being carried out by
Hankey's Secretariat. Adams was convinced of the need for an
administrative intelligence organisation as a permanent and integral
part of government.[15] Not so Hankey, who gave his views in the same
meeting of the committee, on 8 March 1918. At the end of para-
graphs of fulsome praise for the War Cabinet system, and particularly its Secretariat, Hankey remarked that:

> he regarded this organisation as entirely distinct from the personal
> secretariat attached to the Prime Minister of the day. He regarded the
> latter staff as members of the private staff of the Prime Minister, and while
> he was personally in favour of the existence of such an office, he thought
> that its size and organization must depend entirely upon the personal view
> of the Prime Minister. The War Cabinet Secretariat, on the other hand,
> might, in his opinion, be properly called either the Prime Minister's
> Department or the Cabinet Department.[16]

Hankey was always anxious to avoid, or at least to deny, any extension of the functions of the War Cabinet Secretariat into giving
advice or collecting administrative intelligence. He told the committee pointedly that he did not envisage that the Cabinet Secretariat
would be responsible for giving advice; and there is little evidence of
co-operation between the War Cabinet Secretariat and the Garden
Suburb during the war, except when Hankey and Kerr worked
together on the Caxton Hall speech.[17] It is therefore not surprising
that Hankey did nothing to encourage the migration of men or of
functions from the Garden Suburb to the Cabinet Secretariat at the
end of the war. In chapter 1 it was explained how the desire for war
work contributed to the establishment of the Garden Suburb. With
that motive no longer operating, and without encouragement either
from outside or from Lloyd George himself, there was no reason for
the private Secretariat to the Prime Minister to survive when all but
one of its members left Downing Street.

   This account of the origin and working of Lloyd George's
Secretariat can well be concluded with an extract from a memorandum by Haldane, in which he discussed the evidence given by

Hankey and Adams. It is a statement of an ideal, the reality of which has been discussed in this book: but it would be difficult to improve on his analysis of the place of the Prime Minister's Secretariat in the scheme of British Government in the last years of the Great War.

A Prime Minister is chosen as the leader of the nation, largely because of his gifts as its spokesman at the moment, and of his power in Parliamentary debate. But he has to shape policy, and to this end requires the most highly skilled assistance if he is not to be a bungler. He must devolve much of his responsibility, excepting as regards broad principles and general super-intendence. But when he does so devolve he must understand, if he is to remain a real leader, not only what he means to do, but what is actually being done for him. Under the present Prime Minister an attempt has been made for the first time to provide a personal staff for the head of govern-ment which will put him in possession of that knowledge. . .it is significant that the attempt to form it has at last been made, and I doubt whether it would have been possible to avoid the attempt. For the business of govern-ment is not only increasing, but, as standards rise, is becoming more intricate and more dependent on prevision of necessary adaptation and change.[18]

Notes

CHAPTER I. ALL IN A GARDEN FAIR

1. Adams and Kerr to Lloyd George. 1 Jan. 1917. House of Lords Record Office, Beaverbrook Collection, Lloyd George Papers [Hereafter L.G.P.] F/74/2/2.
2. Two n.s. memoranda, 29 and 30 Dec. 1916, L.G.P. F/74/2/9. Cf. Joseph Davies, *The Prime Minister's Secretariat*, (Newport, Mon., 1951), pp. 51–7.
3. 'Proposed statement by Professor Adams' (sec. to the Machinery of Government Committee of the Ministry of Reconstruction chaired by Lord Haldane), 7 Mar. 1918, L.G.P. F/74/10/4.
4. G. W. Jones, 'The Prime Minister's Secretaries: Politicians or Administrators?', in *From Politics to Administration*, ed. J. A. G. Griffith (London, 1976); G. W. Jones, 'The Prime Minister's Advisers', *Political Studies*, xxi (1973).
5. G. D. A. Macdougall, 'The Prime Minister's Statistical Section', in *Lessons of the British War Economy*, ed. D. N. Chester (Cambridge, 1951), pp. 58–68; R. F. Harrod, *The Prof* (London, 1959), pp. 179–237; the Earl of Birkenhead, *The Prof in Two Worlds* (London, 1961), pp. 211–68. Documentary sources in Public Record Office, Cabinet Papers [Hereafter CAB] 21/1366, and in the Cherwell Papers in Nuffield College, Oxford.
6. 'Policy Unit in No. 10', letter to *The Times*, 22 Mar. 1978.
7. Frank Stacey, *British Government, 1966–1975* (Oxford, 1975), pp. 89–92; Joe Haines, *The Politics of Power* (London, 1976), *passim*.
8. John Ehrman, *Cabinet Government in War* (Cambridge, 1958).
9. Andrew Bonar Law (1858–1923). M.P. (Cons.) 1900–22. Leader of Conservative party in the commons, 1911–21. Colonial Secretary 1915–16, Chancellor of the Exchequer 1916–18, Lord Privy Seal 1919–21, Prime Minister 1922–3.
   Arthur Henderson (1863–1935). M.P. (Lab.) 1903–35. Chairman of the Parliamentary Labour party, 1908–10, Chief Whip 1914, 1921–4, 1925–7. President of the Board of Education 1915–16, Paymaster General 1916. War Cabinet Dec. 1916–Aug. 1917. Home Secretary 1924, Foreign Secretary 1929–31. Henderson assumed the leadership of the non-pacifist Labour members after a split with Ramsay Macdonald in late 1914.
   Alfred Milner (1854–1925). Civil servant in Egypt 1889–92. Chairman, Board of Inland Revenue, 1892–7 (introduced Death Duties).

High Commissioner in South Africa 1897–1905. War Cabinet Dec. 1916–Apr. 1918. Secretary of State for War Apr. 1918–Jan. 1919, for Colonies Jan. 1919–Feb. 1921. Knighted 1895, Baron 1901, Viscount 1902. George Nathaniel Curzon (1859–1925). M.P. (Cons.) 1886–98. Viceroy for India 1898–1905. Lord Privy Seal 1915–16. War Cabinet 1916–19. Lord President of the Council 1916–19 and 1925. Foreign Secretary 1919–24. Baron (Irish Peerage) 1898, Earl Curzon of Kedleston (English Peerage) 1911, Marquess 1921.

10. Maurice Pascal Alers Hankey (1877–1963). Royal Marine Artillery 1895–1912. Assistant Secretary, Committee of Imperial Defence 1908, Secretary 1912–38. Secretary of War Council Nov. 1914, Dardanelles Committee May 1915, War Committee Dec. 1915, War Cabinet Dec. 1916. Secretary to the Cabinet 1919–38. Minister without Portfolio Sept. 1939–May 1940, Chancellor of the Duchy of Lancaster 1940–1, Paymaster General 1941–2.

    On the establishment of the War Cabinet Secretariat see John F. Naylor, 'The Establishment of the Cabinet Secretariat', *Historical Journal*, xiv (1971).

11. Franklin A. Johnson, *Defence by Committee* (London, 1960); Nicholas D'Ombrain, *War Machinery and High Policy, Defence Administration in Peacetime Britain, 1902–14* (London, 1973).

12. F. M. G. Willson, *The Organization of British Central Government 1914–1964* (2nd edn, London, 1968), pp. 390–413; R. G. S. Brown, *The Administrative Process in Britain* (London, 1971), pp. 191–215.

13. War Cabinet Minutes [Hereafter W.C.] 97, 15 Mar. 1917, CAB 23/2.

14. *Thomas Jones, Whitehall Diary*, ed. Keith Middlemas (3 vols., London, 1969–71), i, 16.

15. John Thomas Davies (1881–1938), a Welsh speaker, became private secretary to Lloyd George in 1912. Director of the Suez Canal Company 1922–38.

    William Sutherland (1880–1949). Clerk at the Board of Trade 1903–14, then Lloyd George's secretary at the Ministry of Munitions. M.P. (Lib.) 1918–22. Chancellor of the Duchy of Lancaster 1920–22.

    Frances Stevenson (1888–1976). Became Lloyd George's mistress and private secretary in 1912, and married him in 1943.

16. The best starting point is the volumes in the Carnegie Series, published by the Oxford University Press.

17. e.g. Arthur Marwick, *The Deluge* (London, 1965).

18. V. H. Rothwell, *British War Aims and Peace Diplomacy* (Oxford, 1971).

19. J. M. Keynes, *The Economic Consequences of the Peace* (London 1919); Trevor Wilson, *The Downfall of the Liberal Party, 1914–1935* (London, 1966); Peter Rowland, *Lloyd George* (London, 1975).

20. Bernard Semmel, *Imperialism and Social Reform* (New York, 1966).

21. R. J. Scally, *The Origins of Lloyd George's Coalition: The Politics of Social Imperialism, 1900 to 1918* (Princeton, 1975).

22. e.g. P. A. Lockwood, 'Milner's Entry into the War Cabinet, December 1916', *Historical Journal* vii (1964); Paul Guinn, *British Strategy and Politics, 1914–1918* (Oxford, 1965), pp. 191–200.

23. See G. R. Searle, *The Quest for National Efficiency* (London, 1971). The Coefficients Club included the Webbs, Bertrand Russell, H. G. Wells and a number of Tariff Reform Conservatives, and met at dinner; the Compatriots Club, on the same model, was confined to Tariff Reformers.
24. Scally, p. 29.
25. Edward Henry Carson (1854–1935). M.P. (Cons.) 1892–1921. Solicitor-General 1900–5, Attorney-General 1915–16. First Lord of the Admiralty Dec. 1916–Jul. 1917. War Cabinet Jul. 1917–Jan. 1918. Carson led the Ulster Unionists in the commons from 1910 to 1921, then left public life to become a Lord of Appeal.
26. *Op. cit.*, note 22.
27. *Op. cit.*, note 10.
28. A. M. Gollin, *Proconsul in Politics: A study of Lord Milner in Opposition and in Power* (London, 1964).
29. For example he conflates the Garden Suburb and the War Cabinet Secretariat into a body he calls 'The Secretariat', hypothesises a body called the 'Brains Trust' which he staffs with Kerr, the Webbs, Haldane, Lionel Curtis (q.v. below) and William Beveridge, all of whom are described as Milnerites (pp. 347–8), and believes that the removal of Carson from the Admiralty in July 1917 and of Addison from the Ministry of Munitions in the same month represented promotion for influential social-imperialists, rather than the neutralisation of incompetents (pp. 360, 366). Like Lockwood he is unaware that Curtis was in India from 1916 to April 1918.
30. Lionel George Curtis (1872–1955). Served with Milner and Selborne in South Africa 1900–9. Beit Lecturer in Colonial History, Oxford University, from 1912. Staff member, British Delegation at the Paris Peace Conference 1919. Secretary, British Delegation at the Irish Treaty Conference 1921. Colonial Office adviser on Ireland 1921–4.

On the Round Table see J. E. Kendle, *The Round Table Movement and Imperial Union* (Toronto, 1975); Walter Nimocks, *Milner's Young Men: the 'Kindergarten' in Edwardian Imperial Affairs* (Durham, N.C., 1968).
31. James Louis Garvin (1868–1947). Editor of *The Observer* 1908–42. Garvin edited the paper under the proprietorship of W. W. Astor, Waldorf Astor, and earlier of Northcliffe, leaving after a dispute with Astor in 1942.
32. Lockwood, *op. cit.*; J. O. Stubbs, 'Lord Milner and patriotic labour', *English Historical Review*, LXXXVII (1972); Roy Douglas, 'The National Democratic Party and the British Workers' League', *Historical Journal*, XV (1972).
33. Bodleian Library, Addison Diary, 1–2 May 1916. Cf. Christopher Addison, *Four and a Half Years* (London, 1934), I, 202 ff.

Christopher Addison (1869–1951), a doctor and anatomy teacher, was M.P. (Lib.) 1910–22, (Lab.) 1929–31 and 1934–5. Minister of Munitions 1916–July 1917, of Reconstruction 1917–19, of Health 1919–21, without Portfolio 1921. Minister of Agriculture 1930–1.

34. S. Inwood, 'The role of the press in English politics during the first world war, with special reference to the period 1914–1916' (Oxford D.Phil. thesis, 1971), p. 326. Alfred George Gardiner (1865–1946) was editor of the *Daily News* 1902–1919, author of numerous works of 'contemporary history', and after the war a consistent critic of Lloyd George.
35. Davies to Addison, 17 May 1916, Addison Papers 4; Addison to Davies, 23 May 1916, *ibid.*
36. Addison to the chairman of the Liquor Control Board, 22 Jun. 1916, Addison Papers 68.
37. Addison Diary, 17 Jul. 1916; Addison, I, 233; Davies to Thomas Jones, 28 Aug. 1916, Thomas Jones, *Whitehall Diary*, I, 1–2.
38. *Lord Riddell's War Diary 1914–1918* (London, 1933), p. 244.
39. Thomas Jones, *Whitehall Diary*, I, 6. Thomas Jones (1870–1955) went to work at 13, later studied for the Calvinistic Methodist ministry, then at University College, Aberystwyth, and Glasgow University. Lecturer in political economy, Glasgow, 1906–9. Professor, Belfast, 1909–11. Secretary, Welsh National Insurance Commission, 1912–16. Deputy secretary, War Cabinet and Cabinet, 1916–30. Secretary, Pilgrim Trust, 1930–45. President, University College, Aberystwyth, 1945–54.
40. James Henry Thomas (1874–1949). M.P. (Lab.) 1910–36. President, Amalgamated Society of Railway Servants, 1910–16, General Secretary, National Union of Railwaymen, 1916–31. Colonial Secretary 1924, Lord Privy Seal 1929–30, Dominions Secretary 1930–5, Colonial Secretary 1935–6.
41. Davies, pp. 9–11; Thomas Jones, *Whitehall Diary*, I, 6.
42. Jones to E. T. Jones, 10 Dec. 1916, National Library of Wales, Thomas Jones Papers Z/1916, p. 61.
43. Davies to Lloyd George, 10 Dec. 1916, L.G.P. F/83/10/1.
    Frederick Edwin Smith (1879–1930). M.P. (Cons.) 1906–19. Solicitor-General 1915, Attorney-General 1916–19. Created Baron Birkenhead 1919. Lord Chancellor 1920–2. Secretary of State for India 1924–8.
    William Wedgwood Benn (1877–1960). M.P. (Lib.) 1906–27, (Lab.) 1928–31, 1937–42. Parliamentary Private Secretary to Reginald McKenna (q.v. below) at Treasury, Board of Trade, and Admiralty. Junior Whip 1910–15. Secretary for India 1929–31, for Air 1945–6. Benn, who was on active service in Egypt, was offered the Chief Whipship, but turned it down after consultation with his political friends. House of Lords Record Office, Stansgate Papers ST/286.
    David Alfred Thomas (1856–1918). M.P. (Lib.) 1888–1910. President of the Local Government Board Dec. 1916–May 1917, Food Controller May 1917–July 1918. Created Baron Rhondda 1916. A wealthy coal-owner.
44. Jones to E. T. Jones, 10 Dec. 1916. Thomas Jones Papers P1/19.
45. Thomas Jones, *Whitehall Diary*, I, 15–16.
46. Information from Professor N. H. Gibbs.
47. David Lloyd George, *The Truth about the Peace Treaties* (London,

1938), p. 263; Robertson to Lloyd George, 16 Dec. 1916, L.G.P. F/44/3/5.
48. Astor to Garvin, 15 Dec. 1916, University of Texas Humanities Research Center, Garvin Papers.
49. William Maxwell Aitken (1879–1964). Canadian financier. M.P. (Cons.) 1910–16. Purchased *Daily Express* in the interests of the Conservative Party, Dec. 1916. Knighted 1911. Created Baron Beaverbrook Jan. 1917. Chancellor of the Duchy of Lancaster and Minister of Information 1918. Minister for Aircraft Production 1940–1, Minister of State 1941, Minister of Supply 1941–2, Lord Privy Seal 1943–5. A close personal and political friend of Bonar Law.
50. Garvin to Lloyd George, 18 Dec. 1916, L.G.P. F/94/1/39.
51. Thomas Jones, i, *Whitehall Diary*, 17–19. Charles Hubert Montgomery (1875–1942). Entered the Foreign Office 1900. Private Secretary to Campbell-Bannerman as Prime Minister 1908.
52. See pp. 2–3 above and note 1.
53. n.d. memo. by Hankey, Thomas Jones Papers B/1/4/12.
54. Jones to E. T. Jones, 11 Jan. 1917, Thomas Jones Papers Z/1917; testimonials *ibid.* W/1/15–18.
55. *The Times*, 15 Jan. 1917.
56. Davies, p. 62.
57. W.C. 39, 19 Jan. 1917, CAB 23/1.
58. Primrose to Lloyd George, 2 Apr. 1917, L.G.P. F/42/11/7. Neil James Archibald Primrose (1882–1917). M.P. (Lib.) 1910–17. Parliamentary Under-Secretary, Foreign Office, 1915–16. Parliamentary Military Secretary to Minister of Munitions 1916. Killed in action 1917.
59. Davies, pp. 31–7.
60. Edward David, 'The Liberal Party Divided, 1916–1918', *Historical Journal* xiii (1970), 515.
61. Runciman to Mrs Runciman, 24 Apr. 1917, University of Newcastle, Runciman Papers WR 303/2.
Walter Runciman (1870–1949). M.P. (Lib.) 1899–1900, 1902–18, 1924–31, (Lib. Nat.) 1931–7. President of the Board of Education 1908–11, Board of Agriculture 1911–14, Board of Trade 1914–16. President of the Board of Trade 1931–7. Lord President of the Council 1938–9. Ship-owner. Staunch Asquithian.
Reginald McKenna (1863–1943). M.P. (Lib.) 1895–1918. President of the Board of Education 1907–8. First Lord of the Admiralty 1908–11. Home Secretary 1911–15. Chancellor of the Exchequer 1915–16. McKenna was on notoriously bad personal terms with Lloyd George. Retired from politics in favour of banking 1919.
62. Addison Diary, 1 May 1917.
63. Harmsworth to Lloyd George, 1 May 1917, L.G.P. F/87/1/1.
64. Harmsworth to Runciman, 10 May 1917, Runciman Papers WR 169.
65. Frederick Edward Guest (1875–1937). Third son of 1st Viscount Wimborne and cousin of W. S. Churchill. M.P. (Lib.) 1911–22, 1923–9. Joined Conservative party 1930. M.P. (Cons.) 1931–7. Treasurer of the Household 1912–15. Patronage Secretary to the Treasury 1917–21. Secretary of State for Air 1921–2.

66. This paragraph is based on *Who Was Who*, the *Balliol College Record*, Adams's obituary in *The Times* (first drafted by Thomas Jones), and information from Miss K. Digby of the Plunkett Foundation.
67. J. E. Kendle, 'The Round Table Movement and "Home Rule All Round" ', *Historical Journal*, XI (1968) 332–3, 337–40, 344–6.
68. Stephen Roskill, *Hankey, Man of Secrets* (London, 1969–74); I, 184.
69. Cf. J. R. M. Butler, *Lord Lothian* (London, 1960).
70. See Michael Astor, *Tribal Feeling* (London, 1963).
71. Gladstone to Campbell-Bannerman, 21 Jan. 1906. British Library, Addit. MSS. 41217 (Campbell-Bannerman Papers).
72. Information in this paragraph is collected from Jones and Davies, *op. cit.*
73. Donald Maclean (1864–1932). M.P. (Lib.) 1906–18, 1919–32. Chairman of Liberal M.P.s 1919–22. Knighted 1917.
74. William Job Collins (1859–1947). M.P. (Lib.) 1906–10, 1917–18. Chairman of the L.C.C. 1897–8. Doctor and medical teacher. Vice-Chancellor of London University 1907–9, 1911–12. Knighted 1902.
75. See Davies, *op. cit.*, for his own account of himself, and Trevor Wilson, *The Downfall of the Liberal Party 1914–1935* (London, 1966), pp. 128–30, for the context of the Derby by-election.
76. William Martin Murphy (1844–1920). Businessman. M.P. (Nat.) 1885–92. Founder and editor of the *Irish Independent* 1905.
77. Harmsworth to Runciman, 10 Dec. 1916, Runciman Papers WR 153.
78. Rothermere to Northcliffe, 29 Jan. 1919, quoted in Reginald Pound and Geoffrey Harmsworth, *Northcliffe* (London, 1959), p. 696.
    Alfred Charles William Harmsworth (1865–1922). Established the Harmsworth publishing empire and owned at one time or another the *Daily Mail*, the *Evening News*, *The Observer*, the *Daily Mirror*, *The Times*, and other publishing ventures. He was created Baronet 1903, Baron Northcliffe 1905, Viscount 1918. He was chairman, British War Mission to the United States, 1917, Director of Propaganda in Enemy Countries 1918.
    Harold Sidney Harmsworth (1868–1940) was a partner in his brother's ventures. He became Baronet 1912, Baron Rothermere 1914. President of the Air Council 1917–18. Viscount 1919. The other brothers were Cecil, Leicester (1870–1937), Hildebrand (1872–1929).

CHAPTER 2. THE NEW BUREAUCRACY

1. Nicholas D'Ombrain, *War Machinery and High Policy, Defence Administration in Peacetime Britain, 1902–14* (London, 1973); Johnson, *Defence by Committee*.
2. W. K. Hancock and M. M. Gowing, *British War Economy* (Cambridge, 1949), pp. 3–40; E. M. H. Lloyd, *Experiments in State Control* (Oxford, 1924); S. J. Hurwitz, *State Intervention in Great Britain* (New York 1949).
3. Cameron Hazlehurst *Politicians at War* (London 1971) *passim*.

4. William Henry Beveridge (1879–1963). Journalist 1902–8. Entered Board of Trade to run Labour Exchanges 1908. Transferred to Ministry of Munitions 1915. Ministry of Food 1917–19. Director of London School of Economics 1919–37, Master of University College, Oxford, 1937–45. Chairman of Interdepartmental Committee on Social Insurance and author of its report, 1941–2. M.P. (Lib.) 1944–5. Knighted 1919, Baron 1946.

5. Hubert Llewellyn Smith (1864–1945). Entered Board of Trade 1893, Permanent Secretary 1907–19. Chief Economic Adviser to the government 1919–27. Knighted 1908.

6. Ulick Fitzgerald Wintour (1877–1947). Chinese Customs Service 1898–1904. Board of Trade, 1904–14. Director of Army Contracts, 1914–17; First Secretary, Ministry of Food, 1917–18. Controller, Stationery Office, 1918–19.

7. 'We are on the look out for a good, strong businessman with some go in him who will be able to push the thing through.' 70 *H.C. Debs.*, 5s, 9 Mar. 1915, 1277.

8. 'Proposed Statement by Professor Adams' (sec. to the Machinery of Government Committee) 7 Mar. 1918, L.G.P. F/79/10/4.

9. Davies, *The Prime Minister's Secretariat*, p. 64.

10. Files in L.G.P. F/79/29, F/74/1.

11. Adams to Lloyd George, 31 Mar. 1917, and related papers, L.G.P. F/79/13/1–4.

12. W.C. 127, 27 Apr. 1917, CAB 23/2; Papers in L.G.P. F/72/12.

13. Hudson Ewbanke Kearley (1865–1934). Wholesale grocer. M.P. (Lib.) 1892–1910. Parliamentary Secretary, Board of Trade, 1905–9. Chairman, Port of London Authority, 1909–25. Food Controller and Chairman, Royal Commission on Sugar Supply, 1916–17. Baronet 1908, Baron 1910, Viscount 1917.

14. 'Wheat Supplies', G. 141, 11 Apr. 1917, CAB 24/3.

15. Joseph Paton Maclay (1869–1951). Shipowner. Minister of Shipping 1916–21. Baronet 1914, Baron 1922.

16. W.C. 118, 15 Apr. 1917, CAB 23/2.

17. Davies, p. 102.

18. n.d. report by Davies, L.G.P. F/71/17.

19. Harry Gosling (1861–1930). Organised Lightermen's Union. Member of L.C.C. 1898–1925. M.P. (Lab.) 1923–30. President, Transport and General Workers' Union 1927–30.

20. Frederick George Dumayne (1852–1930). Vice-chairman of Commissioners, Port of Calcutta, 1901–13. Chairman, Port and Transit Executive Committee, 1915–18.

21. Gosling to Dumayne, 28 Jul. 1917, Ministry of Transport Papers MT 61/3.

22. Port and Transit Executive Committee to Lloyd George, 15 Aug. 1917, *ibid.*

23. Davies, pp. 162–9; correspondence in L.G.P. F/85/5.

24. Report to War Cabinet, G.T. 2281, 13 Oct. 1917, CAB 24/28; W.C. 252, 18 Oct. 1917, CAB 23/5; Minutes of the Port and Transit Executive Committee, 27 Sept., 11 & 25 Oct. 1917, MT 61/3.

25. Lancelot Grey Hugh Smith (1870–1941). Partner in Rowe & Pitman, stockbrokers. Principal delegate, British Mission to Sweden, 1915. Chairman, Tobacco Control Board, 1917–18.
26. Harmsworth to Lloyd George, 26 Sept. 1917, L.G.P. F/88/22/1.
27. Harmsworth to Bonar Law, 28 Nov. 1917, L.G.P. F/88/21/1.
28. Harmsworth to Lloyd George, 4 Dec. 1917, L.G.P. F/88/21/1.
29. Harmsworth to Bonar Law, 11 Jan. 1918, L.G.P. F/88/22/3.
30. G.T. 3988, 19 Mar. 1918, CAB 24/45.
31. G. I. Gay, *Public Relations of the Commission for the Relief of Belgium* (2 vols., Palo Alto, 1929).
32. I have been unable to identify W. B. Poland in any other context.
33. Walter Hines Page (1855–1918). Journalist and publisher. Editor of *Atlantic Monthly* 1896–9, *The World's Work* 1900–13. Member of Doubleday Page & Co. 1899–1918. Ambassador to Great Britain 1913–18.
34. Page to Astor, 1 Mar. 1918, Harvard University, Houghton Library, Page Papers.
35. Poland to Hoover, 26 Mar. 1918, Hoover Institution Library, Committee for the Relief of Belgium Papers, Poland Correspondence.
36. Harmsworth to Poland, 26 Mar. 1918, *ibid.*, Great Britain Internal Affairs, Prime Minister.
37. Poland to Harmsworth, 19 Apr. 1918, *ibid.*, G.B. Int. Aff., Foreign Office.
38. Harmsworth to Slater (Foreign Office), 22 Apr. 1918, *ibid.*
39. Jan Christian Smuts (1870–1950). Commanded Boer Commando Forces in Cape Province 1901. Minister of Defence, Union of South Africa, 1910–20. South African representative at Imperial War Cabinet 1917 & 1918. Member of the War Cabinet 1917–18. Prime Minister of South Africa 1919–24, Minister of Justice 1933–9, Prime Minister 1939–48.
40. Poland to Harmsworth, 25 May 1918; Poland to Hoover, 6 Jun. 1918, *ibid.* Poland Correspondence.
41. Harmsworth to M. W. Guinness, 17 Jun. 1918, and minutes, FO 382/2027/108718.
42. Cecil, as Minister for Blockade, was responsible for C.R.B. affairs. See chap. 4, note 30.
43. Harmsworth to Guinness, 25 Jun. 1918; minutes and memorandum by Guinness, 9 Jul. 1918, FO 382/2027/112270.
44. Harmsworth to Guinness, 12 Jul. 1918, FO 382/2027/123939.
45. Guinness to Harmsworth, 24 Jul. 1918, *ibid.*; Guinness to Leslie, 4 Jul. 1918, FO 382/2027/121578.
46. Harmsworth to Poland, 21 Oct. 1918, C.R.B. Papers, G.B. Int. Aff., Prime Minister.
47. Davies, pp. 105–31.
48. *Ibid.*, pp. 132–44.
49. *Ibid.*, p. 132.
50. Eric Campbell Geddes (1875–1937). Indian railways engineer. Deputy Director-General, Munitions Supply 1915–16. Inspector-General of Transportation 1916–17. Controller of the Navy 1917. First Lord of

the Admiralty 1917–18, Minister of Transport 1919–21. M.P. (Cons.) 1917–22.
51. Hankey Diary, 11 May 1917.
52. G.T. 1312, 5 Jul. 1917, CAB 24/19.
53. Davies to Lloyd George, 10 Jul. 1917; Davies, p. 145.
54. W.C. 180, 10 Jul. 1917, CAB 23/3.
55. G.T. 1348, 9 Jul. 1917, CAB 24/19.
56. Minutes in Admiralty Papers, ADM 1/8493/164.
57. Alan Garrett Anderson (1877–1952). Director, P. & O. Lines, M.P. (Cons.) 1935–40, chairman, Railway Executive, 1941–5. Director, Suez Canal Company.
58. G.T. 1600, 3 Aug. 1917 CAB 24/20.
59. Churchill to Lloyd George 19 Aug. 1917 quoted Martin Gilbert *Winston S. Churchill* vol. iv (London 1975) 42.
60. Albert Sydney Collard (1876–1938). Railway engineer, Nigeria, 1908–14. Staff Officer, War Office, 1914–17. Deputy Controller for Auxiliary Shipbuilding, Admiralty, 1917–18.
61. Harmsworth to Lloyd George, 20 Sept. 1917, L.G.P. F/87/1/15.
62. Davies, p. 148.
63. Shorthand note in L.G.P. F/215/1.
64. Davies records this, probably misdated, on 10 Oct. 1917. Davies, p. 149.
65. Davies, p. 158.
66. *Ibid.*
67. The original of Harmsworth to Lloyd George, 14 Mar. 1918, is in ADM 116/1608.
68. William James Pirrie (1847–1924). Entered Harland & Wolff 1862, Partner 1874. Lord Mayor of Belfast 1896–7. Controller-General of Merchant Shipbuilding 1918.
69. Davies, p. 149, records the suggestion on 17 Nov.; shorthand notes of conference on 22 Nov. 1917, L.G.P. F/229/7.
70. W.C. 287, 29 Nov. 1917, CAB 23/4; cf. memorandum by L. Macassey, 11 Mar. 1918, ADM 116/1608.
71. Hankey to E. Geddes, 2 Mar. 1918, ADM 116/1806.
72. n.d. draft memorandum 'Government Departments dealing with Labour' by G. N. Barnes [?12 Apr. 1918], ADM 116/1608.
73. Davies, pp. 160–1.
74. Harmsworth to Anderson, 22 Mar. 1918, ADM 116/1807.
75. Anderson to Harmsworth, 23 Mar. 1918, *ibid.*
76. Report in L.G.P. F/85/6/18; notes *ibid.*, F/79/9/1.
77. Harmsworth to Lloyd George, 26 Apr. 1918, L.G.P. F/187/1/8.
78. Cf. Humbert Wolfe, *Labour Supply and Regulation* (Oxford, 1923), *passim.*
79. James Hinton, *The First Shop Steward Movement* (London, 1973).
80. Adams to Lloyd George, 10 May 1917, L.G.P. F/78/20/5.
81. Harmsworth to Lloyd George, 11 Jun. 1917, L.G.P. F/78/6/2.
82. Bonar Law held shipping shares.
83. See e.g. Addison to N. Chamberlain, 19 Mar. 1917, Addison Papers 54.

84. David Lloyd George, *War Memoirs* (London, 1938), I, 801–12; K. Feiling, *The Life of Neville Chamberlain* (London, 1946); Chamberlain's correspondence with Lloyd George, L.G.P. F/7/1.
85. G.T. 1176, 22 Jun. 1917, CAB 24/17.
86. Harmsworth to Lloyd George, 28 Jun. 1917, L.G.P. F/79/29/5.
87. Arthur Cecil Tyrell Beck (1878–1932). Lloyds underwriter. M.P. (Lib.) 1906–22. Junior Whip 1915. Parliamentary Secretary to Department of National Service 1917–19.
88. Kennedy Jones (1865–1921). Journalist, joint founder with Alfred Harmsworth of the *Daily Mail*. Editor of the *Evening News* 1894–1900. M.P. (Ind.) 1916–21. Director, Food Economy Dept., Ministry of Food, 1917.
89. See below, pp. 48, 54–8.
90. Beck to Harmsworth, 26 Jul. 1917, L.G.P. F/87/5/1.
91. Feiling, pp. 71–2.
92. Chamberlain to Lloyd George, 27 Jul. and 8 Aug. 1917, L.G.P. F/7/1.
93. Auckland Campbell Geddes (1879–1954). Brother of E. C. Geddes. Professor of anatomy, Dublin and Canada, 1909–14. Active service 1914–16. Director of Recruiting, War Office, 1916–17. M.P. (Cons.) 1917–20. Minister of National Service 1917–19. President, Local Government Board, 1918. Minister of Reconstruction 1919. President, Board of Trade, 1919–20. Ambassador to Washington 1920–4. Chairman, Rio Tinto Zinc, 1925–47. Baron 1942.
94. Feiling, p. 74.
95. W.C. 179, 9 Jul. 1917, CAB 23/3.
96. Harmsworth to Lloyd George, 28 Jun. 1917, L.G.P. F/87/2/1.
97. Harmsworth to Lloyd George, 10 Jul. 1917, *ibid.*
98. G.T. 1450, [18 Jul. 1917], CAB 24/20.
99. Harmsworth to Lloyd George, 27 Jul. 1917, L.G.P. F/87/2/3.
100. *Ibid.*
101. Harmsworth to Lloyd George, 31 Jul. 1917, L.G.P. F/87/2/4.
102. Stanley Baldwin (1867–1947). M.P. (Cons.) 1908–37. Financial Secretary, Treasury, 1917–21. President, Board of Trade, 1921–2. Chancellor of the Exchequer 1922–3. Prime Minister 1923–4, 1924–9, 1935–7. Earl 1937.
103. Harmsworth to Baldwin, 14 Aug. 1917, L.G.P. F/87/2/7.
104. W.C. 245, 4 Oct. 1917, CAB 23/4; G.T. 2429, 29 Oct. 1917, CAB 24/30.
105. Davies to Smuts 23 June 1917, CAB 21/101. On the establishment of the War Priorities Committee see CAB 21/118. Its records are in CAB 40.

CHAPTER 3. FOOD AND AGRICULTURE

1. Prothero to Lloyd George, 21 Jan. 1917, L.G.P. F/15/8/5.
   Reginald Ernest Prothero (1852–1937). M.P. (Cons.) 1914–19. Barrister and agricultural writer. Fellow of All Souls 1875–91. Editor of the *Quarterly Review* 1894–99. President of the Board of Agriculture 1916–19. Created Baron Ernle 1919.

2. Edward George Villiers Stanley, 14th Earl of Derby (1865–1948). M.P. (Cons.) 1892–1906. Whip 1895–1900, Financial Secretary, War Office, 1900–3, Postmaster-General 1903–5. Director-General of Recruiting 1915–16, Under-Secretary for War, 1915–16, Secretary of State for War 1916–18 and 1922–4. Ambassador to France 1918–20. Derby was Conservative 'boss' of Lancashire. He was dismissed from the War Office in April 1918 to be replaced by Milner. Copies of circulars to his tenants at Knowsley are in Bodleian Library, Milner Papers 161.

3. E. H. Starling, *The Oliver Sharpey Lectures on the Feeding of Nations* (London, 1919).

4. W. H. Beveridge, *British Food Control* (London, 1928), pp. 16–17. Beveridge's volume, part of the Carnegie series on the economic and social effects of the war, is the only full study of the work of the Ministry of Food.

5. Beveridge, p. 105.

6. T. H. Middleton, *Food Production in War* (Oxford, 1923), p. 175.

7. Beveridge, p. 35.

8. *Ibid.*, p. 48. See note 88 to chap. 2.

9. *Ibid.*, p. 45.

10. John Robert Clynes (1869–1949). M.P. (Lab.) 1903–31, 1935–45. Member and sometime President, National Union of General and Municipal Workers. Parliamentary Secretary, Ministry of Food, 1917–18, Food Controller 1918–19. Chairman, Parliamentary Labour Party, 1921–2. Lord Privy Seal 1924. Home Secretary 1929–31.

11. W.C. 5, 13 Dec. 1916, CAB 23/1.

12. 'Report by the Food Controller on Bread, Meat and Sugar', G. 108, 11 Jan. 1917, CAB 24/3.

13. W.C. 33, 12 Jan. 1917, CAB 23/1.

14. W.C. 39, 19 Jan. 1917, CAB 23/1.

15. Lloyd George to Derby, 22 Jan. 1917, L.G.P. F/14/4/16.

16. John Denton Pinkstone French (1852–1925). Chief of the Imperial General Staff 1911–14. Commander-in-Chief, France, 1914–15. C.-in-C. Home Forces 1915–18. Lord Lieutenant for Ireland 1918–21. Knight 1900, Viscount 1915, Earl 1921.

17. W.C. 42, 23 Jan. 1917, CAB 23/1.

18. Transcription of telephone calls from Adams to Sir Arthur Lee and Mr Harling Turner, Feb. 1917, L.G.P. F/70/2/8.

19. Adams to Lloyd George, 16 May, 1917, L.G.P. F/78/20/7; Adams to Lloyd George, 23 May 1917, L.G.P. F/79/20/9.

20. Various correspondence, Jan. to Mar. 1917, L.G.P. F/73/6.

21. Minutes and papers of the Fertilisers Committee, Jan. to Feb. 1917, L.G.P. F/73/8. Cf. 'Proposed Statement by Professor Adams' [sec. to the Machinery of Government Committee of the Ministry of Reconstruction], 7 Mar. 1918, for Adams's responsibility for this committee.

22. Memorandum by Adams, 21 Aug. 1917, L.G.P. F/73/1/1.

23. Prothero to Lloyd George, 31 Jan. 1917, L.G.P. F/15/8/5; G.T. 14. CAB 24/6.

24. Adams to Lloyd George, 14 Mar. 1917, L.G.P. F/71/2.

25. See note 23 above.
26. W.C. 66, 14 Feb. 1917, CAB 23/1. Adams was present.
27. Davies, *The Prime Minister's Secretariat*, p. 89, attributes the price scheme to Adams. I have found no evidence to justify this.
28. W.C. 71, 17 Feb. 1917, CAB 23/1.
29. This decision was reversed by W.C. 76, 21 Feb. 1917, CAB 23/1.
30. Davies to Lloyd George, 18 Feb. 1917, L.G.P. F/70/3/3.
31. Alfred Daniel Hall (1864–1942). Director, Rothamsted Experimental Station, 1902–12. Development Commissioner 1909–17. First Secretary, Board of Agriculture, 1917.
32. A. D. Hall, 'Note on Mr Davies' Memorandum', 20 Feb. 1917, L.G.P. F/70/3/4.
33. Davies, p. 90.
34. On food production, set up in 1915 by Lord Selborne as President of the Board of Agriculture. Prothero had been a member.
35. Adams to Lloyd George, 20 Feb. 1917, L.G.P. F/78/20/1.
36. n.d. drafts, L.G.P. F/70/3/9. Cf. 90 *H.C. Debs.*, 5s, 22 Feb. 1917, 1599ff.
37. W.C. 76, 21 Feb. 1917, CAB 23/1.
38. Adams to Bonar Law, 31 Mar. 1917, L.G.P. F/70/18/1.
39. Adams to Lloyd George, 31 Mar. 1917, L.G.P. F/70/15/1.
40. See L.G.P. F/70/16.
41. W.C. 112, 3 Apr. 1917, CAB 23/2.
42. Thomas Jones Papers, Diary, 8 Apr. 1917.
43. Adams to Lloyd George, 14 Mar. 1917, L.G.P. F/71/2; W.C. 97, 15 Mar. 1917, CAB 23/2.
44. Adams to Lloyd George, 17 Mar. 1917, L.G.P. F/232.
45. W.C. 99, 20 Mar. 1917, CAB 23/2.
46. Charles Bathurst (1867–1958). Barrister 1894–1910. M.P. (Cons.) 1910–18. Parliamentary Secretary, Ministry of Food, 1916–17. Chairman, Royal Commission on the Sugar Supply, 1917–18. Parliamentary Secretary, Ministry of Agriculture, 1924–8. Governor-General of New Zealand 1930–5. Medallist of the Royal Agricultural College, Cirencester. Knighted 1917, created Baron Bledisloe 1918, Viscount 1935.
47. Cf. correspondence 30 Apr. 1917, L.G.P. F/15/2/10–13.
48. Addison to Lloyd George, 21 Mar. 1917, Addison Papers 60.
49. Adams to Lloyd George, 24 Mar. 1917, L.G.P. F/15/2/5.
50. Sutherland to Lloyd George, 24 Mar. 1917, *ibid.*
51. Devonport to Lloyd George, enclosing Adams's report and a letter from Sutherland to Devonport's private secretary, 27 Mar. 1917, L.G.P. F/15/2/5.
52. Lloyd George to Devonport, 13 Apr. 1917, L.G.P. F/15/2/6 & 7.
53. G.T. 345 and 362, 5 Apr. 1917, CAB 24/9.
54. W.C. 114, 5 Apr. 1917, CAB 23/2.
55. 'Wheat Supplies. Notes by Mr Joseph Davies', 11 Apr. 1917, G. 141, CAB 24/3.
56. Davies, p. 101. See above, chap. 2, p. 30.
57. W.C. 133, 7 May 1917, CAB 23/2.
58. Milner Papers 88, Diary, 5 May 1917.

59. Adams to Milner, 7 May 1917, Milner Papers 45.
60. Milner Papers 88, Diary, 10 May 1917.
61. *Ibid.*, 12 May 1917.
62. Adams to Milner, 21 May 1917, Milner Papers 45.
63. W.C. 151, 30 May 1917, CAB 23/2.
64. Minutes in Ministry of Agriculture Papers (P.R.O.) MAF60/54.
65. Harmsworth to Lloyd George, 17 July 1917, L.G.P. F/71/11/2.
66. Beveridge, pp. 51ff.
67. See note 52 above.

CHAPTER 4. FOREIGN AFFAIRS

1. But cf. Roberta M. Warman, 'The Erosion of Foreign Office Influence in the Making of Foreign Policy, 1916–1918', *Historical Journal*, xv (1972).
2. C. J. Lowe and M. L. Dockrill, *The Mirage of Power* (London, 1972), pp. 183–207.
3. Eleutherios Venizelos (1864–1936). Prime Minister of Greece 1910–May 1915, Aug. to Oct. 1915, Jun. 1917–20, 1928–32, 1933. Venizelos represented, both at home and abroad, Greek aspirations to liberal democracy against an autocratic monarch.
4. Constantine of Greece (1868–1923) succeeded as King, 1913. Brother-in-law of the German Kaiser. Forced into exile by the Entente 1917–20. Abdicated 1922.
5. William Robertson (1860–1933). Entered army 1877. Rose from the ranks to become Quartermaster-General, British Expeditionary Force, 1914–15, Chief of Staff, B.E.F., 1915, C.I.G.S. 1915–Feb. 1918, C-in-C Home Forces 1918–19. Knighted 1913, Baronet 1919.
6. Maurice Paul Emmanuele Sarrail (1856–1929). Commanded French 3rd Army at Battle of Marne 1914. Relieved July 1915, sent to command Balkan forces Oct. 1915. Recalled Dec. 1917. Journalist 1919–25. High Commissioner in Syria and the Lebanon 1925. Sarrail's higher military career depended on the strength of the Left in the French government.
7. Guinn, *British Strategy and Politics*, pp. 209–17.
8. See W.C. 1, 9 Dec. 1916, W.C. 4, 13 Dec. 1916, W.C. 16, 23 Dec. 1916, CAB 23/1.
9. W.C. 18, 26 Dec. 1916, CAB 23/1.
10. *Procès-verbaux* in CAB 28/2.
11. W.C. 18, 26 Dec. 1916, W.C. 19, 27 Dec. 1916, CAB 23/1.
12. Churchill College, Cambridge, Hankey Papers, Diary, 26 Dec. 1916.
13. Luigi Cadorna (1850–1928). Commissioned 1868. C-in-C Italian forces from 1915. Dismissed Nov. 1917 after Caporetto.
14. Hankey Diary, 5 Jan. 1917; cf. *Procès-verbaux* in CAB 28/2.
15. W.C. 31, 10 Jan. 1917, CAB 23/1.
16. e.g. W.C. 43, 24 Jan. 1917, CAB 23/1.
17. Conference minutes in CAB 28/2/17.
18. Balfour to Stamfordham, 27 Feb. 1917, CAB 24/6, G.T. 84.
19. Arthur James Balfour (1848–1930). M.P. (Cons.) 1874–1922.

Succeeded his uncle, Lord Salisbury, as Prime Minister 1902, resigned 1905. First Lord of the Admiralty 1915–16, Foreign Secretary 1916–19, Lord President 1919–22, 1925–9. Earl 1922.

20. Cyril Falls, *Military Operations, Macedonia* (London, 1933), I, 294–5.
21. Ferdinand of Bulgaria (1861–1948) was a German prince, born in Saxe-Coburg. Prince of Bulgaria 1887, took title of king on proclaiming independence from Turkey 1908. Allied with Central Powers 1915. Abdicated 1918.
22. Davies to Lloyd George, 5 Apr. 1917, L.G.P. F/83/10/3.
23. Ernest Charles Thomas Troubridge (1860–1926). Entered navy 1875. Chief of Admiralty War Staff 1912. Commander, Mediterranean Cruiser Squadron, 1912–14, court-martialled for failing to engage the German battle-cruiser *Goeben*, and acquitted. Admiral commanding on the Danube 1918, President, International Danube Commission, 1919–24.
24. Troubridge to Carson, 3 Apr. 1917, L.G.P. F/59/4/1.
25. W.C. 116, 10 Apr. 1917, CAB 23/2.
26. Conference records in CAB 28/2/21.
27. Conference records *ibid.*
28. Hankey Diary, 19 Apr. 1917.
29. Minute by Lancelot Oliphant, 19 Mar. 1917, FO 371/2865/58695.
30. Edgar Algernon Robert Cecil (1864–1958). M.P. (Cons.) 1911–23. Under-Secretary of State for Foreign Affairs 1915–16, Minister of Blockade in the Foreign Office 1916–18. Lord Privy Seal 1923–4, Chancellor of the Duchy 1924–7. President of the League of Nations Union 1923–45. 3rd son of Marquess of Salisbury, hence Balfour's cousin.
31. Cecil to Balfour, 22 Apr. 1917, British Library Addit. MSS 49738 (Balfour Papers).
32. George Russell Clerk (1874–1951). Entered Foreign Office 1899. Abyssinia 1903–7, London 1907–10, Turkey 1910–14, War Dept. 1914–18. Later Ambassador in Turkey, Belgium and Paris.
33. Lothian Papers 918; FO 800/384/Bal 17/1.
34. See below, pp. 181–2.
35. Kerr to Lloyd George, n.d. [5–12 May 1917], Lothian Papers 929/1.
36. Ronald Montagu Burrows (1867–1920). Professor of Greek, University College, Cardiff, 1898–1908, Manchester 1908–13. Principal of King's College 1913–20.
37. Kerr to Lloyd George, 18 May 1917, Lothian Papers 919.
38. John Rushworth Jellicoe (1859–1935). Entered navy 1872. Second Sea Lord 1912–14, Commander Grand Fleet 1914–16, First Sea Lord 1916–17. Governor-General of New Zealand 1920–4. Viscount 1918, Earl 1925.
39. G.T. 755, 18 May 1917, CAB 24/13.
40. W.C. 142, 22 May 1917, CAB 23/2.
41. W.C. 144, 23 May 1917, CAB 23/2.
42. Kerr to Cecil, 23 May 1917, Lothian Papers 918/5.
43. Davies to Lloyd George, [27 May] 1917, L.G.P. F/83/10/5. Misitch was the Serbian commander. Buckley was probably Basil Thorold

Buckley (1874– ?), a regular officer who served in South Africa and was in 1917 G.S.O. 1 in the War Office.
George Francis Milne (1866–1948). Entered army 1885, served in South Africa. Brigadier commanding divisional artillery in France 1914. Lt. Gen. commanding British forces at Salonika 1916–18, at Constantinople 1919–20. General 1920. C.I.G.S. 1926–33. Knighted 1918, Field Marshal 1928, Baron 1933.

44. 'Notes of An Anglo-French Conference Held at 10 Downing Street,...on Monday May 28, 1917', CAB 28/2/24; W.C. 148, 28 May, W.C. 149, 29 May 1917, CAB 23/2.
45. Cecil to Lloyd George, 29 May 1917, L.G.P. F/6/5/5.
46. W.C. 150, 30 May 1917, CAB 23/2.
47. Communication from Italian Ambassador, circulated to King and War Cabinet, 30 May 1917, L.G.P. F/163/3/5.
48. Davies to Lloyd George, 31 May 1917, L.G.P. F/83/10/6.
49. Minute by Cecil, 15 Apr. 1917, FO 371/2865/77484.
50. Minute by Hardinge and Granville to F.O., 13 Apr. 1917, FO 371/2866/76399.
51. W.C. 144, 23 May 1917, CAB 23/2.
52. Burrows to Davies and Davies to Lloyd George, 31 May 1917, L.G.P. F/83/10/6.
53. *Ibid.*
54. Kerr to Lloyd George, 1 Jun. 1917, L.G.P. F/89/1/7.
55. *Ibid.*
56. Annotation by Cecil on Kerr to Cecil, 1 Jun. 1917, Lothian Papers 920/2.
57. 'Report by Lieutenant Colonel E. A. Plunkett', 1 Jun. 1917, War Office Papers, WO 106/1360.
58. W.C. 154, 5 Jun. 1917; W.C. 155, 5 Jun. 1917; W.C. 156, 6 Jun. 1917; all CAB 23/3.
59. Henry Norman (1858–1939). Journalist, director of colliery companies. M.P. (Lib.) 1900–23. Liaison officer, Ministry of Munitions to Ministry of Inventions, Paris, 1916. Baronet 1915.
60. Norman to Lloyd George, 7 Jun. 1917, L.G.P. F/41/6/2.
61. W.C. 160, 11 Jun. 1917, CAB 23/3.
62. Davies to Lloyd George, 23 Jun. 1917, L.G.P. F/83/10/7.
63. Henry Wilson (1864–1922). Entered army 1884. Director of Military Operations 1910–14. Liaison officer with French army, 1915. Commanded 4th Corps 1916. C.I.G.S. 1918–22. Field Marshal 1919, Baronet 1919. M.P. (Ulster Unionist) 1922. Assassinated 1922 by Sinn Fein.
64. I am indebted for this information to Miss Stephanie Dee.
65. The presence of such a senior Foreign Office official indicates the importance of political considerations in sending the mission.
66. Clerk to Milner, 7 Feb. 1917, G.134, CAB 24/3.
67. G.131, CAB 24/3.
68. Prince G. E. Lvov (1861–1925). Chairman of the All-Russian Union of Zemstvos 1916. First Prime Minister of the Provisional Government March 1917.

69. Enclosure 3 to Clerk's report, G.143, CAB 24/3.
70. 'Report on Mission to Russia, by Major David Davies, M.P.', 10 Mar. 1917, G.137, CAB 24/3.
71. *Lord Riddell's War Diary*, p. 248.
72. See below, pp. 152–5.
73. W.C. 128a, 1 May 1917 and W.C. 135a, 9 May 1917, CAB 23/14.
74. Kerr to Lloyd George, n.d., [27/28 May, 1917], Lothian Papers 867.
75. n.s. memo., 17 Apr. 1917, ADM 1/8485/75.
76. Commodore Lionel Halsey.
77. n.s. memo. [probably by 4th Sea Lord] 18 Apr. 1917, *ibid.*
78. ADM 1/8491/151. The officers named in this file do not correspond exactly with those named by Davies.
79. e.g. Adams to Lloyd George, 2 Jun. 1917, L.G.P. F/74/1/5.
80. Bodleian Library, H.A.L. Fisher Diary, 4 Jan. 1918.
81. Alexander Feodorovich Kerensky (1881–1970). Member of the Duma 1912. Minister of Justice in the Provisional Government Feb. 1917, Minister for War in May, Prime Minister July–Oct. 1917. Lived in exile in France, United States and finally England.
82. Kerr to Balfour, 22 Jun. 1918, Lothian Papers 821–2.
83. G.T. 4948, 25 Jun. 1918, CAB 24/55, contains Kerr's note of this conversation and of his own talk with Kerensky the next day.
84. K. O. Morgan, "Lloyd George's Premiership: A Study in Prime Ministerial Government', *Historical Journal*, xiii (1970), p. 136.
85. Richard H. Ullman, *Intervention and the War* (Princeton, 1961), pp. 191–229.
86. Ullman, pp. 208–9.
87. Memo., 28 Jun. 1918, Lothian Papers 827.
88. See Ullman; George F. Kennan, *Soviet–American Relations* (2 vols., Princeton, 1956, 1958); Alexander Kerensky, *The Catastrophe* (London, 1927).
89. James Eric Drummond (1876–1951). Entered Foreign Office 1900. Private Secretary to Prime Minister, 1912–15. Private Secretary to Foreign Secretary 1915–19. Secretary-General League of Nations 1919–33. Ambassador to Italy 1933–9. Succeeded half-brother as 16th Earl of Perth 1937.
90. Kerr to Drummond, 19 Jul. 1918, Lothian Papers 55/5.
91. *Lord Riddell's War Diary*, pp. 339–40.
92. W.C. 454, 4 Aug. 1918, CAB 23/7.
93. Rothwell, *British War Aims and Peace Diplomacy*.
94. Albrecht, Count von Mensdorff Pouilly Dietrichstein (1861–1945). Ambassador in London 1910–14.
95. Alexander Skrzynski (1882–1931), who met Kerr in March, entered the Austrian diplomatic service in 1906. Served in Paris 1914. Polish minister in Bucharest 1919–22. Minister for Foreign Affairs, Poland, 1922–3, 1924–5. Prime Minister 1925–6.
96. Rothwell, pp. 177–8.
97. Horace George Montague Rumbold (1869–1941). Entered Diplomatic Service 1891. Chargé d'Affaires, Berlin, 1914. Minister in Berne 1916–

19, in Warsaw 1919–20. High Commissioner, Constantinople, 1920–4. Ambassador to Madrid 1924–8, Berlin 1928–33.
98. Humbert Denis Parodi (1878– ?). Swiss citizen. Inspector-General of Public Instruction, Cairo, 1910–14. Head of Mission Scolaire Egyptienne, Switzerland, 1914–18. Head of Interpreters and Translators Bureau, League of Nations, 1919–21, Interpreter 1922–38.
99. Balfour to Lloyd George, 4 Dec. 1917, FO 800/199.
100. Smuts's report is in Lloyd George, *War Memoirs*, II, 1478–89.
101. *Ibid.*, 1489.
102. Smuts to Rumbold, 19 Dec. 1917, Bodleian Library, Rumbold Papers 24.
   Mahmud Moukhtar Pasha (1867–1935). Commanded Turkish 1st Army 1908–9. Minister of Marine 1912. Ambassador to Berlin 1913–15. Retired to live in Switzerland.
103. Lloyd George, *War Memoirs*, II, 1504–9.
104. Foreign Office to Rumbold (telegram), 21 Dec. 1917, FO 371/3057/241322.
105. Ronald William Graham (1870–1949). Entered Diplomatic Service 1892. Adviser to Ministry of Interior, Egyptian government, 1910–16. Minister Plenipotentiary in Cairo, 1916. War Department, Foreign Office, 1916–19. Acting Permanent Under-Secretary 1919. Minister to Holland 1919–21, Ambassador to Italy 1921–33. Director, Suez Canal Company, 1939–45.
106. Minute by Graham on Rumbold to F.O., 22 Dec. 1917, FO 371/3057/241322; minutes by Graham, Harold Nicholson, and Cecil on Rumbold to F.O., 22 Dec. 1917, FO 371/3057/242085.
107. Martin Gilbert, *Exile and Return: the Emergence of Jewish Statehood* (London, 1978), p. 96.
108. Isaiah Friedman, *The Question of Palestine, 1914–1918* (London, 1973), pp. 265–7.
109. Smuts to Rumbold, 19 Dec. 1917, Rumbold Papers 24.
110. W.C. 311a, 2 Jan. 1918, CAB 23/16.
111. W.C. 318a, 8 Jan. 1918, CAB 23/16.
112. Minute by Cecil, [11 Jan. 1918] FO 371/3133/7760. It appears in fact to have been a *ballon d'essai* by Skrzynski. W. B. Fest, *Peace or Partition* (London, 1978), p. 196.
113. W.C. 331a, 28 Jan. 1918, CAB 23/16; W.C. 338a, 4 Feb. 1918, *ibid.*
114. W.C. 338a, 4 Feb. 1918, CAB 23/16.
115. W.C. 357a, 1 Mar. 1918, CAB 23/16.
116. Milner to Lloyd George, 27 Feb. 1918, L.G.P. F/28/3/16; Bonar Law mode his protest in Cabinet on 1 Mar.
117. W.C. 360a, 6 Mar. 1918, CAB 23/16.
118. Thomas Wodehouse Legh (1857–1942). Entered Diplomatic Service 1880, left 1886. M.P. (Cons.) 1886–91. Succeeded as 2nd Baron Newton 1899. Paymaster-General 1915–16. Assistant Under-Secretary for Foreign Affairs 1916. Controller, Prisoners of War Dept., 1916–19.
119. Rumbold to F.O., 6 Mar. 1918, FO 371/3388/42760.
120. Balfour to Kerr, 6 Mar. 1918, Lothian Papers 1050 and FO 371/3133/41211 give only instructions for Austrian discussions:

W.C. 362a, 8 Mar. 1918, CAB 23/16 discussed Turkish instructions to Kerr.
121. See Kerr's report, 19 Mar. 1918, CAB 1/26; F.O. minutes on Rumbold to F.O., 31 Jan. 1918, FO 371/3388/20082.
122. Minute by Oliphant on Rumbold to F.O., 12 Mar. 1918, FO 371/3133/45538.
123. Fest, p. 206.
124. Kerr's report, CAB 1/26.
125. H. Hanak, 'The Government, the Foreign Office, and Austria–Hungary', *Slavonic Review*, XLVIII, 108 (1969), 187; Rothwell, p. 171.
126. Kerr to Rumbold, 30 Mar. 1918, Rumbold Papers 25.

CHAPTER 5. IRELAND

1. John Edward Redmond (1851–1918). M.P. (Nat.) 1881–1918. Leader of Parnellite wing of the party 1891–1900, then chairman of the party.
2. See below, pp. 115–6.
3. William St John Brodrick (1856–1942). M.P. (Cons.) 1880–1906. Secretary of State for War 1900–3, for India 1903–5. Succeeded as 9th Viscount Midleton 1907.
4. Note by Redmond, 9 Dec. 1916, National Library of Ireland, Redmond Papers 15189.
5. Lord Beaverbrook, *Politicians and the War* (2nd edn, London, 1960), p. 527.
6. John Dillon (1851–1927.) M.P. (Nat.) 1880–1918. Joint leader of the anti-Parnellite wing of the Home Rule party, 1891–1900.
7. *Report by the committee on Irish finances*, P.P., S.P. (Commons) 1912–13, Cd. 6799, xxx.
8. *Political Quarterly*, II (May, 1914).
9. *Ibid.*, I (Feb. 1914).
10. *Ibid.*, II (May 1914).
11. *Ibid.*, VII (Sept. 1916).
12. Adams to Lloyd George, 1 June 1916, L.G.P. D/14/2/1.
13. J. E. Kendle, 'The Round Table Movement and "Home Rule All Round" ', *Historical Journal*, XI (1968).
14. Plunkett Foundation, Oxford, Papers of Sir Horace Plunkett, Diary, 27 June 1918.
15. 'Ireland and the Empire', *The Round Table*, XXIV (Sept. 1916), 623.
16. William Morris Hughes (1864–1952). Born in Wales, emigrated to Australia 1884. Prime Minister (Lab.) 1915–23.
17. Kerr to Lloyd George, 13 Jan. 1917, L.G.P. F/89/1/1.
18. W.C. 61, 10 Feb. 1917, CAB 23/1.
19. Amery to Lloyd George, 16 Feb. 1917, L.G.P. F/2/1/1.
20. Adams to Lloyd George, [3 Mar.] 1917, L.G.P. F/63/1/1.
21. Ian Colvin, *Life of Lord Carson* (London, 1937), p. 593.
22. Carson to Lloyd George, 3 Mar. 1917, L.G.P. F/6/2/18.
23. Kerr to Lloyd George, 3 Mar. 1917, L.G.P. F/89/1/3.

24. Thomas Power O'Connor (1848–1929). M.P. (Nat.) for Liverpool (Scotland) 1885–1929, the only Nationalist to sit for an English constituency.
25. O'Connor to Redmond, 5 Mar. 1917, Redmond Papers 15215.
26. Adams to Lloyd George, 6 Mar. 1917, L.G.P. F/63/1/3.
27. Charles Prestwich Scott (1846–1932). Editor of the *Manchester Guardian* 1872–1929, M.P. (Lib.) 1895–1906.
28. Joseph Devlin (1872–1934). M.P. (Nat.) 1902–22, 1929–34. Devlin occupied a special position as M.P. for West Belfast and leader of Nationalism in Ulster.
29. 'Dillon's private views', 5 Mar. 1917, L.G.P. F/63/1/2.
30. Oliver to Astor, 3 Mar. 1917, L.G.P. F/83/1/2.
31. Astor to Lloyd George, 5 Mar. 1917, L.G.P. F/83/1/2.
32. Astor to Lloyd George, 7 Mar. 1917, L.G.P. F/83/1/3.
33. W.C. 90, 7 Mar. 1917, CAB 23/1.
34. 91 *H.C. Debs.*, 5s, 7 Mar. 1917, 425–500.
35. *The Times*, 9 Mar. 1917.
36. Adams, Astor, and Kerr to Lloyd George, 8 Mar. 1917, L.G.P. F/89/1/4.
37. James Craig (1871–1940). M.P. (Unionist) 1906–21. Parliamentary Secretary, Ministry of Pensions, 1919–20, Financial Secretary, Admiralty, 1920–1. Prime Minister of Northern Ireland 1921–40. Baronet 1918, Viscount Craigavon 1927.
38. Astor to Lloyd George, 10 Mar. 1917, L.G.P. F/83/1/4.
39. Memorandum by Carson, 20 Mar. 1917, Lothian Papers 566.
40. W.C. 101, 22 Mar. 1917, CAB 23/1; cf. Long to Lloyd George, 22 Mar. 1917, L.G.P. F/32/4/54 and Public Archives of Canada, Diary of Sir Robert Borden, 22 Mar. 1917, for the Dominion P.M.s' reaction.
41. O'Connor to Redmond, 29 Mar. 1917, Redmond Papers 15215.
42. Dillon to Redmond, 12 Apr. 1917, Redmond Papers 15182.
43. Adams to Lloyd George, 16 Apr. 1917, L.G.P. F/63/1/4.
44. W.C. 120, 17 Apr. 1917, CAB 23/2.
    Henry Edmund Duke (1855–1939). M.P. (Cons.) 1900–18. Chief Secretary for Ireland July 1916–May 1918. Lord of Appeal 1918–19. President, Probate, Admiralty and Divorce Divisions, 1919–34. Knighted 1918, Baron Merrivale 1925.
45. Astor to Lloyd George, 21 Apr. 1917, L.G.P. F/83/1/6.
46. O'Connor to Redmond, 3 May 1917, Redmond Papers 15215.
47. Draft letter to Redmond (by Adams), 6 May 1917, L.G.P. F/63/1/6.
48. Adams to Lloyd George, 6 May 1917, L.G.P. F/63/1/6.
49. Plunkett Diary, 12 May 1917.
50. Adams to Lloyd George, 13 May 1917, L.G.P. F/63/1/7.
51. Astor to Lloyd George, 14 May 1917, L.G.P. F/83/1/7.
52. O'Connor to Redmond, 10 May 1917, Redmond Papers 15215.
53. Thomas Patrick Gill (1858–1931). M.P. (Nat.) 1885–92. Left parliament after attempts to heal the anti-Parnellite split 1889–92. Secretary of Recess Committee, which founded the Dept. of Agriculture and Technical Instruction, 1895–8. Secretary D.A.T.I. 1900–23.

54. Adams to Lloyd George, 15 May 1917, enclosing Gill's letters, L.G.P. F/63/1/8.
55. Gill to Redmond, 14 May 1917, Redmond Papers 15190.
56. Adams to Lloyd George, 15 May 1917, L.G.P. F/63/1/8.
57. British Library Addit. MSS. 50904 (Scott Papers) Scott Diary, pp. 49–54 (15 May 1917).
58. Robert Offley Ashburton Crewe-Milnes (1858–1945). Viceroy of Ireland 1892–5. Secretary of State for India 1910–15, Lord President 1915–16, President of the Board of Education 1916. Close associate of Asquith after December 1916. Ambassador to Paris 1922–8. Secretary of State for War 1931.
59. Crewe to Asquith, 16 May 1917, Bodleian Library, Asquith Papers 46. Cf. R. B. McDowell, *The Irish Convention 1917–18* (London, 1970), pp. 76–7.
60. Adams to Lloyd George, 16 May 1917, L.G.P. F/63/1/9.
61. W. C. 139, 16 May 1917, CAB 23/2. Cf. Scott Diary, p. 54 (note 57 above).
62. John Brownlee Lonsdale (1850–1924). M.P. (Cons.) 1900–18. Honorary Secretary and Chief Whip, Irish Unionist party 1901–16, chairman of the party 1916–18. Created Baron Armaghdale 1918. Lord Lieutenant of Co. Armagh 1920–4.
63. William O'Brien (1852–1931). M.P. (Nat.) 1883–1918. After 1903 leader with Healy of the All for Ireland League, a splinter party based in Co. Cork. Journalist.
64. Timothy Michael Healy (1855–1931). M.P. (Nat.) 1880–1918. Governor-General, Irish Free State, 1922–8.
65. Redmond to Lloyd George, 17 May 1917, Redmond Papers 15189.
66. O'Brien to Lloyd George, 17 May 1917, L.G.P. F/41/9/2.
67. Lonsdale to Lloyd George, 17 May 1917, L.G.P. F/2/4/1.
68. P. J. Buckland, *Irish Unionism* 1 (Dublin, 1972), pp. 90–5.
69. Adams to Lloyd George, 19 May 1917, L.G.P. F/63/1/11–12.
70. W.C. 141, 21 May 1917, CAB 23/2.
71. W.C. 142, 22 May 1917, CAB 23/2.
72. W.C. 145, 24 May 1917, CAB 23/2.
73. Denis Kelly (1852–1924). Roman Catholic Bishop of Ross 1897–1924. Economist and agricultural expert. Member Agricultural Board for Ireland 1900–21, Royal Commission on the Poor Laws 1906–9, Primrose Committee 1911.
74. Adams to Lloyd George, 24 May 1917, L.G.P. F/63/1/17; cf. same to same, 23 May 1917, L.G.P. F/63/1/15–16.
75. Kelly to Adams, 24 May 1917, L.G.P. F/63/1/17; W.C. 145, 24 May 1917, CAB 23/2.
76. W.C. 146, 25 May 1917, CAB 23/2
77. O'Connor to Redmond, 24 May 1917, Redmond Papers 15215; O'Connor to Devlin, Dillon and Redmond (telegram), 24 May 1917, *ibid.*
78. Dillon to Redmond, 26 May 1917, cited F. S. L. Lyons, *John Dillon* (London, 1968), p. 416.
79. Dillon to Redmond, 26 May 1917, Redmond Papers 15182.

80. O'Connor to Redmond, 26 May 1917, Redmond Papers 15215.
81. Dillon to O'Connor, 25 May 1917, cited Lyons, p. 417.
82. O'Connor to Redmond, 26 May 1917, Redmond Papers 15215.
83. O'Connor to Redmond, 28 May 1917, Redmond Papers 15215.
84. Gill to Adams, 26 May 1917, L.G.P. F/66/1/8; 27 May 1917, L.G.P. F/66/1/12.
85. O'Connor to Redmond, 29 May 1917, Redmond Papers 15215.
86. L.G.P. F/63/1/20.
87. Dillon to Redmond, 31 May 1917, Redmond Papers 15182.
88. W.C. 152, 31 May 1917, CAB 23/2.
89. Adams to Lloyd George, 31 May 1917, L.G.P. F/63/1/20; cf. Appendix II to W.C. 152 (note 88 above).
90. James William Lowther (1855–1949). M.P. (Cons.) 1883–5, 1886–1921. Speaker 1905–21. Created Viscount Ullswater 1921.
    Adams had warned against appointing the Speaker; Adams to Lloyd George, 23 May 1917, L.G.P. F/63/1/15.
91. Francis John Stephen Hopwood (1860–1947). Entered Board of Trade 1885. Permanent Under-Secretary, Colonial Office, 1907–11, Additional Civil Lord of the Admiralty 1912–17.
92. Hopwood was superfluous after the reorganisation of the Admiralty in May, but in recommending him as secretary Carson denied that his motive was to rid himself of an embarrassment. Kerr to Lloyd George, 24 May 1917, L.G.P. F/89/1/6.
93. Buckland, *loc. cit.*
94. McDowell, p. 81.
95. Michael Laffan, 'The Unification of Sinn Fein in 1917', *Irish Historical Studies*, XVII (1971).
96. *The Times*, 20 May 1917.
97. Duke to Lloyd George, 3 Jun. 1917, L.G.P. F/37/4/26.
98. Thomas Aubrey Spring-Rice, 3rd Baron Monteagle of Brandon (1883–1934). Career diplomat 1907–30; in 1917 2nd Secretary in Washington, where his uncle, Sir Cecil Spring-Rice, was Ambassador.
99. George Gavan Duffy (1882–1951). M.P. (Sinn Fein) 1918–23, delegate to negotiate the Irish Treaty 1921, Minister for Foreign Affairs 1922. Judge 1936, President of the High Court of Ireland 1946–51.
100. Monteagle to Adams, 1 Jun. 1917, L.G.P. F/66/1/15; 4 Jun. 1917, L.G.P. F/66/1/18.
101. Adams to Lloyd George, 7 Jun. 1917, L.G.P. F/63/1/22.
102. Plunkett Diary, 10–12 Jun. 1917.
103. W.C. 163, 14 Jun. 1917, CAB 23/2.
104. Monteagle to Adams, 14 Jun. 1917, L.G.P. F/66/1/23.
105. Plunkett to Adams, 16 Jun. 1917, Plunkett Papers.
106. Duke to Lloyd George, 22 Jul. 1917, L.G.P. F/65/1/16.
107. Plunkett Diary, 25 Jun. 1917.
108. Plunkett to Adams, 29 Jun. 1917, L.G.P. F/64/1/13.
109. Adams to Lloyd George, 3 Jul. 1917, L.G.P. F/63/1/24; Plunkett Diary, 3 Jul. 1917.
110. W.C. 190, 19 Jul 1917, CAB 23/3.

111. George William Russell (AE) (1867–1935). Writer, painter, journalist.
112. Edward Anthony MacLysaght (1889–). Publisher, farmer, writer. Senator 1922–5. Publisher and journalist 1916–38. Inspector, Irish Manuscripts Commission, 1939–42. Keeper of MSS, National Library of Ireland, 1943–5.
113. See McDowell, pp. 85–6.
114. Eamon De Valera (1882–1975). A leader of the Easter Rising, released under amnesty June 1917. President of Sinn Fein, 1917–26. President of the 'Irish Republic' 1919–22. Led opposition to Irish Treaty. Leader of Opposition in Free State parliament 1927–32. Head of government 1937–48, 1951–4, 1957–9. President of Ireland 1959–73.
115. W.C. 175, 4 July 1917, CAB 23/3. Midleton and Carson pressed for harsh measures.
116. Bryan Thomas Mahon (1862–1930). Commanded 10th (Irish) Division 1914–15. Commanded Salonika army 1915–16. C-in-C Ireland 1916–18. Senator, Irish Free State, 1922–30.
      Ivor Churchill Guest (1873–1939). M.P. (Cons.) 1900–6 (Lib.) 1906–10. Created Baron 1910. Paymaster-General 1910–12, Lord in Waiting 1913–15, Lord Lieutenant of Ireland 1915–18. Succeeded as 2nd Baron Wimborne 1914, created Viscount 1918.
117. Adams to Lloyd George, n.d., L.G.P. F/63/1/38.
118. W.C. 186, 14 Jul. 1917, CAB 23/3. Cf. G.T. 1261, 3 Jul. 1917, *ibid.*
119. Plunkett to Adams, 20 Aug. 1917, L.G.P. F/63/1/38.
      Horace Plunkett (1854–1932). Emigrated as a youth to ranch in Wyoming. Returned to Ireland 1889 to use his wealth to regenerate Irish agriculture. M.P. (Unionist) 1892–1900. Vice-president (i.e. effective head) Department of Agriculture and Technical Instruction 1899–1907. Founded Irish Agricultural Organisation Society 1908. Senator, Irish Free State, 1922–3.
120. McDowell, pp. 114–16.
121. See above, pp. 83–4.
122. Patrick O'Donnell (1856–1927). R.C. Bishop of Raphoe 1888–1922. Titular Archbishop of Attalia and coadjutor to Cardinal Logue 1922–4. Archbishop of Armagh 1924–7. Cardinal 1925.
123. Arthur Cecil Pigou (1877–1959). Professor of political economy and fellow of King's College, Cambridge, 1908–43.
124. Plunkett to Adams, 12 Nov. 1917, L.G.P. F/64/4/10.
125. Adams to Plunkett, 10 Nov. 1917, L.G.P. F/64/4/6.
126. Adams to Plunkett, 15 Nov. 1917, L.G.P. F/64/4/11.
127. Charles Vane-Tempest-Stewart (1878–1949). M.P. (Cons.) 1906–15. Succeeded as 7th Marquess of Londonderry 1915. Served Western Front 1916–17. Under-Secretary for Air 1920–1. Minister of Education, Northern Ireland, 1921–6. Secretary of State for Air (Westminster) 1931–5.
128. Plunkett to Adams, 16 Nov. 1917, L.G.P. F/64/4/12. Oliver's pamphlet, *A Method of Constitutional Co-operation. Suggestions for the Better Government of the United Kingdom*, was sent to Plunkett, Midleton and Londonderry in October. D. G. Boyce and J. O. Stubbs,

'F. S. Oliver, Lord Selborne and Federalism', *Journal of Imperial and Commonwealth History*, v (1976), 68–70.
129. Plunkett to Adams, 21 Nov. 1917, L.G.P. F/64/4/18.
130. W.C. 280, 22 Nov. 1917, CAB 23/4.
131. Hugh McDowell Pollock (?—1937). Minister of Finance for Northern Ireland 1921–37. M.P. (Unionist) at Stormont, 1921–37.
132. Plunkett Diary, 28–30 Nov. 1917.
133. Adams to Lloyd George, 3 Dec. 1917, L.G.P. F/63/1/40.
134. Adams to Lloyd George, 4 Dec. 1917, L.G.P. F/63/1/42.
135. Adams to Lloyd George, 5 Dec. 1917, L.G.P. F/63/1/44.
136. Kerr to Lloyd George, 5 Dec. 1917, Lothian Papers 573.
137. Plunkett Diary, 5 Dec. 1917.
138. Southborough to Adams, 7 Dec. 1917, L.G.P. F/65/1/22.
139. Plunkett to Adams, 8 Dec. 1917, L.G.P. F/64/5/1.
140. McDowell, p. 130.
141. Midleton to Plunkett, 6 Dec. 1917, Plunkett Papers.
142. Adams to Lloyd George, 10 Dec. 1917, L.G.P. F/63/1/46.
143. Adams to Lloyd George, 10 Dec. 1917, L.G.P. F/63/1/47.
144. Adams to Southborough, 10 Dec. 1917, L.G.P. F/65/1/24; same to same, 11 Dec. 1917, L.G.P. F/65/1/25.
145. Adams to Southborough, 10 Dec. 1917, note 144 above.
146. These letters are in Redmond Papers 15189.
147. Plunkett to Adams, 11 Dec. 1917, L.G.P. F/64/5/2.
148. Lloyd George to Redmond, 11 Dec. 1917, Redmond Papers 15189.
149. Adams to Southborough, 15 Dec. 1917, L.G.P. F/65/1/28.
150. McDowell, pp. 133–4.
151. Plunkett to Adams, 13 Dec. 1917, L.G.P. F/64/5/3.
152. O'Donnell to Redmond, 22 Dec. 1917, Redmond Papers 15217.
153. Gwynn to Redmond, 29 Dec. 1917, Redmond Papers 15192.
    Stephen Lucius Gwynn (1864–1950). M.P. (Nat.) 1906–18. Member of the Dardanelles Commission. Journalist and writer. A protestant.
154. Midleton to Adams, 22 Dec. 1917, L.G.P. F/66/1/56; Gwynn to Adams, 22 Dec. 1917, L.G.P. F/66/1/57; Adams to Gwynn, 27 Dec. 1917, L.G.P. F/66/1/57.
155. Plunkett to Adams, 30 Dec. 1917, L.G.P. F/64/5/10.
156. Redmond to Lloyd George, 4 Jan. 1918, Redmond Papers 15189.
157. Plunkett to Adams, 12 Jan. 1918, L.G.P. F/64/6/5.
158. Thomas Jones, *Whitehall Diary*, I, 45.
159. Adams to Southborough, 14 Jan. 1918, L.G.P. F/65/1/34.
    Hugh T. Barrie (1860–1922). M.P. (Cons.) 1906–22.
160. Southborough to Adams, 15 Jan. 1918, L.G.P. F/65/1/35.
161. McDowell, pp. 149–50.
162. Midleton to Adams, 17 Jan. 1918, L.G.P. F/66/2/3.
163. Antony Patrick Macdonnell (1844–1925). Entered Indian Civil Service 1865. Lt. Governor, N.W. Provinces 1895–1901. Under-Secretary of State in Ireland 1902–8. Created Baron 1908.
164. See note 162 above.
165. Plunkett Diary, 19 Jan. 1918.
166. Adams to Plunkett, 22 Jan. 1918, L.G.P. F/64/6/16: cf. Lloyd George

to Plunkett, 21 Jan. 1918, Redmond to Lloyd George, 21 Jan. 1918, Redmond Papers 15189, Plunkett to Adams 21 Jan. 1918, L.G.P. F/64/6/18, Plunkett to Redmond, 23 Jan. 1918, Redmond Papers 15221.

167. R. J. H. Shaw to Adams, 25 Jan. 1918, L.G.P. F/65/4/2. (See n. 172)
168. Adams to Lloyd George, 2 Feb. 1918, L.G.P. F/63/2/5.
169. Another memorandum, *ibid.*
170. *Ibid.*
171. *Ibid.*
172. Richard James H. Shaw (1885–1946). Secretary, Irish Unionist Alliance, 1913–14. Active Service, Gallipoli, Serbia, Irish Rising, 1915–16. Assistant Press Censor, Ireland, 1916–18. Secretary, Irish Convention, 1917–18. Assistant secretary to Viceroy 1918–19. Journalist, *The Times*, 1919–39.
173. Adams to Lloyd George, 2 Feb. 1918, L.G.P. F/63/2/5.
174. Adams to Lloyd George, 5 Feb. 1918, L.G.P. F/63/2/7.
175. Adams to Lloyd George, n.d., L.G.P. F/63/2/8.
176. 'Heads of Amendments', n.d., L.G.P. F/63/2/9.
177. McDowell, pp. 157–8.
178. W.C. 345, 13 Feb. 1918, CAB 23/5.
179. *Procès-verbal*, L.G.P. F/66/6/1.
180. McDowell, p. 161.
181. Plunkett to Lloyd George, 13 Feb. 1918, L.G.P. F/63/2/11.
182. Plunkett Diary, 14 Feb. 1918.
183. Harmsworth to Plunkett, 16 Feb. 1918, Plunkett Papers.
184. Adams to Lloyd George, 20 Feb. 1918, L.G.P. F/63/2/12.
185. W.C. 351, 22 Feb. 1918, CAB 23/5.
186. Plunkett Diary, 25 Feb. 1918.
187. Southborough to Adams, 27 Feb. 1918, L.G.P. F/65/2/2.
188. Plunkett Diary, 2 Mar. 1918; Plunkett to Adams, 2 Mar. 1918, Plunkett Papers.
189. Midleton to Adams, 1 Mar. 1918, L.G.P. F/66/2/19.
190. Plunkett Diary, 5 Mar. 1918; Plunkett to Adams, 5 Mar. 1918, Plunkett Papers.
191. McDowell, p. 169.
192. *Ibid.*, p. 172.
193. Adams to Plunkett, 7 Mar. 1918, Plunkett Papers.
194. McDowell, p. vii.
195. W.C. 372, 25 Mar. 1918, CAB 23/5.
196. Adams to Lloyd George, 26 Mar. 1918, L.G.P. F/63/2/18.
197. W.C. 375, 27 Mar. 1918, CAB 23/5.
198. Joseph Aloysius Byrne (1874–1942). Entered army 1893, served in South Africa. Deputy Adjutant General, Irish Command, 1916. Inspector-General, Royal Irish Constabulary, 1916–20 (dismissed). Governor of the Seychelles 1922–7, of Sierra Leone 1927–31, of Kenya 1931–7.
199. W.C. 374 and W.C. 375, 27 Mar. 1918, CAB 23/5.
200. W.C. 376, 28 Mar. 1918, CAB 23/5.
201. W.C. 383, 5 Apr. 1918, CAB 23/6.

202. W.C. 385, 6 Apr. 1918, CAB 23/6.
203. Adams to Lloyd George, 28 Mar. 1918, L.G.P. F/63/2/20–1.
204. Gwynn to Adams, 8 Apr. 1918, L.G.P. F/63/2/25.
205. W.C. 388, 10 Apr. 1918, CAB 23/6.
206. Arthur Griffith (1872–1922). Founder and editor of *Sinn Fein* 1906–15. M.P. (Sinn Fein) 1918–22. Chairman of the Mansion House Committee which led Sinn Fein.
207. Lyons, pp. 434–5.
208. W.C. 392, 16 Apr. 1918, CAB 23/6.
209. Adams to Lloyd George, 19 Apr. 1918, L.G.P. F/62/2/30.
210. Memorandum by French, 20 Apr. 1918, CAB 1/26/12.
211. Plunkett Diary, 21 Apr. 1918.
212. *The Political Diaries of C. P. Scott, 1911–1928*, ed. Trevor Wilson (London, 1970) pp. 342–3.
213. W.C. 389, 10 Apr. 1918, CAB 23/6.
214. W.C. 392, 16 Apr. 1918, CAB 23/6.
215. George Cave (1856–1928). M.P. (Cons.) 1906–18. Solicitor-General 1915–16. Home Secretary 1916–18. Lord Chancellor 1922–4, 1924–8. Knighted 1915, created Viscount 1918.
216. Gordon Hewart (1870–1943). M.P. (Lib.) 1913–22. Solicitor-General 1916–19, Attorney-General 1919–22. Knighted 1916, created Baron 1922.
217. Chamberlain to Lloyd George, 10 Apr. 1918, University of Birmingham Library, Austen Chamberlain Papers 18/2/6.
218. J. E. Kendle, 'Federalism and the Irish Problem in 1918', *History*, LVI (1971). Cf. Boyce and Stubbs, *op. cit.*
219. Thomas Jones, *Whitehall Diary*, III, 16; the committee's minutes are in CAB 27/46.
220. CAB 27/46.
221. Adams to Lloyd George, 23 Apr. 1918, L.G.P. F/62/2/32.
222. Bodleian Library, H. A. L. Fisher Papers, 8A, Diary 23 Apr. 1918.
223. Addison Diary, 23 Apr. 1918.
224. W.C. 397, 23 Apr. 1918, CAB 23/6.
225. Plunkett Diary, 5–10 Oct. 1917.
226. Adams to Lloyd George, 22 Feb. 1918, L.G.P. F/63/2/13.
227. Adams to Southborough, 28 Feb. 1918, L.G.P. F/65/2/5.
228. Long to Lloyd George, 3 Mar. 1918, L.G.P. F/32/5/24.
229. Duke to Lloyd George, 22 Mar. 1918, L.G.P. F/37/4/47.
230. Midleton to Bonar Law, 2 May 1918, Bonar Law Papers 83/3/4; memorandum by Midleton, 1 May 1918 and n.d., Bonar Law Papers 85/B/18; cf. Earl of Midleton, *Records and Reactions* (London, 1938), pp. 237–8.
231. Selborne to Lloyd George, 4 May 1918, L.G.P. F/94/3/47; Selborne to Chamberlain, 8 May 1918, Austen Chamberlain Papers 18/2/15.
232. Edward Shortt (1862–1935). M.P. (Lib.) 1910–22. A barrister. Strong Home Ruler who had voted against Irish conscription. Chief Secretary 1918–19. Home Secretary 1919–22.
233. Long to Lloyd George, 7 May 1918, L.G.P. F/32/5/31; same to same, 8 May 1918, L.G.P. F/32/5/34.

234. W.C. 408A, 10 May 1918, CAB 23/14.
235. Harmsworth to Plunkett, 13 May 1918, Plunkett Papers.
236. Harmsworth to Plunkett, 21 May 1918, Plunkett Papers.
237. Long to Balfour, 14 Apr. 1918, British Library Addit. MSS. 49777 (Balfour Papers).
238. Minutes of 3rd Meeting, 9 May 1918, CAB 27/46.
239. Minutes of 4th Meeting, 4 Jun. 1918, CAB 27/46.
240. Astor to Lloyd George, 9 May and n.d. (c. 15 May) 1918, L.G.P. F/83/1/18; Guest to Lloyd George, 3 May 1918, L.G.P. F/21/2/20.
241. Addison Diary (Addison Papers 96), 19 Apr. 1918.
242. Oliver to Carson, 18 Apr. 1918, Austen Chamberlain Papers 14/6/101.
243. Adams to Chamberlain, 4 Jun. 1918, L.G.P. F/67/1/23.
244. Memoranda by Long, G.T. 4728, CAB 24/53, and by Adams, G.T. 4882, CAB 24/54.
245. Adams to Chamberlain, 18 Jun. 1918, L.G.P. F/67/1/23.
246. W.C. 433, 19 Jun. 1918, CAB 23/6. Cf. Adams to Lloyd George, n.d., L.G.P. F/63/2/8.
247. Long to Adams, 20 Jun. 1918, L.G.P. F/67/1/24.
248. They are not in his file of minutes to Lloyd George, L.G.P. F/63/2, but in F/74/26. On the deputation see Kendle 'Federalism and the Irish Problem', 226–7.
249. Adams to Barnes, 27 Jun. 1918, L.G.P. F/67/1/25.
250. Plunkett Diary, 20 Jun. 1918.
251. Adams to Lloyd George, 27 Jul. 1918, L.G.P. F/63/2/38.
252. W.C. 453, 29 Jul. 1918, CAB 23/7.
253. Minutes of 6th Meeting, 6 Aug. 1918, CAB 27/46; cf. Batterbee (Long's secretary) to Adams, 7 Aug. 1918, L.G.P. F/67/1/32.
254. Arthur Cecil Murray (1879–1962). M.P. (Lib.) 1908–23. Parliamentary Private Secretary to Foreign Secretary 1910–14. Served European War 1914–16. Assistant Military Attaché, Washington, 1917–18. Succeeded brother (Gideon Murray) as 3rd Viscount Elibank 1951. Author. Director of L.N.E.R. 1923–48. He was the fourth son of the 1st Viscount Murray of Elibank, and thus the younger brother of Alec Murray, 1st Baron Murray of Elibank (1870–1920), the former Liberal Chief Whip, who retired from politics to concentrate on his business interests in 1912.
255. See above, pp. 90–3.
256. Murray to Sir William Wiseman, 10 Aug. 1918, Yale University Library, Papers of E. M. House.
257. Plunkett Diary, 12–13 Aug. 1918; Plunkett to Adams, 13 Aug. 1918, Plunkett Papers.
258. Plunkett Diary, 2 Sep. 1918.
259. Adams to Lloyd George, 11 Oct. 1918, L.G.P. F/63/2/42.
260. Adams to Lloyd George, 14 Nov. 1918, L.G.P. F/63/2/43.
261. Plunkett Diary, 23 Nov. 1918.

CHAPTER 6. IMPERIAL QUESTIONS

1. D. C. Ellinwood, 'Lord Milner's "Kindergarten", the British Round Table Group, and the movement for Imperial Reform, 1910–1918' (Washington University Ph.D. thesis, 1962), p. 351. But cf. Kendle, *The Round Table Movement and Imperial Union.*
2. Nimocks, *Milner's Young Men*, pp. 138–57.
3. 'The Burden of Victory', *The Round Table*, 19 (June 1915), 517 [written by Kerr]; 'Australia', *ibid.*, 20 (September 1915), 865.
4. Milner to A. J. Glazebrook, 8 Mar. 1916, Milner Papers 44; Vincent Massey, *What's Past is Prologue* (Toronto, 1963), pp. 34 ff.; Max Beloff, *Imperial Sunset* (London, 1969), pp. 212–18; Kendle, pp. 181–205.
5. Cf. Ellinwood, p. 362.
   Robert H. Brand (1878–1963). Served in South Africa 1902–9, then merchant banker. Member, Imperial Munitions Board of Canada, 1915–18. Deputy chairman, British Mission in Washington, 1917–18.
   William Lionel Hichens (1874–1940). Served in South Africa 1902–10. Chairman of Cammell Laird 1910–40.
   Frederick Scott Oliver (1864–1934). Author and pamphleteer, director of Debenham and Freebody's.
   Leopold Stennett Amery (1873–1955). *Times* journalist 1899–1909. M.P. (Cons.) 1911–45. Active service 1914–16. Assistant Secretary, War Cabinet Secretariat, 1917–18. Under-Secretary for Colonies 1919–21, Admiralty 1921–2. First Lord 1922–4.
6. Thomas Jones, *Whitehall Diary*, I, 31 & 216.
7. The resolution was proposed on 28 Mar. 1917 and accepted on 16 Apr. 1917, CAB 32/1, pp. 53 & xii.
8. e.g. Amery to Milner, 10 Jul. 1917, CAB 17/190.
9. 'India and the Empire', *The Round Table*, 8 (September 1912), 587–626 [by Kerr]; cf. D. C. Ellinwood, 'The Round Table Movement and India, 1909–20', *Journal of Commonwealth Political Studies*, IX (1971).
10. William Sinclair Marris (1873–1945). Entered I.C.S. 1895. Lent to Government of Transvaal 1909–10. Acting Secretary, Government of India, Home Dept., 1913–16. Inspector-General of Police, United Provinces, 1916–17. Joint Secretary, Government of India, 1917, Home Secretary 1919–21. Governor of Assam 1921–2, of United Provinces 1922–8. Principal of Armstrong College, Durham University, 1929–37. Vice-chancellor, Durham University, 1932–4.
11. Reginald Coupland (1884–1952). Fellow of Trinity College, Oxford, 1907–14. Beit Lecturer in Colonial History 1913–18. Editor of *The Round Table* 1917–19 and 1939–41. Beit Professor of the History of the British Empire, and fellow of All Souls, 1920–48.
12. Frederick William Duke (1863–1924). Entered I.C.S. 1882. Lt. Governor of Bengal 1911. Member, Council of India, 1914–19. Permanent Under-Secretary of State for India 1919–24.
13. John Morley (1838–1923). Journalist and politician. Editor of *Fort-*

nightly Review 1867–82. M.P. (Lib.) 1883–95, 1896–1908. Chief Secretary for Ireland 1886 and 1892–5. Secretary of State for India 1905–10. Lord Privy Seal 1910–14. Created Viscount Morley of Blackburn 1908. See Stephen E. Koss, *John Morley at the India Office 1905–10* (London, 1969).
14. Gilbert John Murray Kynymond Elliott (1845–1914). Succeeded as 4th Earl of Minto 1891. Soldier and war correspondent 1867–86. Governor-General of Canada 1898–1904. Viceroy of India 1905–10.
15. L. Curtis, *Papers Relating to the Application of the Principle of Dyarchy to the Government of India* (Oxford, 1920), p. 41.
16. Kerr to Curtis, 22 Jul. 1917, Lothian Papers 33/19.
17. Reginald Coupland, *The Indian Problem, 1833–1935* (London, 1942), p. 58; R. Danzig, 'The Many-Layered Cake: A Case Study in the Reform of the Indian Empire', *Modern Asian Studies*, III (1969).
18. Kerr to Milner, 11 Dec. 1916, Bodleian Library, Round Table Papers 814/210–14.
19. W.C. 11, 12, 15, 16, on 19, 20, 22 and 23 Dec. 1916, CAB 23/1.
20. Cf. J. E. Kendle, *The Colonial and Imperial Conferences, 1887–1911* (London, 1967).
21. Austen Chamberlain (1863–1937). M.P. (Cons.) 1892–1937. Chancellor of the Exchequer 1903–6. Secretary of State for India 1915–17. War Cabinet 1918–19. Chancellor of the Exchequer 1919–21, Lord Privy Seal 1921–2. Foreign Secretary 1924–9. W.C. 12, 20 Dec. 1916, CAB 23/1.
22. Diary of Sir Hugh Thornton, Dec. 1916–Jan. 1917, Milner Papers 19, pp. 18–19.
23. Hankey Diary, 12 Jan. 1917.
24. *Ibid.*, 18 Mar. 1917.
25. Long to Bonar Law, 25 Dec. 1916, Bonar Law Papers 81/1/69.
26. Amery to Kerr, 24 Jan. 1917, Lothian Papers 666.
27. Kerr to Lloyd George, n.d., Lothian Papers 668/3.
    Robert Laird Borden (1854–1937). Barrister. Canadian M.P. 1896–1905, 1908–21. Leader of Conservative party 1901–20. Prime Minister of Canada 1911–20. Canadian plenipotentiary at the Washington Naval Conference, 1921–2.
28. *Lloyd George: a diary by Frances Stevenson*, ed. A. J. P. Taylor (London, 1971), p. 145.
29. Long to Balfour, 27 Feb. 1917, FO 800/209/118.
30. Balfour to Kerr, 27 Feb. 1917, FO 800/212/99.
31. Balfour to Long, 1 Mar. 1917, FO 800/209/118.
32. Long to Balfour, 5 Mar. 1917, FO 800/209/121; Balfour to Long, 5 Mar. 1917, *ibid.*
33. Kerr to Lloyd George, 27 Feb. 1917, Lothian Papers 668/1.
34. Louis Botha (1863–1919) Commander-in-Chief Boer forces 1900–02. Prime Minister of Transvaal 1907–10. Prime Minister of the Union of South Africa 1910–19.
35. Joseph Ward (1856–1930). Prime Minister of New Zealand 1906–12, 1928–30.
36. Hankey Diary, 18 Mar. 1917.

37. Borden Diary, 14 & 30 Apr. 1917.
38. Kerr to Curtis, 24 Apr. 1917, Lothian Papers 33/13.
39. Satyendra Prassano Sinha (1864–1928). Barrister. Member Viceroy's Executive Council 1910–15, the first Indian member. Under-Secretary of State for India 1919–20. Governor of Bihar and Orissa 1920–1. Knight 1914, 1st Baron of Raipur 1919.
40. R. A. Huttenback, 'The British Empire as "White Man's Country" – Racial Attitudes and Immigration Legislation in the Colonies of White Settlement', *Journal of British Studies*, XIII (1973).
41. Kerr to Chamberlain, 28 Feb. 1917, Lothian Papers 34.
42. Kerr to Chamberlain, 7 Mar. 1917, *ibid.*
43. Curtis to Chelmsford, 2 Nov. 1916, Lothian Papers 33.
44. Chamberlain to Kerr, 24 Apr. 1917, Lothian Papers 34; Curtis to Kerr, 25 Mar. 1917, *ibid.*
45. James Scorgie Meston (1865–1943). Entered I.C.S. 1885. Adviser on civil service reform in Cape Colony and Transvaal 1904–6. Secretary to Finance Department, Government of India, 1906–12. Lt. Governor, United Provinces, 1912–18. Finance Member, Viceroy's Council, 1919. President, Liberal party organisation 1936–43.
46. M. Ollivier, *The Colonial and Imperial Conferences from 1887 to 1937* (Ottawa, 1954), II, 251–4.
47. Chamberlain to Kerr, 24 Apr. 1917, Lothian Papers, 34/13.
48. Coupland to Curtis, 22 May 1917, Round Table Papers 810/67.
49. 'The New Developments in the Constitution of the Empire', *The Round Table*, 27, June 1917.
50. P. H. Kerr, 'The Imperial Constitution', 1 June 1917, Lothian Papers 33.
51. Charles Hardinge (1858–1944). Entered Diplomatic Service 1880. Assistant Under-Secretary 1903–4, Ambassador at Petrograd 1904–6. Permanent Under-Secretary of State 1906–10 and 1916–20. Viceroy for India 1910–16. Ambassador in Paris 1920–3. Knight 1904, 1st Baron Hardinge of Penshurst 1910.
52. Frederic John Napier Thesiger (1868–1933). Governor of Queensland 1905–9, of New South Wales 1909–13. Viceroy for India 1916–21. First Lord of the Admiralty 1924. Warden of All Souls 1932–3. 3rd Baron Chelmsford, created Viscount 1921.
53. Appendix to G.T. 822, 22 May 1917, CAB 24/14.
54. 'Memorandum by the Secretary of State for India on Indian Reforms', G.T. 822, 22 May 1917, CAB 24/14.
55. Gen. H. H. the Maharajah of Bikanir (1880–1943). Succeeded 1887, assumed ruling powers 1898. Served with 2nd Bengal Lancers in Europe 1914–15. Represented India at 1917 Imperial War Conference and Paris Peace Conference, 1919.
56. Kerr to Curtis, 23 Apr. 1917, Lothian Papers 33/11.
57. Kerr to Lloyd George, n.d., Lothian Papers 741.
58. Hankey to Chamberlain, 6 Jun. 1917, CAB 21/68.
59. G.T. 1199, 27 Jun. 1917, CAB 24/17.
60. W.C. 172, 29 Jun. 1917, CAB 23/3.
61. G.T. 1252, 2 Jul. 1917, CAB 24/18.

62. Kerr to Balfour, 3 Jul. 1917, FO 800/212/101.
63. W.C. 176, 5 Jul. 1917, CAB 23/3.
64. G.T. 1252, p. 1.
65. W.C. 176, 5 Jul. 1917, CAB 23/3.
66. Kerr to Lloyd George, 7 Jul. 1917, Lothian Papers 32/2–9.
67. See note 57 above.
68. See above, p. 124.
69. Kerr to Curtis, 22 Jul. 1917, Lothian Papers, 33/19.
70. See below, pp. 155–7.
71. Kerr to Lloyd George, 30 Jul. 1917, Lothian Papers 644.
72. P.P. 1917–18, Cd. 8610, XVI, 773.
73. Edwin Samuel Montagu (1879–1924). M.P. (Lib.) 1906–22. Financial Secretary to the Treasury 1914–15 and 1915–16. Chancellor of the Duchy of Lancaster 1915 and 1916. Minister of Munitions 1916. Secretary of State for India, 1917–22.
74. S. R. Mehrotra, *India and the Commonwealth, 1885–1929* (London, 1963), pp. 60–3.
75. Montagu to Lloyd George, 5 Jul. 1917, L.G.P. F/39/3/21; 95 *H.C. Debs.*, 5s, 12 Jul. 1917, 2199–2210.
76. 'I enclose the letter for which you ask...' Montagu to Lloyd George, 17 Jul. 1917, L.G.P. F/39/3/23.
77. G.T. 1615, 30 Jul. 1917, CAB 24/22.
78. 97 *H.C. Debs.*, 5s, 20 Aug. 1917, 1695–6.
79. P.P. 1918, Cd. 9109, VIII, 113.
80. Montagu to A. Chamberlain, 15 Aug. 1917, Austen Chamberlain Papers 15/5/8.
81. G.T. 1252, 2 Jul. 1917, CAB 24/22.
82. R. J. Moore, *The Crisis of Indian Unity, 1917–1940* (Oxford, 1974), p. 2.
83. Baptista to the Khilafat committee, 6 Feb. 1918, Lothian Papers 206/62; Kerr to R. H. A. Carter (India Office), 5 Feb. 1918, *ibid.* 206/61.
84. This is the term preferred by Guinn, *British Strategy and Politics.*
85. Kendle, pp. 219–20.
86. S. D. Waley, *Edwin Montagu* (Bombay, 1964), p. 167.

CHAPTER 7. THE POLITICAL CULTURE OF 10 DOWNING STREET

1. *The Nation*, 24 Feb. 1917.
2. Michael Bentley, *The Liberal Mind* (Cambridge, 1977).
3. Lothian Papers, 717.
4. See above, p. 89.
5. Adams to Lloyd George, 25 Apr. 1917, L.G.P. F/70/22/1.
6. Plunkett Diary, 18 May 1917.
7. Kerr to Lady Anne Kerr, his mother, 6 Mar. 1917, Lothian Papers 466/2.
8. *The Political Diaries of C. P. Scott 1911–1928*, ed. Trevor Wilson (London, 1970), pp. 342–3.

9. i.e. 'Ireland and the Empire', *The Round Table*, xxiv (1916); Kerr to Lloyd George, 13 Jan. 1917, L.G.P. F/89/1/1; See above, p. 87.
10. See above, p. 86.
11. *The Oxford Survey of the British Empire* (Oxford, 1914), i, 232–3.
12. *Ibid.*, 222.
13. *Ibid.*, 350.
14. 'European War', *Political Quarterly*, iii (Sept. 1914), 5 & 13.
15. 'International Control', *ibid.*, v (Feb. 1915).
16. 'The Cabinet and the Nation', *ibid.*, vi (May 1915), 3.
17. *Ibid.*, 7.
18. *Ibid.*, 6–7.
19. 'National Organization and National Will', *ibid.*, vii (Mar. 1916), 3.
20. 'The Economic Conference at Paris', *ibid.*, viii (Aug. 1916), 4.
21. 'The Schism of Europe', *The Round Table*, xviii (Mar. 1915), 345–411. Prussian state-worship was also the theme of 'Britain, France and Germany', *ibid.*, v (Dec. 1911) and 'The Balkan Danger and Universal Peace', *ibid.*, vi (Mar. 1912).
22. 'The War in Europe', *The Round Table* xvi (Sept. 1914), 610.
23. 'The Making of Peace', *ibid.*, xxv (Dec. 1916), 4.
24. 'The Schism of Europe', 345.
25. 'The Foundation of Peace', *The Round Table*, xix (June 1915), 612.
26. *Ibid.*, 612–13.
27. *The Round Table*, xviii (Mar. 1915); *ibid.*, xxi (Dec. 1915).
28. 'The Foundation of Peace', 609–10.
29. 'The End of War', *The Round Table*, xx (Sept. 1915).
30. 'The Harvest of War', *The Round Table*, xxi (Dec. 1915), 9, 10.
31. 'War Aims', *ibid.*, xxiv (Sept. 1916), 609.
32. He also lacked the *parti pris* opinions which Namier and Seton-Watson brought to their work on the Austro-Hungarian empire and the successor states.
33. 'The Political Relations between Advanced and Backward Peoples', in A. J. Grant *et al.*, *International Relations* (London, 1916); 'Labour and Industry', in J. Hilton *et al.*, *The Other War* (London, 1916).
34. 'Political Relations...', p. 172.
35. 'Labour and Industry', p. 30.
36. *Ibid.*, p. 35.
37. *Ibid.*, p. 32.
38. Thomas Jones, *Whitehall Diary*, i, 11.
39. *The Diaries of Beatrice Webb, 1912–32*, ed. M. I. Cole (London, 1952), i, 85. In the same passage Adams was condemned as a 'high-browed idealist'.
40. Milner asked him to prepare a reply before he was invited to join the Garden Suburb. Milner Diary, 27 Dec. 1916.
41. Kerr to Lloyd George, 27 Jan. 1917, Lothian Papers 638/4.
42. See Arthur S. Link, *Wilson: Campaigns for Progressivism and Peace* (Princeton, 1965), pp. 249–71.
43. See note 41 above.

44. 'Notes for speech for February 3rd', Kerr to Lloyd George, n.d., Lothian Papers 638/1. Cf. Lloyd George's own notes in L.G.P. F/221 and *The Times*, 5 Feb. 1917.
45. J. C. Smuts, 'The General and Military Situation', 29 Apr. 1917, quoted in Lloyd George, *War Memoirs* I, 911.
46. A short report is in CAB 23/43.
47. Fest, *Peace or Partition*, pp. 80–3 discusses Milner's interview on this subject with Sidney Low for the *Atlantic Monthly*.
48. Thornton Diary, 24 Mar. 1917; Hankey Diary, 23 Mar. 1917.
49. Hankey Diary, 23 Mar. 1917.
50. Milner Diary, 14 Mar. 1917.
51. Kerr to Lloyd George, n.d., [Mar. 1917], Lothian Papers 670.
52. Kerr to Balfour, 20 Mar. 1917, FO 800/213/233.
53. Kerr to Lloyd George, n.d., [20 Mar. 1917], Lothian Papers 865.
54. Minutes in CAB 23/43. Speech reprinted in Lloyd George, *War Memoirs*, I, 1047–57.
55. See note 53 above.
56. For example it was proposed to relinquish Duala, which the Admiralty wanted as a coaling station, rather than German South West Africa, which South Africa wanted as a colony. Report in CAB 21/77.
57. See Rothwell, *British War Aims and Peace Diplomacy.*
58. Kerr to Lloyd George, n.d., [Apr. 1917], Lothian Papers 866.
59. Reported in *The Times*, 13 Apr. 1917. Lloyd George's notes are in L.G.P. F/232.
60. Kerr to Lloyd George, n.d., [May, 1917], Lothian Papers 929/1.
61. 'The Peace Settlement in Europe', 4 Oct. 1916, quoted in Lloyd George, *War Memoirs*, I, 524.
62. W.C. 128a, 1 May 1917, CAB 23/14.
63. W.C. 133a, 9 May 1917, CAB 23/14.
64. Kerr to Lloyd George, n.d., Lothian Papers 867.
65. Kerr to Lloyd George, 1 Jun. 1917, L.G.P. F/89/1/7 and Lothian Papers 920/3. See pp. 61–71 above for the Serbian question.
66. Kerr to Lloyd George, 26 Jun. 1917, Lothian Papers 640. Disposal of the colonies was prominent in Lloyd George's speech in Glasgow on 29 Jun. *The Times*, 30 Jun. 1917; Lloyd George's notes, L.G.P. F/232.
67. Kerr to Lloyd George, 20 Jul. 1917, Lothian Papers 642/1.
68. Kerr to Curtis, 22 Jul. 1917, Lothian Papers 33/19.
69. Kerr to Lloyd George, 26 Jun. 1917, note 66 above.
70. See above, pp. 39–40.
71. Kerr to Lloyd George, 30 Jul. 1917, Lothian Papers 644. The speech was delivered at the Queen's Hall on 5 Aug. *The Times*, 6 Aug. 1917.
72. Kerr to Lloyd George, 18 Oct. 1917, Lothian Papers 646. The Albert Hall speech, on War Savings on 22 Oct., is reported in *The Times*, 23 Oct. 1917. Notes in L.G.P. F/233.
73. Kerr to Lloyd George, 18 Oct. 1917, Lothian Papers 646.
74. *The History of The Times* (London, 1952), IV, I, 340; Evelyn Wrench, *Geoffrey Dawson and our Times* (London, 1955), pp. 156–7.
75. W.C. 290a, 4 Dec. 1917, CAB 23/13; Charles Seymour, *The Intimate Papers of Colonel House*, III (London, 1928), 237, 284–91.

76. *The Times*, 30 Nov. 1917; Cecil to Bonar Law, 1 Dec. 1917, Bonar Law Papers 82/7/1.
77. Kerr to Lloyd George, n.d. [August 1917], Lothian Papers 645/2.
78. n.s. memorandum to Lloyd George, 4 Dec. 1917, L.G.P. F/89/1/9.
79. Astor to Lloyd George, 5 Dec. 1917, Astor Papers 40/756.
80. Kerr to Lloyd George, n.d. [5/7 Dec. 1917], L.G.P. F/89/1/11 and Lothian Papers 648/2.
81. Kerr to Lloyd George, 4 Dec. 1917, L.G.P. F/89/1/10.
82. *The Times*, 15 Dec. 1917.
83. n.d. memo. by Smuts [11–12 Dec. 1917], FO 800/214/362–9; memo. by Balfour, 15 Dec. 1917, FO 800/214/370–2; Cecil to Balfour, 25 Dec. 1917, FO 800/207/132.
84. See Rothwell, pp. 158–71; Fest, pp. 151–3; above, p. 77.
85. Hankey to Balfour, 5 Dec. 1917, FO 371/3086/231940.
86. Smuts, *op. cit.*; memo. by Drummond, 10 Dec. 1917, G.T. 2976, CAB 24/35.
87. Kerr to Smuts, 14 Dec. 1917, Lothian Papers 219/750.
88. Cecil to Lloyd George, 5 Dec. 1917, L.G.P. F/6/5/10.
89. Lloyd George, *War Memoirs*, II. 1486.
90. *Ibid.*, II, 1504–9.
91. The current state of British knowledge is best seen in J. W. Wheeler-Bennett, *Brest-Litovsk: The Forgotten Peace, March 1918* (London, 1938), pp. 116–22.
92. Cecil to Balfour, 25 Dec. 1917, FO 800/207/132.
93. It is this view which distinguishes him from Lansdowne.
94. Balfour to Cecil, 29 Dec. 1917, British Library Addit. MSS. 49738 (Balfour Papers).
95. Hankey Diary, 2 Jan. 1917.
96. This would suggest that Kerr was unaware of the treaty's secret clauses.
97. Kerr to Lloyd George, 29 Dec. 1917, L.G.P. F/89/1/12.
98. Lloyd George, *War Memoirs*, II, 1515.
99. *The Nation*, 12 Jan. 1918.
100. G.T. 3180 (Smuts), G.T. 3181 (Cecil), both 3 Jan. 1918, CAB 24/37.
101. Hankey Diary, 5 Jan. 1918.
102. *Ibid.*, 4 Jan. 1918; Grey to Runciman, 5 Jan. 1918, Runciman Papers WR 300. Both Asquith and Grey approved of the content.
103. Printed in *The Left and the War: the British Labour Party and World War I*, ed. Peter Stansky (New York, 1969), pp. 318–26.
104. Draft in W.C. 314, 4 Jan. 1918, CAB 23/5; Lloyd George, *War Memoirs*, II, 1511, 1513.
105. Newton Diary, 8 Jan. 1918. Extract seen by courtesy of Dr Cameron Hazlehurst.
106. *The Nation*, 12 Jan. 1918.
107. L. Maxse to H. Page Croft, 9 Jan. 1918, Page Croft Papers 1/10/37.
108. Cf. D. R. Woodward, 'The Origins and Intent of David Lloyd George's January 5 War Aims Speech', *The Historian*, XXXIV (1971), 22–39.

109. William Dudley Ward (1877–1946). M.P. (Lib.) 1906–22. Treasurer of the Household 1909–12. Vice-Chamberlain 1917–22.
110. Guest to Addison, 17 Aug. 1918, Addison Papers 72.
111. Guest to Lloyd George, 16 Aug. 1918, L.G.P. F/21/2/31.
112. 'Manchester Speech', Kerr to Lloyd George, 6 Sept. 1918, Lothian Papers 653/1; *The Times*, 13 Sept. 1918.
113. 'Notes for Leeds Speech', 6 Dec. 1918, Lothian Papers 654/1.
114. *Ibid.* and 'Notes for Newcastle Speech', n.d., Lothian Papers 655.
115. 'Notes for Newcastle Speech'.
116. Kerr to Lloyd George, 20 Nov. 1918, Lothian Papers 1026.
117. Addison Diary, 24 May 1917; L.G.P. F/192/6/2 & 3; Sutherland to Addison, 23 May 1917, Addison Papers 70.
118. Hankey Diary, 21 Jun. 1918.
119. *Address by Mr Hall Caine on the Prime Minister, Parliament and the Parties* (privately printed, 1918), p. 6.
120. Hapgood to Colonel E. M. House, 9 Mar. 1917, E. M. House Papers.
121. 'The Irish Crisis', *The Round Table*, XXXI (June 1918).
122. Thomas Jones, *Whitehall Diary*, I, 39.
123. Addison Diary, 8 & 15 Oct. 1917, Addison, *Four and a Half Years*, II, 435, 437–8.
124. P.P. 1918, Cd. 9005, XIV, 383.
125. *Ibid.*, 393.
126. *Ibid.*, 394.
127. *Ibid.*, 395.
128. *Ibid.*, 398.
129. P.P. 1919, Cd. 325, XXX, 454. Circular letters and working papers for the 1918 Report are in L.G.P. F/75 and 76. Materials for the 1917 Report are apparently not in the Lloyd George Papers.

CHAPTER 8. TWO MALCONTENTS

1. Michael Rose, 'The Success of Social Reform: the Central Control Board (Liquor Traffic) 1915–1920' in *War and Society* ed. M. R. D. Foot (London, 1973). Cf. Henry Carter, *The Control of the Drink Trade* (2nd edn, London, 1919); Arthur Shadwell, *Drink in 1914–22 – A Lesson in Control* (London, 1923); and the Board's own reports, P.P. 1914–16, Cd. 8117, XXV, 1; 1916, Cd. 8243, XII, 493; 1917–18, Cd. 8558, XV, 669; 1918, Cd. 9055, XI, 119.
2. John Turner, 'State Purchase of the Liquor Trade in the First World War', *Historical Journal*, in press.
3. W.C. 12, 20 Dec. 1916, CAB 23/1.
4. G. 107, 16 Dec. 1916, CAB 24/3.
5. W.C. 33, 12 Jan. 1917, CAB 23/1.
6. Edgar Algernon Vincent (1857–1941). Financial adviser to the Egyptian government 1883–9. Governor of the Imperial Ottoman Bank 1889–97. M.P. (Cons.) 1899–1906, a Unionist Free Trader. Chairman of the Liquor Control Board 1915–20. Ambassador to Berlin 1920–6. Knighted 1887, created Baron D'Abernon 1914, Viscount 1926.

7. G. 116, 19 Jan. 1917, CAB 24/3; D'Abernon to Lloyd George, 18 Jan. 1917, Home Office Papers HO 185/263.
8. W.C. 42, 23 Jan. 1917, CAB 23/1.
9. Astor to J. T. Davies, 2 Feb. 1917, Astor Papers 40/756.
10. George Cave (1856–1928). M.P. 1906–18. Solicitor-General 1915–16. Home Secretary 1916–19. Lord Chancellor 1922–4, 1924–8. Knighted 1915, created Viscount 1918.
11. W.C. 65, 14 Feb. 1917, CAB 23/1.
12. W.C. 70, 16 Feb. 1917, CAB 23/1.
13. Astor to Lloyd George, n.d. [Feb. 1917], L.G.P. F/83/2/3.
14. G.T. 241, 21 Mar. 1917, CAB 24/8.
15. W.C. 106, 27 Mar. 1917, CAB 23/2.
16. File of letters, 23 Mar. 1917, Astor Papers 24/398.
17. 'Lloyd George' to Joseph Rowntree, 22 Mar. 1917, Astor Papers 56/1055. There is no evidence that this letter was ever sent.
    Joseph Rowntree (1836–1925). A member of the large Quaker family of philanthropists, Joseph Rowntree concentrated on temperance, championing municipalisation in numerous works, especially *The Temperance Problem and Social Reform* (London, 1901).
18. G. 144, Apr. 1917, CAB 24/3.
19. G. 143, 6 Apr. 1917, CAB 24/3.
20. G.T. 526, 23 Apr. 1917, CAB 24/11.
21. W.C. 132, 4 May 1917, CAB 23/2.
22. G.T. 643, n.d., CAB 24/12.
23. W.C. 134, 8 May 1917, CAB 23/2.
24. Shorthand note of the interview, 11 May 1917, L.G.P. F/228. Cf. Turner, 'State Purchase', in press.
25. G.T. 885, n.d., CAB 24/14.
26. Turner, 'State Purchase', in press.
27. W.C. 153, 31 May 1917, CAB 23/2.
28. G.T. 1008 (Munitions), G.T. 1070 (Milner), G.T. 1092 (The Board), 19 Jun. 1917, CAB 24/16.
29. W.C. 165, 19 Jun. 1917, CAB 23/3.
30. W.C. 167, 21 Jun. 1917, CAB 23/3.
31. Astor to Thomas Jones, 21 Feb. 1949, Jones Papers A/2/12.
32. 'State Purchase of the Liquor Trade: Reports of the English, Scotch and Irish Committees', P.P. 1918, Cd. 9042, XI, 145.
33. Milner to Astor, 22 Jun. 1917, Garvin Papers.
34. Cf. Addison, *Four and a half Years*, II, 359.
35. D'Abernon's notes on G.T. 885, HO 185/266.
36. For a fuller discussion of the logic of State Purchase, see Turner, 'State Purchase...', in press.
37. John Gretton (1867–1947). M.P. (Cons.) 1895–1943. Chairman of Bass, Ratcliffe and Gretton 1908–45.
38. Astor to Jones, 21 Feb. 1949, cited above note 31.
39. Thornton Diary, 25 Jun. 1917, Milner Papers 23.
40. Jones to E. T. Jones, 2 Jan. 1917, Jones Papers Z/1917, p. 3.
41. Owen, *Tempestuous Journey* (London, 1954), p. 380.
42. Imperial War Museum, Diary of Sir Henry Wilson, 17 Jan. 1917.

43. Jones to E. T. Jones, n.d. [Mar. 1917], Jones Papers Z/1917, p. 37, The 'Nursing Home' was a sanatorium which Davies had founded in Montgomeryshire.
44. Addison Diary, 22 Mar. 1917.
45. Davies to Lloyd George, 10 Apr. 1917, L.G.P. F/83/10/4.
46. Derby to Lloyd George, 28 Apr. 1917, enclosing Davies's memorandum of 23 Apr., L.G.P. F/14/4/38.
47. Massingham to Runciman, 14 Apr. 1917, Runciman Papers 161/1; *The Nation*, 21 Apr. 1917.
48. *H.C. Debs.*, 5s, 17 Apr. 1917, 1607–14.
49. Thomas Jones, *Whitehall Diary*, 1, 31.
50. Jones to E. T. Jones, 18 Apr. 1917, Jones Papers Z/1917, pp. 54–5.
51. See above, pp. 68–71.
52. Davies to Lloyd George, [27 May 1917], L.G.P. F/83/10/5.
53. See above, p. 70.
54. Davies to Lloyd George, 23 Jun. 1917, L.G.P. F/83/10/7, cited by Owen, p. 381.
55. Geoffrey Robinson to Northcliffe, 28 Jun. 1917, British Library, Northcliffe Deposit 4890/93.
56. Lloyd George to Davies, 24 Jun. 1917, L.G.P. F/83/10/8.
57. Davies to Lloyd George, 25 Jun. 1917, L.G.P. F/83/10/9.
58. Lord Beaverbrook, *Men and Power* (London, 1956), pp. 71–2; Owen, p. 382.
59. D'Abernon to Lady D'Abernon, n.d. [Jun. 1917], British Library Addit. MSS. 48936 (D'Abernon Papers), 18; same to same, n.d. [Aug. 1917], *ibid.*, 21.
60. Astor to Garvin, 18 Feb., 12 Mar., 27 Aug. 1917, Garvin Papers.
61. Garvin to Astor, 21 Sept. 1917, Garvin Papers.
62. Astor to Garvin, 18 Dec. 1917, Garvin Papers.
63. W.C. 241, 28 Sept. 1917, CAB 23/4; Sykes, *Nancy: The Life of Lady Astor* (London, 1972), p. 176.
64. Astor to Canon Perowne, 26 Dec. 1917, Astor Papers 24/403.
65. W.C. 309, 1 Jan. 1918, CAB 23/5.
66. Astor to Garvin, 2 Jan. 1918, Garvin Papers.
67. Garvin to Astor, 4 Jan. 1918, Garvin Papers.
68. Astor to Garvin, 16 Jan. 1918, Garvin Papers; Astor to Lloyd George, 18 Jan. 1918, G.T. 3375, CAB 24/39.
69. Astor to Lloyd George, 1 Feb. 1918, Astor Papers 40/756.
70. Hedworth Lambton (1856–1929). Naval officer 1870–1916. Promoted Admiral and changed name to Meux, 1911. C-in-C Portsmouth 1912–16. M.P. (Cons.) 1916–18. Knighted 1906.
71. Meux to Astor, 7 Feb. 1918, Garvin Papers; answering Astor to Meux, 5 Feb. 1918, King's College, London, Military Archives Centre, Robertson Papers 1/36/93/2.
72. Robertson to Astor, 16 Feb. 1918, Robertson Papers 1/36/94.
73. 102 *H.C. Debs.*, 5s, 656–7, 19 Feb. 1918.
74. Astor to Lloyd George, 20 Feb. 1918, L.G.P. F/83/1/11.
75. Goulding to Garvin, 26 Feb. 1918, Garvin Papers.
76. Guest to Lloyd George, 26 Feb. 1918, L.G.P. F/21/2/12.

77. He used *The Observer* to promote it; Astor to Garvin, 18 Mar. 1918, Garvin Papers.
78. W.C. 400, 26 Apr. 1918, CAB 23/6.
79. Astor to Lloyd George, 6 May 1918, L.G.P. F/83/1/12.
80. Garvin to Astor, 18 Mar. 1918, Garvin Papers.
81. Astor to Goulding, 15 Mar. 1918, Garvin Papers.
82. Goulding to Garvin, 20 Mar. 1918, Garvin Papers.
83. Goulding to Garvin, 21 Apr. 1918, Garvin Papers.
84. e.g. Astor to Garvin, 31 May 1918, Garvin Papers, pressing for a condemnation of delay in preparing a register of electors.
85. Long to Bonar Law, 16 Jul. 1918, L.G.P. F/30/2/37.
86. Goulding to Garvin, 15 Jul. 1918, Garvin Papers.
87. Goulding to Garvin, 18 Jul. 1918, Garvin Papers.

CHAPTER 9. CONCLUSION

1. Untitled memo. by Adams and Kerr, 1 Jan. 1917, L.G.P. F/74/2/2.
2. 'Proposed Statement by Professor Adams', 7 Mar. 1917, L.G.P. F/74/2/2.
3. Harmsworth to Lloyd George, 28 Jun. 1917, L.G.P. F/79/29/5.
4. See, e.g., *The Nation*, 24 Feb. 1917.
5. Stephen Roskill, *Hankey, Man of Secrets*, II, 276–7.
6. *Lord Riddell's Intimate Diary of the Peace Conference and After* (London, 1933), p. 223; *Field Marshal Sir Henry Wilson, His Life and Diaries*, ed. C. E. Callwell (London, 1927), II, 344; Thomas Jones, *Whitehall Diary*, I, 203;
   Edward William Macleay Grigg (1879–1955). Journalist, *The Times*, 1903–13. Active Service 1914–18. Military Secretary to the Prince of Wales 1919. Private secretary to Lloyd George 1921–2. M.P. (Nat. Lib.) 1922–5. Governor of Kenya 1925–31. M.P. (Nat. Cons.) 1933–45. Parliamentary Secretary, Ministry of Information 1939–40, Financial Secretary, War Office, 1940, Parliamentary Under-Secretary of State for War 1940–4. Minister Resident in the Middle East 1944–5. Editor of *National Review* 1948–55. Knighted 1920, created Baron Altrincham 1945.
7. Jones, 'The Prime Minister's Advisers', *Political Studies*, XXI, 363.
8. Willson, *The Organization of British Central Government, 1914–1964*, pp. 288–91 and 325.
9. K. O. Morgan, 'Lloyd George's Stage Army: The Coalition Liberals', in *Lloyd George: Twelve Essays*, ed. A. J. P. Taylor (London, 1971).
10. Plunkett Diary, 23 June 1918; Sir Henry Jones to Thomas Jones, 4 May 1918, Jones Papers V/1/58.
11. I have been unable to see Harmsworth's diary, which might contain some useful insight: his comments at the time, recorded by Plunkett, were moderately favourable. Plunkett Diary, 4 Sept. 1918.
12. Astor to Captain J. Astor, 6 May 1918. Astor Papers WA 1/12.
13. David Davies to D. Maclean, 23 Sept. 1918, Asquith Papers 145; Spender to Maclean, 8 Oct. 1918, *ibid*.
14. Adams to Thomas Jones, 31 Jan. 1948, Jones Papers A/2/24.

15. 'Proposed Statement...', L.G.P. F/74/2/2.
16. Minutes of 29th Meeting of the Machinery of Government Committee, 8 Mar. 1918, L.G.P. F/74/10/1.
17. See above, pp. 160–6.
18. Undated, untitled memorandum by Haldane, L.G.P. F/74/12/1.

Bibliography

UNPRINTED SOURCES

1. Private Papers

The principal source for this study was the collection of Lloyd George Papers which forms part of the Beaverbrook Library collection and is now housed in the House of Lords Record Office. Besides correspondence between Lloyd George and other public figures, it includes many files of the Secretariat's working papers. Other working papers were found in the Lothian Papers in the Scottish Record Office and the Astor Papers in Reading University Library. Extracts from the Newton Diary were seen by courtesy of Dr Cameron Hazlehurst. The Joseph Davies Papers and the David Davies of Llandinam Papers, both in the National Library of Wales, appeared to hold nothing relevant to this study. No papers were located for W. G. S. Adams, whose working papers in the Lloyd George Papers are however very full; the author was unable to use the Cecil Harmsworth Papers.

The following collections were also used:

Addison Papers   Bodleian Library, Oxford
Asquith Papers   Bodleian Library, Oxford
Balfour Papers   British Library, London
Balfour (Foreign Office) Papers   Public Record Office, Kew
Borden Papers   Public Archives of Canada
Buckler Papers   Sterling Library, Yale University
Campbell-Bannerman Papers   British Library, London
Austen Chamberlain Papers   Birmingham University Library
Cecil of Chelwood Papers   British Library, London
Cecil of Chelwood (Foreign Office) Papers   Public Record Office, Kew
Cherwell Papers   Nuffield College, Oxford
Commission for the Relief of Belgium Papers   Hoover Library, Stanford
  University
D'Abernon Papers   British Library, London
H. A. L. Fisher Papers   Bodleian Library, Oxford
Garvin Papers   Humanities Research Center, The University of Texas at
  Austin
Hankey Papers   Churchill College, Cambridge
Hardinge Papers   Cambridge University Library

E. M. House Papers   Sterling Library, Yale University
Thomas Jones Papers   National Library of Wales, Aberystwyth
Bonar Law Papers   Beaverbrook Collection, House of Lords Record Office
Milner Papers   Bodleian Library, Oxford
Northcliffe Papers   British Library, London
W. H. Page Papers   Houghton Library, Harvard University
Page Croft Papers   Churchill College, Cambridge
Plunkett Papers   Plunkett House, Oxford
Redmond Papers   National Library of Ireland, Dublin
Robertson Papers   Military Archives Centre, King's College, London
Round Table Papers   Bodleian Library, Oxford
Rumbold Papers   Bodleian Library, Oxford
Runciman Papers   Newcastle University Library
C. P. Scott Papers   British Library, London
J. C. Smuts Papers   Microfilm, Cambridge University Library
Stansgate Papers   House of Lords Record Office
Henry Wilson Diary   Imperial War Museum
Wiseman Papers   Sterling Library, Yale University

2. Official Records

The following Record Classes, all now kept at the Public Record Office, Kew, were consulted:
Admiralty Papers   ADM 1, 116
Cabinet Papers   CAB 1, 21, 23, 24, 27, 28
Foreign Office Papers   FO 371, 382, 800
Home Office Papers   HO 185
Ministry of Agriculture, Fisheries, and Food Papers   MAF 60
Ministry of Transport Papers   MT 61
War Office Papers   WO 106

PRINTED SOURCES

It is tendentious to maintain a distinction between primary and secondary printed sources for the history of politics and administration in the First World War, since much 'secondary' material was written by participants. A different classification is therefore adopted in the following list, which includes only the printed material found most useful for this study. Place of publication is London except where shown.

1. Autobiography, memoirs, edited diaries and documents

Addison, Christopher   *Four and a Half Years* (2 vols., 1934)
Lord Beaverbrook   *Politicians and the War* (first one vol. edn, 1960)
Lord Beaverbrook   *Men and power* (1956)
Curtis, Lionel   *Papers Relating to the Application of the Principle of Dyarchy to the Government of India* (Oxford, 1920)
Davies, Joseph   *The Prime Minister's Secretariat* (Newport, Mon., 1951)
Gay, G. I.   *Public Relations of the Commission for the Relief of Belgium* (2 vols., Palo Alto, 1929)

The Intimate Papers of Colonel House, ed. Charles Seymour, vol. III (1928)
Thomas Jones, Whitehall Diary, ed. Keith Middlemas (3 vols., 1969–71)
Kerensky, Alexander *The Catastrophe* (1927)
Lloyd George, David *The Truth about the Peace Treaties* (2 vols., 1938)
Lloyd George, David *War Memoirs* (Cheap edn, 2 vols., 1938)
Massey, Vincent *What's Past is Prologue* (Toronto, 1963)
Earl of Midleton *Records and Reactions* (1938)
Ollivier, Maurice (ed.) *The Colonial and Imperial Conference from 1887 to 1937* (3 vols., Ottawa, 1954)
Lord Riddell's War Diary 1914–1918 (1933)
The Political Diaries of C. P. Scott 1911–1928, ed. Trevor Wilson (1970)
Lloyd George: A Diary by Frances Stevenson, ed. A. J. P. Taylor (1971)
Stansky, Peter (ed.) *The Left and the War: the British Labour Party and World War I* (New York, 1969)
The Diaries of Beatrice Webb, 1912–32, ed. M. I. Cole (2 vols., 1952–6)
Field Marshal Sir Henry Wilson, His Life and Diaries, ed. C. E. Callwell (2 vols., 1927)

2. Publications which include writings by members of the Secretariat before 1916

Adams
    The Oxford Survey of the British Empire (Oxford, 1914)
    The Political Quarterly, nos. 1 to 8
Kerr
    The Round Table
    Grant, A. J., et al. *International Relations* (1916)
    Hilton, J., et al. *The Other War* (1916)
Harmsworth
    Harmsworth, Cecil *Pleasure and Problem in South Africa* (1908)

3. Biographies

Astor, Michael *Tribal Feeling* (1963)
Earl of Birkenhead *The Prof in Two Worlds* (1961)
Butler, J. R. M. *Lord Lothian* (Philip Kerr) 1882–1940 (1960)
Colvin, Ian *Life of Lord Carson* (1937)
Feiling, Keith *The Life of Neville Chamberlain* (1946)
Gilbert, Martin *Winston S. Churchill*, vol. IV, 1917–1922 (1975)
Gollin, A. M. *Proconsul in Politics: A study of Lord Milner in Opposition and in Power* (1964)
Harrod, R. F. *The Prof* (1959)
Lyons, F. S. L. *John Dillon, a biography* (1968)
Owen, Frank *Tempestuous Journey* (1954)
Pound, Reginald, and Harmsworth, Geoffrey *Northcliffe* (1959)
Roskill, Stephen *Hankey, Man of Secrets* (3 vols., 1969–72)
Rowland, Peter *Lloyd George* (1975)
Sykes, Christopher *Nancy: The Life of Lady Astor* (1972)

240   *Bibliography*

Waley, S. D.   *Edwin Montagu* (Bombay, 1964)
Wrench, J. E.   *Geoffrey Dawson and our Times* (1955)

4. Other works

i. Books
Beloff, Max   *Imperial Sunset* (1969)
Beveridge, W. H.   *British Food Control* (1928)
Brown, R. G. S.   *The Administrative Process in Britain* (1971)
Buckland, P. J.   *Irish Unionism* I (Dublin, 1972)
Carter, Henry   *The Control of the Drink Trade* (2nd edn, 1919)
Coupland, Reginald   *The Indian Problem, 1833–1935* (1942)
Ehrman, John   *Cabinet Government in War* (Cambridge, 1958)
Falls, Cyril   *The History of the Great War: Military Operations, Macedonia*, vol. I (1933)
Fest, W. B.   *Peace or Partition* (1978)
Friedman, Isaiah   *The Question of Palestine, 1914–1918* (1973)
Guinn, Paul   *British Strategy and Politics, 1914–1918* (Oxford, 1965)
Haines, Joe   *The Politics of Power* (1976)
Hancock, W. K. and Gowing, M. M.   *British War Economy* (Cambridge, 1949)
Hazlehurst, Cameron   *Politicians at War* (1971)
Hinton, James   *The First Shop Steward Movement* (1973)
The History of The Times, vol. IV, pt. I (1952)
Hurwitz, S. J.   *State Intervention in Great Britain* (New York, 1949)
Kendle, J. E.   *The Round Table Movement and Imperial Union* (Toronto, 1975)
Kennan, George F.   *Soviet–American Relations* (2 vols., Princeton, 1956, 1958)
Lloyd, E. M. H.   *Experiments in State Control at the War Office and the Ministry of Food* (Oxford, 1924)
Link, Arthur S.   *Wilson: Campaign for Progressivism and Peace* (Princeton, 1965)
Lowe, C. J. and Dockrill, M. L.   *The Mirage of Power* (1972)
Marwick, Arthur   *The Deluge* (1965)
McDowell, R. B.   *The Irish Convention 1917–1918* (1970)
Mehrotra, S. R.   *India and the Commonwealth, 1885–1929* (1963)
Middleton, T. H.   *Food Production in War* (Oxford, 1923)
Moore, R. J.   *The Crisis of Indian Unity, 1917–1940* (Oxford, 1974)
Nimocks, Walter   *Milner's Young Men: the 'Kindergarten' in Edwardian Imperial Affairs* (Durham, N.C., 1968)
Rothwell, V. H.   *British War Aims and Peace Diplomacy 1914–1918* (Oxford, 1971)
Scally, R. J.   *The Origins of Lloyd George's Coalition: The Politics of Social Imperialism, 1900 to 1918* (Princeton, 1975)
Searle, G. R.   *The Quest for National Efficiency* (1971)
Semmel, Bernard   *Imperialism and Social Reform* (New York, 1966)
Shadwell, Arthur   *Drink in 1914–22 – A Lesson in Control* (1923)
Stacey, Frank   *British Government, 1966 to 1975* (Oxford, 1975)

Bibliography   241

Starling, E. H.   *The Oliver Sharpey Lectures on the Feeding of Nations* (1919)
Ullman, Richard H.   *Intervention and the War* (Princeton, 1961)
Wheeler-Bennett, J. W.   *Brest-Litovsk: The Forgotten Peace, March 1918* (1938)
Willson, F. M. G.   *The Organization of British Central Government, 1914–1964* (2nd edn, 1968)
Wilson, T.   *The Downfall of the Liberal Party, 1914–1935* (1966)
Wolfe, Humbert   *Labour Supply and Regulation* (Oxford, 1923)

ii. Articles

Boyce, D. G. and Stubbs, J. O.   'F. S. Oliver, Lord Selborne and Federalism', *Journal of Imperial and Commonwealth History*, v (1976)
Danzig, R.   'The Many-Layered Cake: A Case Study in the Reform of the Indian Empire', *Modern Asian Studies*, iii (1969)
David, Edward   'The Liberal Party Divided, 1916–1918', *Historical Journal*, xiii (1970)
Douglas, Roy   'The National Democratic Party and the British Workers' League', *Historical Journal*, xv (1972)
Ellinwood, D. C.   'The Round Table Movement and India, 1909–20', *Journal of Commonwealth Political Studies*, ix (1971)
Hanak, H.   'The Government, the Foreign Office, and Austria–Hungary', *Slavonic Review*, xlviii (1969)
Huttenback, R. A.   'The British Empire as "White Man's Country" – Racial Attitudes and Immigration Legislation in the Colonies of White Settlement', *Journal of British Studies*, xiii (1973)
Jones, G. W.   'The Prime Minister's Advisers', *Political Studies*, xxi (1973)
Jones, G. W.   'The Prime Minister's Secretaries: Politicians or Administrators?', in *From Politics to Administration*, ed. J. A. G. Griffith (1976)
Kendle, J. E.   'The Round Table Movement and "Home Rule All Round"', *Historical Journal*, xi (1968)
Kendle, J. E.   'Federalism and the Irish Problem in 1918', *History*, lvi (1971)
Laffan, Michael   'The Unification of Sinn Fein in 1917', *Irish Historical Studies*, xvii (1971)
Lockwood, P. A.   'Milner's Entry into the War Cabinet, December 1916', *Historical Journal*, vii (1964)
Macdougall, G. D. A.   'The Prime Minister's Statistical Section', in *Lessons of the British War Economy*, ed. D. N. Chester (Cambridge, 1951)
Morgan, K. O.   'Lloyd George's Premiership: A Study in Prime Ministerial Government, *Historical Journal*, xiii (1970)
Morgan, K. O.   'Lloyd George's Stage Army: The Coalition Liberals', in *Lloyd George: Twelve Essays*, ed. A. J. P. Taylor (1971)
Naylor, John F.   'The Establishment of the Cabinet Secretariat', *Historical Journal*, xiv (1971)
Rose, Michael   'The Success of Social Reform: the Central Control Board

(Liquor Traffic) 1915–1920', in *War and Society*, ed. M. R. D. Foot (1973)

Stubbs, J. O. 'Lord Milner and patriotic labour', *English Historical Review*, LXXXVII (1972)

Warman, Roberta M. 'The Erosion of Foreign Office Influence in the Making of Foreign Policy, 1916–1918', *Historical Journal*, XV (1972)

Woodward, D. R. 'The Origins and Intent of David Lloyd George's January 5 War Aims Speech', *The Historian*, XXXIV (1971)

iii. Theses

Ellinwood, D. C. 'Lord Milner's "Kindergarten", the British Round Table Group, and the movement for Imperial Reform, 1910–1918' (Washington University Ph.D. thesis, 1962)

Inwood, S. 'The role of the press in English politics during the first world war, with special reference to the period 1914–1916' (Oxford D.Phil. thesis, 1971)

Index

Devonport, Lord, 28, 30, 47–9, 54–8, 183, 205 n13; and brewers' materials, 175

Dillon, John, 85, 89–91, 93–4, 96–7, 114–15, 120, 121, 216 n6

Dominions: at Imperial War Conference (1917), 125–30, 134, 137–8; and Indian emigration, 130; Prime Ministers to settle Irish question, 88–92; war aims, 156, 151–3, 161

Donoughue, Bernard, 4

drink control, 2, 3, 8, 10, 23, 174–80, 183, 185, 187; *see also* Central Control Board

Drummond, Sir Eric, 76, 161, 214 n89

Dublin, Lord Mayor of, 101

Duke, Henry, 103, 109, 217 n44; drafts 1917 Home Rule Bill, 92; and Irish conscription, 113–15; and Convention, 95–100; resigns, 116–17

Duke, Sir William, 124, 131, 137, 225 n12

Dumayne, Sir Frederick, 31, 205 n20

dyarchy, 124, 125, 135

Easter Rising (1916), 83, 88, 98, 115

Education Bill (1917), 171

Egypt, British prestige in, 79

Empire, British: and British trade, 144; security of, 146–7, 167, 171; *see also* Dominions, imperial federation, Imperial War Conference

Engineers, Amalgamated Society of, 39, 168

Entente, 163, 164; and Balkans, 61–71; and peace negotiations, 77–8, 80–2; war aims incompatible with Russian aims, 72–6

Fabianism, 11–12

federalism, 86, 88, 92; in Home Rule Bill (1918), 116–21; in Irish Convention, 102–3, 107, 111–12; Round Table proposals (1914), 90

Ferdinand, King of Bulgaria, 63, 212 n21

Fertilisers Committee, 51

fiscal autonomy, 101–6, 108–12, 121; *see also* Primrose Committee

Fisher, H. A. L., 22; on Home Rule Bill committee, 116–17, 119

Fisher, Admiral Lord, 184

Food, Ministry of, 2, 33, 46–9, 52, 54–8, 188

Food Controller, 28, 40, 47; *see also* Devonport, Lord, and Rhondda, Lord

Food Production Department, 28, 46, 58

food supply, 2–3, 29–30, 46–59, 156, 169, 170, 192

Foreign Office, 127; Balkan policy (1917), 63–6; and Belgian relief, 3–4, 32–5; and Caxton Hall speech, 163; Harmsworth appointed to, 26; and peace negotiations, 77–82, 153; and Russia, 72, 76; contacts with Secretariat, 2, 75, 190, 193; Secretariat as 'the other Foreign Office', 60

foreign policy in Secretariat: *re* Balkans, 10, 61–71; peace negotiations, 77–82; Russia, 71–6

France: Balkan policy of, 10, 61–71, 183; British obligations to, 144, 147, 161; fear of British intentions, 158; liberation of, 152, 153; war aims, 9, 156, 163

French, Lord, 50, 85, 115, 117–18, 209 n16

Gaelic League, 98–9

Garden Suburb, *see* Prime Minister's Secretariat

Gardiner, A. G., 11, 16, 202 n34

Garvin, J. L., 13–14, 18, 184–9, 201 n31

Gavan Duffy, George, 98–9, 219 n99

Geddes, A. C., 42, 208 n93

Geddes, E. C., 35–7, 206 n50

general election (1918), 8, 85, 122, 166–7, 171–2

General Staff, British, 61; *see also* Robertson, Sir William

Germany: Balkan alliances, 61;
British policy towards, 81–2, 145,
147, 151–60, 166; blockade of, 33;
competition with Britain before
1914, 12, 146; empire, British
attitudes to, 128–9, 151, 153, 155,
161–3; *Mitteleuropa* policy, 151;
offensives, 82, 113, 117, 135, 156;
Russian attitude to, 76; war aims,
69–70, 78, 144, 146–7, 151, 154,
156, 161
Gill, T. P., 93–7, 114–15, 217 n53
'ginger group' (1916), 14, 23
Gollin, Prof. A. M., 13
Gosling, Harry, 31, 205 n19
Goulding, Sir E., 187–9
Graham, Ronald, 79, 215 n105
Greece, 10, 61–71, 170
Gretton, John, 180, 233 n37
Grey of Fallodon, Lord, 165
Griffith, Arthur, 115, 223 n206
Grigg, Sir Edward, 193, 235 n6
Guest, Frederick, 20–1, 119, 166,
169, 187, 193, 203 n65
Gwynn, Stephen, 105, 111–12, 115,
118, 221 n153

Haig, Sir Douglas, 182
Haldane, Lord, 197–8, 201 n29;
see also Machinery of Government
Committee
Hall, A. D., 53, 210 n31
Halsey, Commodore Lionel, 75
Hanak, Harry: opinion of Kerr's
Swiss mission, 81
Hankey, Lt. Col. Sir Maurice, 5, 17,
62, 168, 193; and Caxton Hall
speech, 160, 163, 165; and
Imperial War Conference, 126,
127, 151; and Irish conscription,
118; and Secretariat, 18, 19, 191,
197; *see also* War Cabinet Secretariat
Hardinge of Penshurst, Lord, 131,
227 n51
Harmsworth, Cecil, 2, 3, 4, 14, 173,
174, 190, 191, 195, 196; and air-
raid insurance, 42–4; and Belgian
relief, 32–4; and food policy, 48,

56–8; and Ireland, 86, 110–11,
117, 118; and labour, 29, 38–42,
156, 193; joins Secretariat, 20–1,
25–6; and shipbuilding, 30, 35–8;
and tobacco, 31–2; and War
Cabinet Report, 10, 169
Health, Ministry of, 4, 18, 187, 195
Healy, Tim, 95, 99, 115
Henderson, Arthur, 5, 39, 48, 56,
178, 199 n9; and Stockholm
conference, 158, 167
Hewart, Sir Gordon, 116, 223 n216
Hichens, Lionel, 124, 225 n5
Hodge, John, 41
Home Office, 2, 25, 193
Home Rule, *see* Ireland
Hoover, Herbert, 33, 177
Hopwood, Sir Francis (later Lord
Southborough), 98, 101, 104, 106,
109–11, 219 nn91 & 92
House, Col. E. M., 158
Hughes, William, 87, 216 n16

imperial affairs, 123–38; Kerr's
background in, 3, 10, 13, 22
imperial federation, 123–4, 126–8,
130–1, 138
Imperial War Cabinet, 125–7, 151–
3, 157; committees on the
desiderata of peace, 153
Imperial War Conference (1917), 15,
124, 125–6, 127–30, 132, 151;
(1918), 138, 154
India: British prestige in, 79;
constitutional reform, 10, 123,
124–5, 131–8; emigration from,
127, 128–30, 149; Government of,
131, 136, 140; Government of
India Act (1919), 125; Montagu's
Declaration of 20 Aug. 1917, 136,
137, 171; represented at Imperial
War Conference, 126
India Office, 2, 131, 133, 136, 138,
190, 195
Indian Civil Service, 125
Indian Cotton Duties debate, 20,
140
Indian Moot, of Round Table, 124–5
Independent Labour party, 14

Industrial Unrest, Commission of
Inquiry on, 39–40, 156
international organisation: Adams's
views, 15, 145–6, 171; Kerr's
views, 15, 147–8, 158–9, 164, 171;
see also League of Nations
Ireland, 3, 9, 15, 25, 83–122, 133,
140, 142, 166, 169, 192, 194
Ireland, Government of, 83, 85, 92,
101, 117, 120
Ireland, Home Rule Bill (1914), 12,
14, 83, 87, 103; Home Rule proposals (1916), 101; Home Rule
proposals (1917), 90–5, 121–2;
Home Rule proposals (1918), 3,
85, 116–22
Irish Agricultural Organisation
Society, 98
Irish Convention, 3, 84–5, 88, 91,
114, 137, 171; establishment,
93–9; proceedings, 100–13;
report, 112, 116–17, 119–22
Irish Department of Agriculture and
Technical Instruction, 2, 51, 54,
93, 96, 144
Irish Independent, 25; *see also*
Murphy, W. M.
Irish Land Purchase Scheme, 89, 105
Irish Nationalist party, 192; split
over conscription, 85, 114–15, 118;
and establishment of Convention,
94–8; in Convention, 100–12;
decline of, 88; and Home Rule
before 1917, 83–5, 87; and Home
Rule proposals (1917), 89–95; and
Home Rule proposals (1918), 120–
2; *see also* All for Ireland League
Irish Unionist Alliance, *see* Southern
Unionists
Irish Volunteers, 83
Italy, 160; Balkan policy of, 62, 64,
68; British policy towards, 80, 167;
war aims, 77, 161, 163

Japan, 76, 128
Jellicoe, Admiral Sir John, 65, 66,
67, 212 n38
Jones, Kennedy, 41, 55, 208 n88
Jones, Thomas, 23, 54, 181, 182–3,

202 n39; and establishment of
Secretariat, 15–19

Kaiser, trial of, 167
Kelly, Dr Denis, 96–7, 218 n73
Kendle, Prof. J. E., 138
Kerensky, Alexander, 75–6, 214 n81
Kerr, Philip, 2, 3, 173, 174, 188, 193,
195, 196; and agricultural policy,
53; and Caxton Hall speech, 9,
160–6; as ideologue, 140–1, 143,
146, 172, 192; and imperial expansion, 161–2, 165; and imperial
federation, 123–4, 127–8; and
India, 124–5, 128–30, 132–8; and
Ireland, 85–7, 89–91, 94, 103, 111,
115–16, 169; and labour questions, 149–50, 156, 157, 171; and
Lansdowne letter, 157–60; and
League of Nations, 15, 146–8,
158–9, 164, 166, 171; as Milner's
disciple, 141, 142, 149–50, 194;
and morale of British people, 156;
and peace negotiations (Austria),
77, 80, 81–2, 153, 161, (Turkey),
77, 78–81, 162; religious belief, 22,
87; and Round Table policies,
123–5, 127, 129, 130, 138; and
Serbian question, 10, 60, 65–70,
156; as social-imperialist, 11, 13–
15, 138, 141, 194; and establishment of Secretariat, 18–19, 21–2,
190; Swiss mission, *see* peace
negotiations; and War Aims, 9–10,
60, 139, 140–1, 150–68, 171; and
war, interpretation of, 146–68;
and War Cabinet Report, 169–72
Keynes, J. M., interprets Lloyd
George, 11
Kindergarten, Milner's, 14, 22, 123–4
Kühlmann, Richard von, German
Secretary of State, 157, 162

Labour, Ministry of, 2, 6, 19, 28, 30,
38, 41; *for* Minister of Labour,
see Hodge, John
labour exchanges, 40–1
Labour Mission to the United States,
35

Cambridge Studies in the History and Theory of Politics

Editors: Maurice Cowling, G. R. Elton, E. Kedourie, J. G. A. Pocock, J. R. Pole and Walter Ullmann

A series in two parts, studies and original texts. The studies are original works on political history and political philosophy while the texts are modern, critical editions of major texts in political thought. The titles include:

TEXTS

Liberty, Equality, Fraternity, by James Fitzjames Stephen, edited with an introduction and notes by R. J. White

Vladimir Akimov on the Dilemmas of Russian Marxism 1895–1903. An English edition of 'A Short History of the Social Democratic Movement in Russia' and 'The Second Congress of the Russian Social Democratic Labour Party', with an introduction and notes by Jonathan Frankel

J. G. Herder on Social and Political Culture, translated, edited and with an introduction by F. M. Barnard

The Limits of State Action, by Wilhelm von Humboldt, edited with an introduction and notes by J. W. Burrow

Kant's Political Writings, edited with an introduction and notes by Hans Reiss: translated by H. B. Nisbet

Karl Marx's Critique of Hegel's 'Philosophy of Right', edited with an introduction and notes by Joseph O'Malley; translated by Annette Jolin and Joseph O'Malley

Lord Salisbury on Politics. A Selection from His Articles in 'The Quarterly Review' 1860–1883, edited by Paul Smith

Francogallia, by François Hotman. Latin text edited by Ralph E. Giesey. English translation by J. H. M. Salmon

The Political Writings of Leibniz, edited and translated by Patrick Riley

Turgot on Progress, Sociology and Economics: A Philosophical Review of the Successive Advances of the Human Mind on Universal History. Reflections on the Formation and Distribution of Wealth, edited, translated and introduced by Ronald L. Meek

Texts concerning the Revolt of the Netherlands, edited with an introduction by E. H. Kossmann and A. F. Mellink

Regicide and Revolution: Speeches at the Trial of Louis XVI, edited with an introduction by Michael Walzer; translated by Marian Rothstein

George Wilhelm Friedrich Hegel: Lectures on the Philosophy of World History: Reason in History, translated from the German edition of Johannes Hoffmeister by H. B. Nisbet and with an introduction by Duncan Forbes

A Machiavellian Treatise by Stephen Gardiner, edited and translated by Peter S. Donaldson

The Political Works of James Harrington, edited by J. G. A. Pocock

STUDIES

1867: Disraeli, Gladstone and Revolution: The Passing of the Second Reform Bill, by Maurice Cowling

The Social and Political Thought of Karl Marx, by Shlomo Avineri

Men and Citizens: A Study of Rousseau's Social Theory, by Judith Shklar

Idealism, Politics and History: Sources of Hegelian Thought, by George Armstrong Kelly

The Impact of Labour 1920–1924: The Beginnings of Modern British Politics, by Maurice Cowling

Alienation: Marx's Conception of Man in Capitalist Society, by Bertell Ollman

The Politics of Reform 1884, by Andrew Jones

Hegel's Theory of the Modern State, by Shlomo Avineri

Jean Bodin and the Rise of Absolutist Theory, by Julian H. Franklin

The Social Problem in the Philosophy of Rousseau, by John Charvet

The Impact of Hitler: British Politics and British Policy 1933–1940, by Maurice Cowling

Social Science and the Ignoble Savage, by Ronald L. Meek

Freedom and Independence: A Study of the Political Ideas of Hegel's 'Phenomenology of Mind', by Judith Shklar

In the Anglo-Arab Labyrinth: The McMahon-Husayn Correspondence and Its Interpretations 1914–1939, by Elie Kedourie

The Liberal Mind 1914–1929, by Michael Bentley

Political Philosophy and Rhetoric: A Study of the Origins of American Party Politics, by John Zvesper

Revolution Principles: The Politics of Party 1689–1720, by J. P. Kenyon

John Locke and the Theory of Sovereignty: Mixed Monarchy and the Right of Resistance in the Political Thought of the English Revolution, by Julian H. Franklin

Adam Smith's Politics: An Essay in Historiographic Revision, by Donald Winch

For EU product safety concerns, contact us at Calle de José Abascal, 56–1°,
28003 Madrid, Spain or eugpsr@cambridge.org.

www.ingramcontent.com/pod-product-compliance
Ingram Content Group UK Ltd.
Pitfield, Milton Keynes, MK11 3LW, UK
UKHW010342140625
459647UK00010B/772